Naething Dauntit

Naething Dauntit

The Collected Poems
of
Douglas Young

Edited
with an Introduction and Notes
by Emma Dymock
and a Foreword
by Clara Young

humming earth

Published by

Humming Earth
an imprint of
Zeticula Ltd
Unit 13
196 Rose Street
Edinburgh
EH2 4AT
Scotland

http://www.hummingearth.com
admin@hummingearth.com

First published in 2016
Text Copyright © Clara Young 2016
Introduction and Notes Copyright © Emma Dymock 2016
Appendix Copyright © Estate of Hugh MacDiarmid 2016
Illustrations by George Bain Copyright © Clara Young 2016
Photographs and holograph poems Copyright © Clara Young 2016

ISBN 978-1-84622-062-3 Hardback
ISBN 978-1-84622-169-9 Paperback

All rights reserved. No part of this publication may be reproduced, stored in a retrieval system, or transmitted in any form or by any means, electronic, mechanical, photocopying, recording or otherwise, without the prior permission of the publishers.

*He was eident, he was blye
in Scotland's cause.*

Contents

Acknowledgements	xv
Foreword	xvii
'The ferlies ye ha seen': Vision and Commitment in the Poetry of Douglas Young	xix
Douglas Young: A Biographical Outline	xxxv

Naething Dauntit

Poems by Douglas Young	**3**
Thesaurus Paleo-Scoticus	5
Traveller's Tale	6
Attic Noon	7
On the Akropolis at Skoplje, July 1936	8
Austrian Scene	10
To Gillian in Vienna	12
On the Death of Wallace Martin Lindsay	13
22 St Giles Street, Oxford. February Midnight	15
Lines on a Gaelic Poet at an Oxford Party	16
Sonnet Peu Probable	17
After Lunch, Ekali	18
Leaving Athens	20
For Deòrsa and his *Calum Thonder*	22
London Midnight	23
Fife Equinox	24
December Night: The Aesthete in the House	25
Ardlogie, Christmas Eve, 1939	26
Winter Pool	27
Quatorzain in an Entr'acte: His Majesty's Theatre Aberdeen	28
Speculation	29
The Cat in the Rock-Garden	30
August Night	31
Autumn Fire	32

Letter to Hugh MacDiarmid, 1940	33
Sonnet for a Phone-Call	39
To a Friend on a Campaign	40
For Alasdair	41
For a Scotsman Slain	42
Dulce et Decorum...	43
Carmen In Patriam Suam	44
For the Old Highlands	45
Winter Homily on the Calton Hill	46
Simplon Tunnel	47
Epilogue to Theokritos	48
Sang by the Sea	49
Whiles	50
Sabbath i the Mearns	51
Confluence	52
W.B. Yeats	53
Russian Thought	54
The Roots of Love	55
May Nocturne	56
A Love	57
For Willie Soutar, October 1943	59
D. til H.	60
For a Wife in Jizzen	61
Obair-Bhrothaig	62
For D. D-H	63
Requiem	64
Fermer's Deein	65
Sainless	66
Ice-Flumes Owregie Their Lades	67
Hielant Colloguy	70
Last Lauch	71
A Cameronian Cat	72
A Ballad o Saughton Jail	73
Thochts Anent Bluid and Roses	75
Thomas Joseph Williams	76
Du Bellay in Fife	79
Til the *Andantino* frae Gluck's *Orpheus*	80
Reconciliation	81
Luve	82
On an Auld Map o Scotland	83

Bairn-Music	85
On A North British Devolutionary	86
Duncan the Joiner	87
The Ballant o the Laird's Bath	89
Jessie o Balronald	91
Kintra Couplin	95
Aisling na h-Alba	96
Pious Ejaculation in Aberdeen	97
Eternitie	98
Vishnu	99
Duncan the Joiner and the Laird of Jura	100
Rabbie in Plastics	101
Snaw Thochts	105
Thow Thochts	106
The Shepherd's Dochter	109
For Edwin & Willa, Bannockburn Day 1947	110
Naomi Mitchison	111
Young Kilkerran	112
Maurice Lindsay	113
Hugh MacDiarmid	114
London, 1948	115
Ane Acrostich Sonnet in the auld Scots for the Queen's Grace in Embro, on Bannockburn Day 1953	116
Maister John Knox's First Blast o the Trumpet again the Yerl o Balcarres	117
A Ballad of the Plockton Hay-Drier	119
Garlic in Colinton Dell	121
The Fleurs of Embro	122
Van Gogh – *The Starry Night*	123
Passing Poet	124
Crail Harbour	124
St Andrews Castle	124
Photo from Pitlour Towards East Lomond	125
Falkland Palace (floodlit photo)	125
Dunfermline Abbey	126
St Andrews Castle	127

Political and Social Comment in Verse Form by Douglas Young   129

Scotlann, Awauk	131
Scotland's Complaynt to his Mistress Industry	132
Scotsmen, Wake Up!	133
Pious Canticle	135
The French are surrounded	136
Prognostication, April 1939	137
Chain Stores	138
Timor belli ne nos conturbet	139
It's Easy Sperin'	140
Crusade	141
Mr E. Brown's Highland Tour, or Muckle Cry and Little Oo	142
The Bold Sloganeer	143
Moral Problem	145
The Umpteenth Forefront	146
To the Hymn Tune "Veni Immanuel"	147
Lady Grant	148
Fiscal and Advocate	149
The Glesca Muckers: An Againflytin tae George Todd's "The Embro Makars"	150
Anthem for the Primrose League	151
Labour's Call to Rally	152

Translations   153

TRANSLATIONS FROM GAELIC   154
Frae the Gaelic o Sorley MacLean   154

Dàin do Eimhir XXVIII:	The Ghaists	154
Dàin do Eimhir XXXIII:	The weird o makars	155
Dàin do Eimhir XXXIV:	When I am talkan o the face and natur...	156
Dàin do Eimhir XLII:	Were we thegither, me and you...	157
Dàin do Eimhir XLIII:	Were't no for ye	158
Dàin do Eimhir LI:	I the connachan time	159
Dàin do Eimhir LIII:	I fashna masel for the grand revolution...	160
Dàin do Eimhir LIV:	Ye were the dawn	161
Dàin do Eimhir LV:	I dinna ken the sense o ma trauchlan...	162

Dàin do Eimhir LVII	163
Dàin Eile XVII	167
Wald ye be atween a lassie's houghs	167
Hielant Woman	168
My een are nae on Calvary	169
Gealach Ùr:	170
Reothairt	171
Frae the Gaelic o George Campbell Hay	*172*
Thonder they ligg	172
Guestless Howff	174
Lass wi the Keekin-Gless	175
Frae the Scots Gaelic o William Livingstone	*176*
Eirinn ag Gul. Ireland Greitan	176
Frae the Erse, Eichteenth Yearhunder	*178*
Do Threasgair an Saol	178
Frae the Gaelic.	*179*
An t-Iarla Diurach – by *a MacLaine Lady of Lochbuie to a Campbell of Jura.*	*179*
From the traditional Gaelic	*180*
Raasay Lament – *"Cumha Mhic' ille Chaluim"*	*180*
FRAE THE LALLANS OF BURNS	181
"Caa the Yowes" intil Bioitian [Greek]	181
"Ae Fond Kiss" i the Doric [Greek]	182
CLASSICAL TRANSLATIONS	183
Frae the Aiolic o Psappho	*183*
Thon time we aa wonned	183
Til Anaktoria	184
Frae the Aiolic o Psappho	185
Frae the Greek	*187*
Frae the Greek o Theognis o Megara	*188*
Fowr Epigrams	188
Frae Homer's Iliad, VI, 392-496.	*189*
Hektor's Twynan frae Andromacha	189
Frae Catullus, V. "Vivamus, Mea Lesbia, Atque Amemus…"	*193*
Lassie, c'wa	193
Frae Catullus, VIII, "Miser Catulle, Desinas Ineptire…"	*194*
Catullus man, ye maunna	194

Frae the Latin o Sulpicia, Elegidion VI	195
I wish, my jo	195
Frae Propertius. Elegies II, xi.	196
Ithers may scryve	196
Frae the Latin o Emperor Gallienus	197
Lasses and Lads	197
Frae the Greek of Aeschylus, Agamemnon 429-455	198
Choric Threnody	198
Aristophanes in Scots: Frae Choruses o The Birdies	199
TRANSLATIONS FROM ITALIAN	200
Frae the Second Canzone o Dante's "Vita Nuova"	200
"Mentre Io Pensava La Mia Frale Vita..."	200
TRANSLATIONS FROM FRENCH	202
Frae the French o Paul Valéry, "Le Bois Amical"	202
The Couthy Wuid	202
Frae the French o Paul Valéry, "Le Cimetière Marin"	203
The Kirkyaird by the Sea	203
TRANSLATIONS FROM GERMAN	208
Frae Hugo Von Hofmannsthal: "Wo kleine Felsen, kleine Fichten..."	208
Whaur monie a wee bit spruce and craid	208
Frae Theodor Storm: "Die Stadt"	209
Grey are the sands	209
Frae the German o Emanuel Geibel	210
The mowdie	210
Frae the German o Erich Fried	211
Hame frae Stalingrad	211
Frae the German o Erich Fried eftir the portraict by Pieter Breughel	212
The Bairns' Slauchter o Bethlehem	212
Frae a German owreset by Lili du Bois-Reymond o an English Sonnet o the First World War whas autour isna kent	213
On the Daith o a Young German Scholar	213
Frae the German o Ludwig Uhland	214
On a Bairn's Daith	214

Frae Paul Heyse	216
Eftir the Daith o a Bairn	216
Frae Christian Morgenstern	217
Frae the German o Heine	218
I loe a fleur	218
Frae the German o Goethe	219
Travesty in Lallans: Mignon's Song, "Kennst du das Land…"	219
TRANSLATIONS FROM LITHUANIAN	220
Kościuszko's son	220
The Gods' buss, epple-ringie	221
Britherly Fareweel	222
TRANSLATIONS FROM CHINESE	223
"Shi King": The Second o the Odes o T'Ang	223
"Shi King": The Second o the Odes o Wei	224
"Shi King": The Ninth o the Odes o Wei	225
The Rich Spinster's Sang	225
The Auchtand o the Odes o P'ei	226
The phaisant cock has flown awa	226
TRANSLATIONS FROM RUSSIAN	227
Frae the Russian o Pushkin	227
I loed ye yince	227
The Black Shawl	228
To A.P. Kyern	230
Frae the Russian o Kondrati Fyedorovitch Rileyev	231
Octobrist Manifesto	231
Frae the Russian of Nyekrasov	232
A Mother's Tears	232
TRANSLATION FROM THE WELSH	233
Frae the Welsh hymn by D. Gwenallt Jones	233
Wales	233
TRANSLATION FROM THE HEBREW	235
Frae the Hebrew	235
The 23rd Psalm o King Dauvit	235

The Coolin: An Assonantal Projection into English,
from the original Gaelic of Sorley MacLean's
  'An Cuilithionn' **237**

Notes **287**
Poems by Douglas Young 289
Political and Social Comment in Verse Form by Douglas Young 311
Translations by Douglas Young 319

Appendix: Foreword to *Auntran Blads* by Hugh MacDiarmid 341
Bibliography 347

Index of Titles and First Lines **353**

Acknowledgements

This book would not have been possible without the help and support given to me by Clara Young. Throughout the editing and writing process, she has tirelessly supplied useful information and the more personal accounts of Douglas Young and his poetry, which could never have been gleaned from manuscripts alone. Her enthusiasm for this project has matched my own. Clara's discovery of a previously inaccessible bookcase in her father's study, containing manuscripts, notebooks and letters, is just one example of how she has succeeded in sustaining my excitement in this work. She is a true and faithful custodian of her father's poetry and legacy.

I am grateful to the Trustees of the National Library of Scotland for permission to reproduce material in their possession. The continuing assistance of staff at this institution in relation to my research is always appreciated.

George Reid and George Sutherland provided crucial advice and expertise on the Latin and Greek pieces, an area in which I am more than aware of my inexperience. However, all remaining inaccuracies are my own responsibility. I am also grateful to Professor Wilson McLeod (University of Edinburgh) for his advice during the book's preparation and Dr. Anja Gunderloch (University of Edinburgh) for her guidance in relation to Young's Gaelic translations.

Thanks also go to all at the Association for Scottish Literary Studies, who have been supportive of my work for many years. It was at an ASLS event that I was first introduced to both Clara Young and the publisher, so the ASLS is partly responsible for this book's inception.

Finally, I wish to thank my parents, Craig and Janette, for their love and encouragement in all my literary passions, and my husband Peter, who generously shared the first two years of our marriage with Douglas Young.

Emma Dymock,
1 May 2016

Foreword

I am delighted that my father's collected poems are now being launched on to the world more than forty years after his untimely death in 1973. Much earlier *Auntran Blads: An Outwale o Verses by Douglas Young* came out in 1943, shortly after his eight month stay as "a guest of His Britannic Majesty" in Saughton gaol. He was at the height of his fame or notoriety as the Chairman of the Scottish National Party who had refused to be conscripted. This slim volume was well reviewed at the time by the critics.

Aberdeen Press and Journal: "*Auntran Blads* is a book of unique flavour, written by a man of brilliant talents, whose sophisticated intellectual approach is something new in the annals of our country's poetry. His verse is as vigorous in form as it is sensible in content. One finds oneself muttering, 'Ay man, here's a poet.'"

Poetry Review: "Douglas Young is more Scottish than Burns."

Ivor Brown in *The Observer*: "*Auntran Blads* proves the author to be as good an internationalist as he is a localist. Most of it is in Scots, which he can set 'whummlan' along like a burn in noble spate (e.g. in his magnificent war-epitaph 'For Alasdair'). In his translations from the Gaelic of Sorley Maclean, the words sing and plash like Hebridean winds and waters. There is grand writing of all kinds here, epigrammatic as well as emotional, rich in wit, taste and sensibility."

The title of this collection, *Naething Dauntit*, comes from 'Last Lauch', Douglas's best known and perhaps funniest poem. Published in numerous anthologies and frequently quoted on the Internet, it even came top in a list of favourite short poems.

Douglas Young was rather modest about calling himself a poet. In the introduction to his book, *Scottish Verse 1851-1951*, he maintains that there are only about six writers in his anthology who are "poets in the higher sense", describing himself as an "accomplished versifier".

An outstanding Classical scholar, he was a brilliant linguist and had a great facility for learning foreign languages, notably mastering German in three weeks with the aid of newspapers and a dictionary while walking through the Dolomites in 1933. He was passionate about "Lallans" (Lowland Scots) which he absorbed while working on his uncle's farm in Fife during the 1920s.

Notably *Auntran Blads* was dedicated to Sorley MacLean and George Campbell Hay, both included among the "poets in the higher sense", whose Gaelic poems translated into Lallans were given pride of place in the layout. While not a lyric poet himself, Douglas had tremendous empathy with other poets who were; these translations were greatly admired as being "alive with the pith of Scots" (*Glasgow Herald*) and "exhibiting a superb and well-justified confidence in his native Lallans" (Helen Parry Eden).

As well as writing much of his own poetry in Lallans, Douglas gave lectures, later produced as pamphlets, on the Scots language. *"PLASTIC SCOTS and the Scottish Literary Tradition"* was an address given in Glasgow in December 1946 with Hugh MacDiarmid in the chair. *The Use of Scots for Prose* was the John Galt Lecture for 1949, given in Greenock. It's interesting to speculate how his career would have developed if he had accepted Glasgow University's offer of a lectureship in Scottish literature.

I am most grateful to Dr Emma Dymock not only for her scholarship and critical awareness but also for the phenomenal energy and enthusiasm she has brought to the task of editing this collection of poems and verses. When this project was first mooted, we thought that the bulk of the work would be found in the two volumes published by MacLellan in 1943 and 1947 — but Emma discovered a great many more pieces among the huge archive of the Douglas Young papers in the National Library of Scotland. One surprise was the discovery of Douglas's version of Sorley MacLean's epic poem, *The Coolin*, which is notable for its sense of rhythm and visceral energy.

Our family and friends recently sponsored a Douglas Young memorial paving stone in Makars' Court, Edinburgh, quoting lines from his poem, 'For Willie Soutar'.

> *He was eident, he was blye*
> *in Scotland's cause.*

These words equally apply to my father.

Clara Young, Tayport, 10 April 2016

'The ferlies ye ha seen': Vision and Commitment in the Poetry of Douglas Young

I

In recent years there has been a sustained reassessment of Scottish poetry of the 1930s and 1940s. Part of this reassessment has involved a deeper appreciation and a dawning understanding that Gaelic and Scots poets from this period will benefit from being studied in conjunction with each other rather than as completely separate entities. This is not a new concept; rather, it is a rediscovered and remembered vision. Figures such as Hugh MacDiarmid and Douglas Young had already crossed that most challenging of borders – the Highland-Lowland divide – and become all the richer for it. Likewise, the Gaels had benefitted greatly from this literary alliance. The Gaelic poets, Sorley MacLean and George Campbell Hay, were in active service in the British Army during World War II, and it was a certain classicist and politician, Douglas Young, who championed these poets, keeping safe material which was ground-breaking in scope, and assisting in the publication process of some of this work, most famously, MacLean's *Dàin do Eimhir* (*Poems to Eimhir*).[1] What is perhaps less widely recognised is that during this same period and beyond, Douglas Young was himself a poet. Sorley MacLean was well aware of this fact, showing great respect for Young's work when he corresponded with him during the war. On more than one occasion MacLean laments Young's unwavering support for his Gaelic poetry, hoping that this commitment is not to the detriment of his friend's own work.[2] Young has rightly been cast in the role of father figure and

---

1 MacLean 1943 and 2002.
2 See for example MacLean's letter to Young, dated 18 December 1941, in which MacLean writes 'I think again and again how your work for my poetry must be hindering so much of your other work and sometimes I have uncomfortable feelings that my stuff is not worth your trouble, especially when I feel flat and think that I may never write another poem worth a damn and that your fellow Classicists may deprecate your

champion of writers and poets – Gaelic and otherwise – who can be loosely associated with MacDiarmid's Scottish Literary Renaissance, but to view him in this role alone would be to do a disservice to such a multi-dimensional literary figure.

Douglas Young's poetic output was not insufficient for a man who was also an academic researcher and active political figure. His *Auntran Blads* was published in 1943, followed by a second collection, *A Braird o Thristles*, in 1947. Both collections were published by William MacLellan of Glasgow and articulated the Scottish Literary Renaissance values of the period in both their style and execution. The collections include original poems in Scots and English, Scots translations of Greek, Latin, French, German, Lithuanian, Chinese and Russian poetry, Scots translations of the Gaelic poetry of Sorley MacLean and George Campbell Hay as well as translations of earlier poetry from the Scottish and Irish Gaelic tradition, and polyglot pieces including translations of Burns into Greek. Praising *Auntran Blads* in the collection's foreword, Hugh MacDiarmid describes it as a 'significant book', manifesting 'all the chief characteristics of the independent Scottish tradition in its differences from English tradition.'[3] *A Braird o Thristles* develops these elements even further; there are significantly more poems in Scots in the second collection requiring, in some cases, detailed glossaries to explain Young's use of different registers of Scots, which ranged from the familiar to the archaic. Visually, the collection also endorses the characteristics of the Renaissance, with poems embellished with the Celtic knotwork and other designs of the artist, George Bain (1881-1968), who was greatly influential in the revival of interest in Celtic and Insular art. Derrick McClure has written that in these collections 'a boldly enterprising approach to the Scots language is applied in the service of a poetic vision combining tradition and innovation, nationalism and cosmopolitanism, as deliberately and as convincingly as the Renaissance ideals required.'[4] As well as his poetry collections, Young's poetic contributions to small magazines and journals should not be underestimated as they also reveal a poet who was involved in the political and literary life of Scotland from the 1940s onwards.[5]

---

spending on my stuff time you might have spent on Theognis.' National Library of Scotland, Accession 6419, Box 38b.
3   See Appendix 1 for a full transcript of MacDiarmid's foreword.
4   McClure 2000: 116.
5   *The Scots Independent, The Scots Magazine, The Voice of Scotland,*

II

This new edited collection of his work should go some way to proving that Douglas Young's poetry deserves a firmer place in Scottish literary history. One reason for this assertion is quite simply that many of the poems included in this book chart the social and political history, like no other poetry of the period, of a young man living (and attempting to work) during World War II. What makes Young unique is that unlike many of his literary compatriots, he did not take up arms during the war. Young was no pacifist. He would have fought on the side of a Scottish Army if one had existed, and his subsequent nationalist stance in court has been well-documented.[6] Nevertheless, this political objector has documented the war in both Scots and English poetry. A poetic response such as this is perhaps more possible in World War II poetry than it could ever have been in relation to World War I; definitions of war poetry in World War II are certainly complicated with the absence of conscription in Northern Ireland and the neutral stance taken by the Irish Republic. Peter Mackay has suggested that Young's experience of war had more in common with the Irish Nationalists who were interred in the Curragh for the duration of the war.[7] Poets such as Young are proof that there was no singularly appropriate reaction to the conflict. One could argue that it was actually Young's largely unmatched position as a political spokesperson for Scottish independence during its most unfashionable and unpopular phase, which afforded him the ability to scrutinise the problems with British wartime policy and the ordinary concerns of people attempting to survive extraordinary circumstances. He was a dissenting voice during a time when the established position was one of unity and national agreement in the face of foreign aggression and threat. This, of course, may be the very reason why Scottish Nationalists such as Young have been accused of ambivalence towards fascism. Gavin Bowd's reading of correspondence between Young, George Campbell Hay and R.E. Muirhead is that there was a vein of revenge against England running through the letters and a sense of opportunism relating to the furthering of Scottish Nationalism in the wake of a possible

---

The New Alliance and *Scottish Art and Letters* were among the many magazines to which Young contributed work.

6 Young 1942.
7 Mackay 2011: 94.

Nazi occupation[8], although one could also argue that early in the conflict, with the outcome far from clear, these men were attempting to imagine every eventuality and how they would have to adapt to possible momentous changes in the organisation and control of their country. Richie McCaffery has argued convincingly that Young was not attempting to downplay the need for a military response to fascism – 'Instead he wanted to wage an internal war of liberty, bolstered by rhetoric, tracts and poetry, even if this meant a losing battle, an act of martyrdom... Young's 'auld enemy' argument is something of a pose, designed to ignite feelings of Scottish independence and its post-War potential, over demonising England and calling for its ruin.'[9]

It may be that when viewed through this lens, Young's nationalism is not even the most prevalent force in his poetry. Rather, it is his internationalism which provides the most poignant and powerful notes, particularly in his wartime poetry. Young was a scholar at ease in the company of people of many nationalities, conversing with them in their own languages during his Classical research around Europe, and nowhere is this more accurately caught than the 'moment in time' poem, 'After Lunch, Ekali'. This poem centres on 1 September 1939, evocatively describing a late summer afternoon in Greece. Young is sitting with his German hosts when it is announced on the wireless that Germany has invaded Poland. The reactions that follow the announcement both symbolise and anticipate the fracturing of Europe that will ensue.

> *Vous allez revenir après la guerre*,
>   they said, and beamed, but with a hopeless look.
> *En peu de temps*, I answered, *je l'espère*,

From a personal perspective, this poem heralds a disruption in Young's research, as the war means that he can no longer freely travel around the libraries of Europe, studying manuscripts. However, the underlying issues are more far-reaching; the number of languages used in 'After Lunch, Ekali' and the ease in which the voices in the poem understand and are understood in these languages symbolise

---

8   Bowd 2013: 160.
9   McCaffery 2015. I am grateful to Richie McCaffery for allowing me access to his article ahead of its publication. In this article, he provides the first sustained discussion and defence of Young's poetry against suspicions of fascist sympathies.

the lack of borders in Young's vision of Europe and indeed, the world. 'A deep cold gulph has sprung' despite the goodwill shared between Young and his hosts, and by extension, between nations. In the poem, 'Leaving Athens', composed on 2 September 1939, Young cannot help but prophesy what the future may hold – 'Ruin of empires, cities skyward flaring, / massacred millions, mark the march of History' while 'Epilogue to Theokritos' is a deliberately self-conscious monologue about the perceived futility of education and scholarship in a time of war.

> I dinna ken the sense of ma trauchlan
> owresettan thochts frae a by-gane leid
> nou that amang the ruins of Europe
> me and my students micht sune be deid.

The chord of fatalism which is struck in the earlier stanzas of the poem does not pervade in the last stanza. The wrestling with death being likened to struggling with the notoriously difficult 'Antinoe papyrus' shows that Young's joy in intellectual inquiry and learning can never be separated from his overall sense of self.

It could be argued that much more of Young's original poetry and his translations are coloured by European politics and the ever-constant threat of war during this period than is first apparent. In an (unsuccessful) application for the Chair of Greek at the University of Glasgow in 1946, Young rightly intuits that the readers of his application may take a dim view of his, by then infamous, political choices in World War II. He writes

> In view of the possibility that my political activities may be misunderstood or regarded as a disqualification for academic work, I should like to recall that the ancient Greeks were notoriously a politically-minded people, and went so far as to term 'idiots' all those among them who took no part in public affairs. Accordingly some experience of political life may be thought useful to an exponent of Greek culture.
> Further, as the ancient Greeks were especially zealous for Constitutionalism in politics, it may be worth mentioning that my own participation in public life has arisen mainly through my interest in democratic Constitutionalism... Moreover, my

constitutional principles have received widespread public support, reflected partly in Parliamentary elections. In this connection the Regius Professor of Greek in the University of Aberdeen is willing to testify that while I served as his Assistant, I never extended my political activities to the class-room.

Rather on the contrary, I have been accused of extending the class-room into my political activities. When His Majesty's Judges committed me to prison I did not permit that to interfere with my Greek researches, but actively pursued my commentary on Theognis, evidence of which is kindly supplied by the Right Hon'ble Thomas Johnston, at that time H.M. Secretary of State for Scotland, in the accompanying Testimonial.[10]

The reasoning behind this statement could easily be applied to Young's poetic vision, as well as his academic code of practice. To take his words a stage further, Young could be accused of regularly extending poetry into his political activities, particularly in relation to his translations of poetry into Scots. He is certainly not the first poet to mix poetry with political commitment; the Scottish Renaissance poets were well-aware of the power that literary symbolism had had during the 1916 Easter Rising in Ireland, with many of those who participated in the struggle being poets as well as political rebels. McClure has noted that 'the translation of literature is an act in which individual motives are liable to play an important role.'[11] Young's choice of subject in the translations that he published, as well as those translations that have remained unpublished until now, could be interpreted as being political actions in their own right and are far from random 'exercises'. When studied as a complete body of work, they reveal themes of war, loss, injustice and a pervading sense of doom, which are surely understandable responses to living during a time of war. Thus 'Hektor's Twynan frae Andromacha', translated from Homer's *Iliad*, VI, 392-496, takes on a powerful immediacy when it is considered how many wives had to say goodbye to husbands who then never returned from war. Likewise, Young's translation from the *Shi King*, has war and famine as its main focus, a theme and context understood as much by a 20th century readership as it would have been by audiences or readers in the 11th to 7th centuries BC. 'A Mother's Tears' from the Russian of Nyekrasov, with the lines

---

10 National Library of Scotland, MS 29540 f. 126.
11 McClure 2004: 216.

'They can't forget their children's dying / among the battle's bloody maze' is undoubtedly universal in its scope, while his translation from Gaelic of 'Cumha Mhic'ille Chaluim', with its tragedy at sea, could easily be transplanted into a setting in which losses at sea and the constant threat of u-boats were a weekly occurrence.

> From that day of the drowning,
>   lost the boat and the hero,
> Gille Calum, Iain Mor,
>   the young lord, my tale is grievous.

Young also composed wartime verses for publication in magazines such as the *Scots Independent*, which are certainly less literary in their composition but have been included in this new collected edition because they exhibit yet another facet of Young's work. They were clearly never meant to be serious poems in the style of his 'For Alasdair' or 'Dulce et Decorum', which incidentally both deal with the reality of the loss of life during war from a personal and public viewpoint respectively. In contrast, the 'magazine poems' are often irreverent, with a simple metre and rhyme scheme, and deal with subjects and issues that Young has heard on the wireless or read in the newspaper that day. As such, they provide excellent social commentary to the developing war and, after World War II, the machinations of government and local authorities. They also exhibit Young's wickedly humorous side and, in some cases such as 'The Bold Sloganeer', they also show his uncanny ability for political prophesying.

III

When viewing both *Auntran Blads* and *A Braird o Thristles* as complete collections, with interlinking themes and common threads, it becomes apparent that Douglas Young can also be classed as a nature poet. He effectively captures the natural world, its placenames, landscape features and weather. Descriptions of foreign summers and, in a few cases, Scottish summers aside, Young seems to revel mostly in descriptions of wintery landscapes and the autumnal dying back of the year. There may be several reasons for this; the language of Scots, which is the language of choice in a number of his nature poems, is perhaps richest in scope when describing the extremes of weather and season. Words like 'cauldruif', 'wastlan winds', and 'yowden-druft' are remarkably common in Young's poetry and it is perfectly reasonable that it is this sort of favoured vocabulary that informed the type of poetry composed in Scots by Young. He was keen to capture the descriptions of his native countryside in the Scots language, perhaps again strengthening the bond of language and landscape, a skill which the 20th century Scottish Renaissance poets greatly admired in the Gaelic poetic tradition. On a more subtle psychological level, the autumn and winter seasons can reveal far more of the human condition, testing the mettle of ordinary folk who are attempting to make a living off the land, and stripping back the metaphorical layers of personality and character trait to reveal what is at the core. For a poet such as Young, this stripping back is an attractive possibility which can herald a recovery or renewal of what has been lost or forgotten, an attitude which was central to the philosophy of the Scottish Renaissance writers in the 1930s and 1940s, who were effectively calling for a reassessment of Scottish culture, literature and politics. In his 'Ice-Flumes Owregie Their Lades', the stark sublimity of glaciers, with their slow movement and eventual revealing of the long-lost but perfectly preserved bodies of climbers, are used as a metaphor for the state of Scotland and Young's hopes for his country's future.

> Sae sall it be wi Scotland. She was free,
>   throu aa the warld weel kent, a sonsy lass,
> whill whummlet in Historie's flume. But sune we'll see
> her livan bouk back i the licht. Juist byde a wee.

Likewise, in 'Requiem', with its extremes of freezing conditions and stormy weather which 'can whammle the body's bruckil fleur', there is still a 'ruit' which 'bydes stieve i the yird'. Young is conscious that he may be living in Scotland's winter but in this severe landscape he foresees the promise and wisdom of spring.

> the luift carries the seed,
> a braird o bairns renews the true and aefauld breed,
> and memorie lives and grows when aa that can dee is deid.

In his most famous poem, 'Last Lauch', which has inspired the title of this present edition of Young's poems, Young also articulates the constancy and resilience of nature compared with the perceived more fleeting mark of mankind on the world.

> The Minister said it wad dee,
>   the cypress buss I plantit.
> But the buss grew til a tree,
>   naething dauntit.
>
> Hit's growan stark and heich,
>   derk and straucht and sinister,
> kirkyairdie-like and dreich.
>   But whaur's the Minister?

It is a clever poem, despite its apparent simplicity. The features of the minister are mirrored in the 'cypress buss' but it is the bush rather than the minister which prevails, showing Young's respect for nature while also ensuring that the perceived closeness between the natural world and humanity means that Young's nature poems never deal solely with a landscape devoid of people. In a poem such as 'Fife Equinox', Young employs a comment overheard by a servant-girl at Ardlogie, thus populating nature with living voices.

> the wind-faan epples 'll hae to be cuikit
> afore they get waur.
> The plooms are aa wersh, they're that sair droukit
> and clortit wi glaur.

His observational skills can be connected to a tradition of articulating the rhythms of the landscape, including its flesh-and-blood inhabitants, which has Robert Burns as one of its most famous proponents. The use of language used by the Fife farmers and their ilk and the careful descriptions of their everyday experiences in relation to the landscape ensure that the overall execution of Young's poetry is authentic. Like George Campbell Hay, who learned much of his Gaelic from the fishermen of Tarbert, Young gleaned much of his vernacular Scots by working on his uncle's farm in Fife where he and his brother spent all their school holidays. The farm workers spoke nothing but Scots and allowed Young a window into this culture, which he also supplemented with his voracious reading of Scots literature. Thus, Young, in a similar way to Hay, is an observer of life and accessed a number of societal groups which added richness to the portrayal of speech patterns in his poetry. This would not have been difficult for someone like Young who is described by David Murison, in his memoir published in *A Clear Voice*, as 'a polymath...with a fantastically well-stored mind, enriched by the widest reading, constant travel, and contacts with people of all lands and of all conditions...He lived according to Terence's maxim, that he was a man and there was nothing human which did not interest him.'[12] This ability fuels his objective stance, which has its roots in a Classical rather than a Romantic tradition of literature, and is a major characteristic in his work.

Young's objectivity can also be linked to his use of language as he moves between an authentic depiction of the vernacular language of Scots speakers and a more literary, 'plastic' Scots in his work, favoured by writers such as Hugh MacDiarmid. Derick McClure has pointed out that this mixing of plain registers of Scots with synthetic Scots is not particularly surprising – modern poets in other languages are at ease in writing poetry which is linguistically difficult and poetry is never written in the language of popular speech.[13] In his poetry and his other writing, Young is an advocate of synthetic Scots. In his pamphlet, *Plastic Scots and the Scottish Literary Tradition*, he traces the roots of the Scots language, Lallans. This 32 page pamphlet was based on a lecture he gave in Glasgow on 22 December 1946, with Hugh MacDiarmid in the chair. Referring to remarks by J. Logie Robertson (Hugh Haliburton) he writes

> Now, Ladies and Gentlemen, here we are up against one of the worst features of the *Kailyard* mentality, even in its best figures, — the defeatism regarding the potential of Lallans for serious themes and consequent recourse to English.[14]

This attitude towards the Lallans vocabulary is both refreshing and indicative of the techniques he employs in his own work.

> It seems to me ridiculous to restrict oneself to words heard. It is important to keep contact with the living racy language

---

12 Young 1977: 31-32.
13 McClure 2000: 122.
14 Young 1947b: 21.

of all sorts and conditions of Scots, but no literary creator in English, Russian or French would restrict himself to words heard. Words read may be as good as words heard, and even a Methuselah would never hear all the words which are still used. I even adopt words read in a dictionary, or words I make up for myself from Scots and kindred roots by old Scots principles, such as my words "Ice-flumes" for glaciers.[15]

Young elicits excitement and pleasure in his purpose and commitment to restoring Scots to the status of a national language, independent of English, and with the capacity to be linked to other cultures in the process. However, he always remains realistic about the poetry which was emerging from this tradition, avoiding the trap of praising all poetry in Scots simply because it was composed in that language. In his foreword to *Scottish Verse 1851-1951 - selected for the general reader*, he writes that probably only six of his chosen 'cultivators' in the 100 years selection 'are poets in the higher sense'. He lists some more 'good minor poets' and describes himself as 'an accomplished versifier'.[16]

IV

Young's poetry articulates the joy of experience, in both a linguistic and more physical sense. The first poem in *Auntran Blads*, 'Thesaurus Paleo-Scoticus', is both a blueprint and a celebration of his Scottish Renaissance-inspired aims. Language is viewed as a treasure-chest ('ferlies I thocht them') and the simplest of registers (the childhood recollection 'I mind when I was a bairnie') mingles with the ancient Scots of Jamieson's *Dictionary*, which provides Young with the inspiration and resources to birth a living Scots language into being. It may have been a subconscious decision on the part of Young or a fitting coincidence but either way, it is both significant and apt that the first poem in Young's next collection deals with 'ferlies' of a different kind. 'For a Wife in Jizzen', a poem to his wife after the birth of their first child, deals with the mystery of real childbirth, rather than the birth of a language, and by the poet's own admission, this experience is less easy to verbalise – 'whaur ye ha come frae, / whatna ferlies seen?'. It is a woman's country, 'dern frae aa men'.

---

15 Young 1947b: 22-23.
16 Young 1952: 3.

The emergence of a language was perhaps more familiar territory for Young than childbirth and can be closely tied to the friendship between himself and Sorley MacLean and George Campbell Hay; these three writers, amongst others, were part of a second wave of cultural energy, coming after MacDiarmid's first wave in the 1920s. Michel Byrne has emphasised the importance of Young's *Auntran Blads*, which 'highlights the close communication, the support and mutual inspiration binding some of the key literary figures of mid-twentieth century Scotland.'[17] MacDiarmid's poem, 'On Receiving the Gaelic Poems of Somhairle MacLean and George Campbell Hay', composed in 1940 and first sent to Douglas Young, is proof of these close ties but Young's own poetry also provides evidence of the warmth of mutual artistic and socio-political values and holds the key to a fuller understanding of Young's overall belief in the literary potential of Scotland. Young's poetry exudes generosity and inclusiveness in relation, not only to his fellow poets, but other scholars, political figures, and colleagues. He dedicates no less than fourteen of his poems in this collection to friends and associates; this is not including the acrostic poems, which are the most extreme examples of dedicatory poems (and are also proof that Young can be as scathing as he can be kind, if the 'Young Kilkerran' is taken into consideration). However, it is the content of a number of his other poems that reveal Young's far-sightedness regarding the place of his circle of friends in the Scottish literary landscape of the mid-20th century. Coincidentally, this generous attitude extended to a worldwide platform of literature with his dedication to the role he played in PEN, an organisation which was focussed on the bringing together of writers from all countries. David Murison emphasises Young's importance in this organisation when he writes that 'to many a foreign writer...Douglas *was* Scottish PEN'[18]

Young's enthusiasm for a Scottish literati of which he himself was part, is the guiding inspiration in 'Letter to MacDiarmid, 1940'. The poem is little-known, not having been included in either of Young's poetry collections, but it is proof that what can be classed as personal to one man can nevertheless hold universal truths regarding human nature and the creative impulse. It would be unfortunate to depict this poem as simply a window into an elite group of friends or a self-

---

17 Byrne 2002.
18 Young 1977: 21.

congratulatory exercise in literary history, written from the point of view of an insider. It does indeed capture a moment in 1940, when MacDiarmid was welcoming and encouraging the younger poets of the Renaissance into the fold, and Young's poem not only acknowledges this fact but returns the compliment by describing in poetic terms, the excitement that MacDiarmid's poetry had affected in him, specifically reminiscing about his feelings when he first saw *A Drunk Man Looks at the Thistle* in a shop:

> \- and I coft a copy,
> and was kind o dumbfoundert a wee as gin I'd been drinkan
> to see in prent a chiel thinkan as I'd been thinkan,
> to hear at last the authentic voice o Scotland,
> *la voix du sang, de mon sang,*
> and nae the muffin-mouit mummle o Saxonie and Jutland
> that had threepit at me sae lang.

Fittingly, Young's poem has something of the atmosphere of *A Drunk Man* with the late night musings and stream of consciousness of the speaker that characterises MacDiarmid's poem. However, the speaker in 'A Letter to MacDiarmid, 1940' is no drunk man but a decidedly focussed Young after a literary gathering in the city.

> ...The mornan at fowr
>   I was bydan on a train at the Waverley station,
> at Embro, ye ken, eftir lea'an a *soiree*
>   wi Davie and Hay, maist talkan o yersel.

It is possibly an even more self-conscious poem than *A Drunk Man* with Young providing a dichotomy between himself and the sleeping soldiers and sailors in the Waverley waiting-room who were presumably anticipating the train to take them back to their barracks or quarters. When one sailor wakes from his sleep and asks Young for the time, the question triggers a much greater question regarding the state of Scotland for the poet.

> Scotland's been sleepan, that's what's the matter,
> and nou she's in a yirth-mair, the puir dozent cratur.
> But she'll wauk ae day, she'll wauk ae day. I ken by mysel.
> She's warsslan nou, she's waukan nou, at the chappan o the bell.

Young's vision for the future of Scotland is one in which the country finds its own voice and authentic 'language'. He seems to view himself and MacDiarmid as John the Baptist figures, preparing the way for something greater when 'this Not-land, cretinized-sot-land, land fit for heroes, be a land fit for men.' Certainly, his belief that this vision may at least partly lie with the Gaelic poets and the Gaelic language is far from understated, but perhaps the real key to the poem, and by extension, the key to Young's whole vision, is the hope and potential that many voices and many languages can bring to the country. Even in 1940 he was looking past the war to what could come next – a renewed British identity or confidence in a 'land fit for heroes' was not an option for him. He was evading a narrow sense of nationalism in favour of a European-wide vision of multilingual potentials. Bill Findlay has suggested that 'the fruits of [Young's] multilingualism served a nationalist purpose in reasserting Scotland's independent links with the world and demonstrating the potentialities that still resided in Scots as a literary medium capable of translating effectively a variety of languages and writerly styles.'[19] Findlay has likened Young to the 16th century Scots humanists who also made genuine efforts to establish cross-relations with other cultures.[20] It is clear in Young's 'Letter to MacDiarmid, 1940' that his vision, even at this relatively early stage in his work, was going beyond the testing of limits and potential of a Scots language, although that was always going to be an important objective for him. However, on a greater scale, Young seems to be positively encouraging the imbibing of heady languages, perhaps simply in order to see what will come of the experiment.

> When a Scotsman boozes
> siccan a polyphloisboisterous language he uses.
> *Quel* Mischmasch *di luath-bheulachd. Lugeret Democritus.*

It is this tendency towards a playfulness with language and his encouragement for his close literary circle of friends to indulge in this same endeavour, that suggests that Young, even as early as 1940, was capable of transcending serious modernism. There is the possibility that he may have been even more at home in this present postmodern period of Scottish literature, in which minority languages are celebrated and translation can provide potential for

---

19 Findlay 2005: 176.
20 Findlay 2005: 176.

further meaning and possibilities for literature rather than hindering it. This playfulness, inherent in much of Young's work, could only come from being confident and 'undauntit' among many languages and shows the progressiveness of Young's vision and commitment to Scotland's place in a literary world.

Douglas Young: A Biographical Outline

1913 Douglas Young is born on 5 June 1913 at Tayport in Fife, the son of Stephen Young, a jute salesman and mercantile clerk, and his wife, Margaret Smart, *née* Black. He has a brother and twin sisters. His father worked for twenty six years in India and Margaret makes a special trip back to Scotland for the birth of Douglas, on Stephen's insistence that all the children would be natives of Tayport.

1921-1930 He attends Merchiston Castle School in Edinburgh. He has a serious accident which involves a severe head injury. While recuperating, he discovers the delights of reading. In 1929, while at school, he is appointed Company Quartermaster Sergeant of the O.T.C.

1930-1934 He studies Classics at the University of St Andrews. His achievements are considerable; he will earn the Miller Prize for the most distinguished graduate of the year in arts, the Guthrie Scholarship, and the Lewis Campbell Medal for Greek. He also becomes president of the Conservative Club, explaining later that politics had never been taken seriously in St Andrews since the Jacobite Rising of 1715. It is during his time at St Andrews that he also first earns the nickname 'God' or 'the Deity'.

1933 During Eric Linklater's candidature on behalf of the Scottish National Party in an East Fife by-election, Young becomes involved in the campaign. He is also, by this time, president of the Scottish Nationalist Society at the University. He participates in a walking tour through the Dolomites and in July/August he attends the Salzburg Festival.

1934 In June Young is in Munich during the Night of the Long Knives.

1934-1938 He continues his studies at the University of Oxford.

1935 Young joins the Labour Party and helps to canvas for their candidate in a local by-election.

1936 In August Young visits Vienna.

1938 He gains the first Craven Research Fellowship at the University of Oxford.

1938-1941 Despite having the chance to take a teaching post in the USA, remain at Oxford with the Craven Scholarship or work with the archaeologist, Leonard Woolley, in Syria, Young chooses to begin his professional academic career as an assistant in Greek at King's College, Aberdeen, where his fellow assistant is David Murison, later a leading lexicographer in Scotland. This decision is based on his love of teaching the Classics. Between 1935 and 1939, Edwin and Willa Muir are living in Aberdeen and Young spends time with the couple, who read and comment on the poetry that Young is composing.

1939 When Germany invades Poland in September, Young is in Greece. In mid-September he arrives back in Britain. He goes to the Clarendon buildings in Oxford to volunteer to help and is told that being over 25 years of age he is in reserved occupation and can do nothing.

1940 In May Young begins a correspondence with the Gaelic poet, Sorley MacLean, which will continue throughout the years of World War II and beyond. In November, Young goes to Perth to introduce himself to William Souter.

1941 His contract at the University of Aberdeen expires and is not renewed. He is in defiance of the authorities over conscription and lives for some months in Lochwinnoch, Renfrewshire, at Meikle Cloak, the farm of the veteran Scottish nationalist, R.E. Muirhead. During this time he contributes to various periodicals and continues his Greek studies and the composition of verse. He also meets his future wife, Helena Auchterlonie, who was born in South Africa to a Basque mother.

1942 After being tried for refusal of military conscription on 13 April at Glasgow Sheriff Court, Young is out on bail while awaiting his appeal to the High Court. At the SNP annual conference held in May, he is elected to the post of Chairman of the Party. Soon after, his able trial defence fails (published as *The free-minded Scot: Trial and Defence of Douglas Young*) and he is imprisoned in Saughton Jail for eight months. Robert MacIntyre organises a procession with bagpipes to serenade Young at the prison gates. Hugh MacDiarmid is one of the demonstrators.

1943 Young marries Hella Auchterlonie on 24 August. William MacLellan of Glasgow publishes his *Auntran Blads: An Outwale o Verses*.

1944 In February Young contests the Kirkcaldy Burghs by-election. He loses to the Labour Coalition candidate who has 52% of the votes to Young's 42%. In August his daughter Clara is born.

Still Party Chairman, he drafts a statement of Scotland's claim for Dominion status, which the SNP council submit to the Dominion Prime Ministers. A new prosecution is brought against him on the grounds of industrial rather than military conscription and the trial is held at Edinburgh High Court. He is given a prison sentence of three months, serving two.

1945-1946 Young is editor of the *Scots Independent*.

1946 In March, he applies for the Chair of Greek at Glasgow. Among his glowing references from dons at Oxford and St Andrews, is one from Professor Rose, who wrote: 'Mr Young is without exception or doubt the most brilliant student I have ever taught.' Anticipating a lukewarm reception from the University due to his political activities during World War II, he provides a letter of explanation in order to answer expected criticisms. In the event, the Chair is given to A.W. Gomme, a senior member of the Glasgow Classics Department.

In June Douglas and Hella with Clara move from Meikle Cloak, Lochwinnoch, to Ardlogie, by Leuchars, to look after his widowed mother. Their second daughter Joanna is born on 1 September.

1947 The Youngs buy a house in Newington, Edinburgh and enjoy the first year of the International Festival. Almost simultaneously Young is offered lectureships by the Universities of Glasgow and St Andrews – Glasgow offers one in Scottish literature, a new creation. However, he accepts a post in Latin at University College Dundee, then an off-shoot of St Andrews.

After becoming a member of PEN, he attends its conference in Zurich as a representative of Scotland. His *A Braird o Thristles: Scots Poems* is published by MacLellan. Saltire's *Modern Poets Series,* edited by Young and Maurice Lindsay, is also published.

1948 The SNP changes its constitution to exclude members of any other parties from its membership and Young leaves the Party. He canvasses for the Labour Party for 'Barr's Bill'. In the same year he attends the PEN conference in Copenhagen.

1949 The Youngs buy a house in Tayport, re-named Makarsbield. Young attends the PEN conference in Venice, taking time to also inspect some manuscripts of Theognis there.

1950 *Chasing and Ancient Greek: Discursive Reminiscences of a European Journey*, a book about Young's search for manuscripts of Theognis, and the nearest he will come to an autobiography, is published.

1953 He visits Russia with a party of six British writers – supporters of the Authors' World Peace Appeal – at the invitation of the Union of Soviet writers. At Yasnaya Polyana he meets Valentin Bulgakov, Tolstoy's last secretary.

1953-1968 He takes up a post as lecturer in Greek at St Andrews University.

1955 With the retirement of W L. Lorimer from the Chair of Greek, Young applies for the vacancy but is turned down in favour of K. J. Dover.

1957 Young is appointed the Scottish PEN President. He holds the post for four years. In the same year his *The Puddocks: A Verse Play in Scots from the Greek of Aristophanes* is first published.

1958 *The Puddocks* is performed by the students of St Andrews at the Byre Theatre, St Andrews. It is performed at the Edinburgh Fringe later in the year, in the Braidburn Open Air Theatre.

1959 Young composes *The Burdies: A Comedy in Scots Verse by Aristophanes and Douglas Young* for the Edinburgh Fringe. On 25 January, BBC TV broadcasts a special Burns Supper to celebrate the poet's Bicentenary, with Young proposing the Immortal Memory. Later in the same year, he attends the PEN Conference in Frankfurt.

1960 Young is promoted to Senior Lecturer of Greek at St Andrews.

1962 Young's thesis on Theognis earns him the degree of D.Litt.

1963-1964 Young spends a sabbatical year as a visiting professor of Classics at the University of Minnesota. He is invited to give lectures across America to great acclaim and subsequently receives job offers from various universities.

1966 *The Burdies* is revived for the Edinburgh International Festival and performed at the Lyceum Theatre.

1968-1970 In March 1968, one of Young's best books, *St Andrews, Town and Gown, Royal and Ancient,* is published.

After his strong candidature for the vacant Greek chair in Aberdeen is unsuccessful, Young feels free to consider a post further afield. In September 1968, he takes up the post of Professor of Classics at McMaster University in Hamilton, Ontario.

1970-1973 Young becomes the Paddison Professor of Greek at the University of North Carolina at Chapel Hill, canvassing successfully for his successor at McMaster University to be W. J. Slater, his old St Andrews student.

1971 Young hunts manuscripts in Italy, Spain and Greece in relation to his work on Aeschylus. These travels include one memorable visit to Mount Athos with Prof. W. J. Slater.

1973 On 23 October, Young writes home to his wife about arrangements for her to fly to North Carolina in mid-November. Referring to the proposal to cast the words of 'Last Lauch' on a paving slab at a Glenrothes bus stop, he writes, 'Pindar's odes were set up in golden letters on the walls of temples, so I don't see why the Fifers should not have one of mine available to the public gaze, even if underfoot.'

On 24 October, Young dies suddenly; he is found at his desk with his Homer in front of him. A memorial service is held for him at Chapel Hill.

1974 On 12 January, a memorial service is held for Young at the University of St Andrews. Readings at the service include an extract from Plato's Apology of Socrates and two works of Young's – 'The 23rd Psalm O King Dauvit (frae the Hebrew)' and 'Sainless'. The Douglas Young Memorial Volume Appeal Fund is formed. In the same year there is the posthumous publication of *Aeschylus: The Oresteia* (University of Oklahoma Press).

1977 *A Clear Voice: Douglas Young, Poet and Polymath*, edited by Clara Young and David Murison, is published, funded by subscriptions to Douglas Young's Memorial Volume Appeal Fund and the Scottish Arts Council.

This account is based on information kindly supplied by Young's daughter Clara, the 'Memoir' essay by David Murison in Young 1977 and relevant chapters in Young 1950.

A Note on the Text

It has been the aim of the editor to retain the original layout of Young's poems, including notes in Scots and English by Young, which add to the character of the poems and, in some instances, emphasise the poet's humour, political stance and intention. Further editor's notes are included in the separate section following the poems.

Glossaries accompany each of the Scots poems; they are given separately rather than collected into one overall glossary because often the meaning of specific words can vary substantially between poems. In *Auntran Blads* and some of the previously uncollected poems, Young had provided very sparse glossaries compared with the much more detailed ones included in *A Braird o Thristles*, perhaps responding to a readerships' demand for knowledge and appreciation of Scots. The editor has thus expanded the glossaries where appropriate, attempting to provide consistency across all of the poems.

The Dictionary of the Scots Language is available online at www.dsl.ac.uk

Naething Dauntit:

The Collected Poems of Douglas Young

Poems by Douglas Young

Thesaurus Paleo-Scoticus

I mind when I was a bairnie hou ma mither
brocht out ae day a kist o skinklan things,
ferlies I thocht them, ilk mair rare nor anither,
aa kind o gowdies, stanes and chains and rings,
braw orleges that made her guidsire vauntie,
auld fallals that belanged her grannie's auntie.
I thocht ma forebears maun be queens and kings,
sic sma delytes can mak a bairnie canty.

I'm canty yet wi sma delytes, albeid
ma baird's sae black and swack. I ken a thing   10
that's like a kist o ferlies gif ye read.
Frae Jamieson's muckle buik the words tak wing,
auld douce or ramstam, lown or virrfu words,
for musardry o thocht or grame o dirds,
our forebears useit, to flyte or scryve or sing.
I'd wuss to be a falkner o sic birds.

skinklan: glittering *ferlies:* marvels *gowdies:* jewels *orleges:* watches
guidsire: grandfather *vauntie:* proud, boastful *canty:* cheerful *swack:*
abundant *douce:* sedate, sober *ramstam:* rash *lown:* calm, quiet
virrfu: vigorous *flyte:* scold *musardry:* pensiveness *grame:* passion,
rage *dirds:* blows *scryve:* write *wuss:* wish

Traveller's Tale

In Athens once a Macedonian Jew,
going down Statheeoo, said to me, "We Greeks
were famous, great, and civilised, when you
English ran round in rabbit-skins for breeks.
Have you any old building to compare
with our wonderful Parthenon there?"

"Hell's bells," I cried, "don't think I'm any more
a Sassenach than you're an ancient Greek.
In bonny Scotland I could show a score
of brochs as good's your architectural freak.   10
Besides, the Greeks are decadent, but not, –
far from decadent the modern Scot."

(I'm bound to say that I
was telling him a lie.)

(l. 2) *Statheeoo*: a main street in Athens.

The brochs of Scotland seem to me examples of an architecture as remarkable as ancient Greek temple-building, and no more absurd.

Attic Noon

"Bright city, violet-wreathed and songful," chanted
ancient Pindar, – words not vainly vaunted.
   In shattered pediment and riven column
   beauty lingers, intimate and solemn,
purple-shadowed, dapple-lizard-haunted,
cypress-towered, myriad-flower-flaunted.

Thirsty meadows, shrill-cicala-teeming,
marbled screes, loud cataracts white-streaming,
   amethystine heaven's tremulous spaces,
   dark promontories the shining sea embraces,   10
odorous thickets, precipices gleaming:
slumbers the noon, of ancient splendours dreaming.

On the Akropolis at Skoplje, July 1936

Here on the hillside garden the dusk closes;
elderly gardeners shuffle about, watering
green graves of old Turkish pashas among the roses, –
bones and dust after their lust and slaughtering.

Down there in the vaporous street the crowds are strolling
in the evening coolness; a brass band booming and battering
blares on the square by the bridge, where elegant officers are lolling
with their would-be Parisian dames sipping and whiffing and chattering.

With long red fingers caressing, the bright day leaves
that stark fortress piled on its swart precipice,   10
where Serbian serfs skewered the veal and bay-leaves
for epicure pashas, wise in delicate recipes.

The pashas moulder, their vast empire vanished;
their Skoplje castle shelters a Serb garrison;
from the lands of their conquest the conquering race is banished.
(A wandering Scot gets pleasure from this comparison.)

The Shar Planina is pink now, the anonymous eastern highlands'
harsh dun contours flush with the hot sun's flattering.
The Vardar swirls amethystine round shimmering shingle islands
where the hooves of the cavalry rattle, Homerically clattering.   20

From the dim garden of the roses where the twilight glimmers
I see the men and the horses rush into the Vardar's eddying.
The floating manes of the horses and the flash of the splashing swimmers
kindle a tingling excitement that is quite unsteadying.

I must go down from this hill and swim in the swirling Vardar,
Homer's "fair-eddying Axios." Leaving the modern, habitual,
aesthetic, neurotic perhaps, I must seek the older and harder
barbarous primitivity, the swimmer's strengthening ritual.

It is three thousand years from Homer to me, his scholar,
who read him on India paper, an aesthetical Oxonian,   30
in my grey linen trousers and coat, my shirt and my tie and my collar,
him with his wreath and his lyre, a trailing-tunicked Ionian.

But if he were here now, looking down from this hillside garden,
we would both have the same excitement, the heart heavily battering,
the urge to strip and to plunge in the waters that soothe and harden,
to race and shout on the shingle to the rhythm of the hard hooves' clattering.

(l. 17) The Shar Planina is the main mountain range of Macedonia.

Austrian Scene

Grey-green the Danube flows, grey-green the willows
weep on the stream, clear-blue the morning air
shines on the white foam-breaking of the billows
spread from the stern, that wash the shingles bare.
Dark-green on rocky walls the spruces tower,
bright-green the pastures lie, their hay new-mown;
with silver sheen frail birchen stems embower
the gentler slopes with maize and barley sown.
Fast flows the stream, by tower and church and village,
Passau, Linz, Melk down to Vienna's walls;   10
Through forest dark, vine slope, and laughing tillage,
cloisters and castles, woods and waterfalls.

Flow, Danube, flow, of rivers far the fairest
to loveliest lands the traveller thou bearest.

        July 1936, in a Byronic moment on the
Erste Donau Dampfschiffahrtsgesellschaft Steamer.

Austrian Scene.

Grey-green the Danube flows, grey-green the willows
weep on the stream, clear-blue the morning air
shines on the white foam-breaking of the billows
spread from the stern, that wash the shingles bare.
Dark-green on rocky walls the spruces tower,
bright-green the pastures lie, their hay new-mown;
with silver sheen frail birchen stems embower
the gentler slopes with maize and barley sown.
Fast flows the stream, by tower & church & village,
Passau, Linz, Melk, down to Vienna's walls;
through forest dark, vine slope, and laughing tillage,
cloisters & castles, woods and waterfalls.

Flow, Danube, flow, of rivers far the fairest;
to loveliest lands the traveller thou bearest.

    July, 1936. in a Byronic moment on the
Erste Donau Dampfschifffahrtsgesellschaft steamer.

To Gillian in Vienna

    We walked together in the Belvedere,
and glanced at paintings, and I looked at you.
      It was the Orangery of Prince Eugene,
        who strolled there in a wig and with a cane.
    You had no hat, my beard was doubtless queer,
and there was lots to say between us two.

    We saw Cézanne, Renoir. I looked at you.
You said, "Van Gogh has such a sense of line."
      We went into the garden and sat down,
        you gazed at me with a half-smile, half-frown.   10
    I opened my mouth to speak a word or two,
when the porter cried, "Jetzt sollt's geschlossen sein."

And then we went across the Schwarzenbergplatz
and consumed Eiskaffee among the Jews on the Ringstrasse.

On the Death of Wallace Martin Lindsay

I knew that learned man when he was old,
white-haired, but young in spirit. Red ripe cheek,
keen eye, straight back, firm tread would often seek
boulders of Lairig Ghru' and where the cold
spurs of the mountains reach the glittering Spey.
He climbed the peaks, scanned the high eagle-flights,
an eagle among scholars loved the heights,
strong pinions shining in that steepest day.

Much had he travelled in the classic land,
Buchanan's heir, to Milan, Naples, Rome;   10
but our St Andrews was his dearest home.
Witty and earnest, quick to understand –
we mourn him, warm of heart as keen of mind.
Cruel his death, that leaves no like behind.

22 St Giles St. Oxford.   February Midnight.   aetatis 23.

Brown vermouth in a glaucous glass,
and the black peats burning low;
rare cars that in the darkness pass,
foot-steps that come and go,
the policeman stalking slow.
Brown vermouth in a glaucous glass,
the saddest fool that ever was,
and the black peats burning low.

Dimly-mirrored white-panelled wall,
candle-flame and the peat-fire's glow;
on the high green chair a tartan shawl,
ferns, recorders, and row upon row
books, books, my joy and woe.
Dimly-mirrored white-panelled wall,
me restless and lonely in spite of all,
candle-flame and the peat-fire's glow.

~~Sleep now~~...

Unsatisfactoriness of the green-dressing-gown-Weltanschauung.

14

22 St Giles Street, Oxford. February Midnight.

Brown vermouth in a glaucous glass,
   and the black peats burning low.
Rare cars that in the darkness pass,
   footsteps that come and go,
   the policeman stalking slow.
Brown vermouth in a glaucous glass,
the saddest fool that ever was,
   and the black peats burning low.

Dimly-mirrored white panelled wall,
   candle-flame and the peat-fire's glow.   10
On the high green chair a tartan shawl,
   ferns, recorders, and row upon row
   books, books, my joy and woe.
Dimly-mirrored white-panelled wall,
me restless and lonely in spite of all,
   candle-flame and the peat-fire's glow.

Lines on a Gaelic Poet at an Oxford Party

Deòrsa, the peat-fire
that smoulders darkling,
with sudden rapture
flaring and sparkling, –
striving to capture
with quick intuition
the joy of desire, –
tasting forgotten
lang-syne rotten
Makaris' songs, and giving 10
birth to new jewels, dusky resilient
yew-boughs' bright brief corralled fruition.

Wrapped in the breacan waves
blue-green, the Bright of Eye
lives in an older realm
than our dull narrow Scotland of dull slaves.
Banners that flap on high,
trusty sharp sword on thigh,
heart that all danger braves,
skilled hand on helm; 20
galleys of hundred oars,
wrecks on the ocean floors,
blood that the death-wound pours,
glory and doom;
chants that fierce hate inspires,
lilting of dear desires,
croons by the island fires
in the twilit room;
cèilidh and lichtsome dance,
red-brimming wine of France, 30
love and the gallant chance,
splendour and gloom.

Heart-whole he sits, and still,
and smokes and drinks his fill;
sits still and smile serene,
oblivious of the Dean.

Sonnet Peu Probable

A Monsieur et Madame G. G. Garden-Coie, Fionnay. août 1939
An experiment with 'sprung rhythm' *in French*

Je vois les eaux qui se frottent dans le désableur,
   la cataracte de la Drance tombée du Grand Combin,
   à travers ces roches sauvages sous ces énormes sapins,
de sa force élémentaire faisant tumulte d' horreur.
Mais ce chaos s'ordonne, peu à peu la fureur
   du torrent entravé dans le hérissement de brins
   d'acier dur qui pullulent rigides et fins
s'apaise, et la masse en sort uniforme en vigueur.
La brutalité des eaux, adoucie sans peine,
   se rend aux desseins aimables d'électrisation,   10
et peut-être sortira-t-il de l'âme humaine
   un dessin simple enfin pour régler les nations,
qui se plongent maintenant dans tel abîme immonde
où s'étouffera noyé le clair esprit du monde.

After Lunch, Ekali

September 1ˢᵗ, 1939.

Cicalas burst the air, a heat-haze quivers
   on the pale plain, the glittering olive-trees.
The aerodrome vibrates, Mount Parnes shivers,
   the tamarisks squirm like flames waved in a breeze.
In that fierce blaze the scorched rock-garden shimmers,
   even the white verandah dazzles our sight.
We step inside, where Dresden china glimmers
   and ivories gleam in this green-shaded light.

I became peeved outside. Too hot ... As hot as
   Dante's Inferno. Now I can indulge   10
coolly in nick-nacks. Tanagra terra-cottas
   smile from their shelves, archaic vases bulge
seductively. My host displays his treasures, –
   rare coins, fine books, quaint bits of this and that.
We settle down and reminisce of pleasures
   had here and there... But Madame will not chat.

There is an awkward silence. Harsh and tireless
   choirs of cicalas make a shattering din.
Madame is restless, crosses to the wireless,
   twiddles the knobs, and gets, at last, Berlin.   20
𝔐𝔢𝔦𝔫𝔢 𝔈𝔫𝔱𝔰𝔠𝔥𝔢𝔦𝔡𝔲𝔫𝔤 𝔥𝔞𝔟' 𝔦𝔠𝔥 𝔧𝔢𝔱𝔷𝔱 𝔤𝔢𝔱𝔯𝔬𝔣𝔣𝔢𝔫
   𝔡𝔦𝔢 𝔓𝔬𝔩𝔢𝔫 𝔞𝔲𝔰𝔷𝔲𝔯𝔬𝔱𝔱𝔢𝔫. Then 𝔖𝔦𝔢𝔤 ℌ𝔢𝔦𝔩! 𝔖𝔦𝔢𝔤 ℌ𝔢𝔦𝔩!
Did I hear right? Or am I 𝔤𝔞𝔫𝔷 𝔟𝔢𝔰𝔬𝔣𝔣𝔢𝔫?
   This to the Reichstag... Well, it's done in style.

We do not speak, nor look at one another;
   between us now a deep cold gulph has sprung.
My hosts are German... It is hard to smother
   excited words that throng upon the tongue...
Now I am calm, and contemplate a glaucous
   columnar cypress by the garden fence.   30
I hardly hear the individual raucous
   shouts of the Fuehrer, but I know the sense.

My hostess says, **Gott sei Dank! Du bist Schotte.**
  Du bist kein Feind. Technically not so,
in view of 1707, I thought. But not a
  symptom of contradiction did I show.
Vous allez revenir après la guerre,
  they said, and beamed, but with a hopeless look.
En peu de temps, I answered, *je l' espère,*
  And wrote in Doric in their visitors' book: 40

  Κόλπῳ ἐν Ἀδριακῷ καὶ αἱμασιαῖσιν Ἑκάλας
    Σκωτὸς Γερμανοῖν συγγενόμαν φιλικῶς.
  Νῦν δ' ὁ χρόνος δεινός, καὶ ἐπὶ ξυροῦ ἵσταται ἀκμᾶς
    εἰράνα πόλεμός θ' · ἁ δὲ μενεῖ φιλία.

Leaving Athens

2nd September, 1939

Parnes, Pentelikon, Hymettos, glowing
rose-red with sunset, violet waters flowing
   north from the stern, long furrows outward whitening –
this twilit coolness soothes our troubled going.
   Through the hot day new rumours vague and frightening
of ruinous war alarmed us, never knowing.

Now with light hearts our Odyssey is started
into a sea of dangers yet uncharted.
   There may be peace for all the war-storm's blackening.
Remember how Odysseus, lion-hearted,   1
   passed through a hundred perils without slackening,
and found his home as safe as when he parted.

More likely home to ruins. That old jurist
Servius Sulpicius Rufus, as a tourist
   among the wrecks of Greece serenely pondering,
wrote to his Cicero what seemed the surest
   anodyne for his grief. And in our wandering
we have a consolation, not the poorest.

*Nos homunculi indignamur si quis nostrum interiit aut occisus est, quorum
vita brevior esse debet, cum uno loco tot oppidum cadavera projecta jacent?*   2

The carcases of ancient cities lying
may teach a man the smallness of his dying.
   Berlin and Warsaw bombed, and men in chiliads
shattered and choking – legless children crying
   round headless mothers – themes for modern Iliads!
Some gas-blind Homer hymn the bombers' flying!

Horrors may turn to beauty. Not despairing
of human progress, nor too greatly caring
   how soon or how, we watch the myriad mystery.
Ruin of empires, cities skyward flaring,   30
   massacred millions, mark the march of History.
Success will crown at last Man's skill and daring.

Enough of Stoicism, enough of moping.
Enjoy the limestone ridges seaward sloping,
   the moonlit surges and the white gulls' hovering.
After long months' uncertainty and groping
   for peace and safety, now at last uncovering
the face of war we smile and go on hoping.

For Deòrsa and his *Calum Thonder*

There is no poem in language like Deòrsa's poem for Calum,
nothing with that free fresh vivid childlike directness,
the intimate and total apperception of a wondering child.

It gives you all Calum, and all that was ever about him,
night and day on loch and moor, and the home hills,
and all that is there to mould and excite man or boy.

Och, it's just Calum, you said. But Deòrsa, you're in it too.

London Midnight

For Maurice Lindsay

I can't lie still in my bed
   nor sit still in a chair
      nor be in the house at all
since the thought has come into my head
      of moorland and waterfall
   and the hills and the Highland air.

I'll take a stick for the walking,
   the big plaid for the sleeping,
      bread and cheese for the eating.
No English creatures talking,
   but old Gaelic folk to be meeting,
   and mountainy waters leaping.

On ptarmigan-haunted screes,
   lichen and heather and grass,
      I'll sleep at the night's coming,
high and sublimely at ease,
      burns murmuring, winds humming,
   till the grief of the world pass.

Fife Equinox

Ae day and ae nicht a yowden-druft
fae the cauld nor-aist has whusslit and pufft
and blawn the craws about the luft,
blatteran sairlie;
it reeshlit the wuids and gart them shuft
like a breer o barley.

The cypress-busses are aa blawn cruikit,
the greens are as clorty as onie doocot;
the wind-faan epples 'll hae to be cuikit
afore they get waur. 10
The plooms are aa wersh, they're that sair droukit
and clortit wi glaur.

yowden-druft: downwards driving rain-storm   *luft:* the sky, firmament
reeshlit: rustled   *gart:* made   breer: first shoot (of grain)   *waur:* worse
wersh: tasteless, waterlogged   *droukit:* drenched   *clortit:* filthied

December Night: The Aesthete in the House

(23rd December 1939)
For Henry Page III

Outside is cold and rain and gloom;
here warm and calm in the drawing-room.

I'm seeing the things I've seen before:
the red-blue rugs from Mirzapore,
the old red desk with a Chippendale chair,
"The Artist's Studio" of Jan Vermeer,
a Constable landscape with corn and trees,
and the black piano with ivory keys;
the log-fire, soothing to eye and nose,
a crystal vase with a Christmas rose;   10
three swans as lovely as ever was seen, –
mulberry, amber, and aquamarine, –
that float on a round mahogany mere, –
glass birds, wooden water, shining and clear.

The walnut wireless talks of wars,
bombs on Chungking and Helsingfors,
snow and frost on the Maginot Line...
"Wann der Krieg ist beendet wird's gluecklich sein."
"À bas la guerre et le pas de oie.
Tout près du feu c'est mieux, chez soi."   20

Peace and quiet in the drawing-room.
But the rhyme that runs in my head is "Doom".

Ardlogie, Christmas Eve, 1939

The mild midwinter evening ebbs, leaving
wreckage of gold and purple on the hill.
The full round moon sails up from eastward, cleaving
dim veils of star-split cloud, tenuous and still.

Winter has jewels yet, leaf, flower, and berry,
berberis, holly, crab, and many more;
wych-hazels' golden straps, a starry cherry,
primroses, heaths, a purple hellebore.

There's a viburnum by the porch, some vagrant
botanist found in western Yunnan. 10
It's flowering now, exquisitely fragrant,
waxy white umbels, scent of marzipan.

Moon-white the naked beeches tower, wreathing
lichened limbs above the laurel glooms;
beyond the lawn a ground-air faintly breathing
stirs the white torches of the pampas plumes.

About me as I walk an odour lingers
of cypress logs I sawed; the pungent scent
clings in my tweeds, and when I raise my fingers
I get the resinous smell, and am content. 20

Cock-pheasants from the neighbouring pinewood chortle,
a blackbird whistles from the red-twigged lime.
There's enough pleasure here for any mortal
with eyes, ears, nose, this mild midwinter-time.

Winter Pool

The pool in the dark rocks reflects the sky no longer,
   no more ripples with wind, nor mirrors the sunlight flicker
through air-swept fronds of fern. The ice nightly stronger
   settles upon it tight, each morning tighter and thicker.

Brown and flaccid now the polypodies dangle,
   mahogany-red beech-leaves freeze to the ice-cover;
under the clear black ice the pondweed tresses tangle,
   and black-green rotting buds of the waterlilies hover.

Out of the litter of leaves in those slimy dull recesses
   three goldfish glide, torpidly gaping and squinting,   10
to patrol their gloomy world that the prisoning ice compresses.
   I come daily and watch, and am glad at their golden glinting.

Quatorzain in an Entr'acte
His Majesty's Theatre Aberdeen. 2nd February 1940

In the theatre-bar three officers laughing and drinking
   with a party of smart dames, all hearty and tough.
   velvet and khaki, fur and the pleated rough
tartans, and brass stars beside diamonds blinking.

A toast is proposed. The glasses flashing and clinking
   mingle with eyes' gleaming and shrill or gruff
   voices. I look and listen. It's all gay enough.
But some second-sight in my mind has set me thinking.

And if I think it's utterly crushing and shattering.
   Blank lonely women's faces loom in mind...   10
Poisonous seeping vapour, bren-guns pattering...
   Hot-blooded man-flesh broken, choking, blind...
But I echo that mocking toast and the gay chattering.
   "On with the show: Let joy be unrefined!"

Speculation

Gin the firmament was nearer
or the lyft whiles clearer
wald we ken the starns mair certainlie, or less?

Aiblins the universalitie
and unco mathematicalitie
o Astronomie's naebut kenners' pretentiousness.

The wey it is wi men
it's the masses that we ken,
but never ae man kens anither's consciousness.

And why suldna the starns   10
hae ilk their ain harns
and sclents o their ain that we dinna see wi the gless?

lyft: the sky, firmament   *whiles:* sometimes   *starns:* stars   *aiblins:* perhaps   *unco:* unusual, excessive   *harns:* brains   *sclents:* inclinations

The Cat in the Rock-Garden

Ha! the blue trumpets blowing triumphantly,
brilliant, gem-like, blooms of gentian,
and yellow hoop-petticoats poising prettily,
where the white puss wonderingly wanders.

Look! she's away, the white tail waving,
archly bounding on the brown andesite,
red-brown rocks where aubrietias cataract,
pale purple, pink, vivid violet.

Now she pauses and poises a paw
at a flaunting tulip from far Turkmenistan,　　　　10
sniffs the pink daphne from Dolomite screes,
peers in the pool at her own white whiskers.

August Night

What is thatt? What iz it? Swish-swishing about me in the dark,
fluttering and twittering in the hot empty night?
God! I'm sweating, my heart thumps, thumps, and a stark
terror bristles my hair. Christ! let me put on the light.
Hell! It's dazzling, I can't see, it's hellishly bright.
My glasses. Ah, that's better. It's only a bat.
It can't hurt. No need to be in such a fright.
I don't care, I'm going to kill him. I'll squash him flat.

So I got up and took a towel and began swiping crazily
at the maddening creature, and the light swayed dizzily,   10
and the curtains flapped and the papers on the table fluttered
and the bat flew frantically about and shrilly twittered,
and I sweated and swore and got nearly hysterical,
swiped... missed... swiped... missed... and at last by a miracle hit him.

He fell on a shelf, on Farnéll's Pindar,
volume III, and clung a second. I was struck with wonder
at his gleaming eyes and his silk-and-velvety softness.
Then he fell on the rug, dead. With hideous swiftness
the lustre faded off. I felt myself a criminal
when I saw calmly the dusty corpse of the frail animal.   20
Out of the window I threw it with a shuddering horror,
and ran to wash my hands, and there in the mirror
saw my face, and was shocked at my own terror.

Autumn Fire

For Bernard Babington Smith

Day-light-long in the woodland penumbra,
lichened boles of beech and pines columnar,
silver ash and birches gold-autumnal,

I made a fire and tended well his burning,
felled and chopped among the shrubs, returning
loaded high with lilacs and laburnum,

holly and thorn and laurel sharply-cracking,
yellow grass and bronze-brown fronds of bracken,
lest the bright beast should lack his food and slacken

belching gloom and myriad sparks upflinging,   10
till smoke and sweat and odorous mould commingling
set the eyes blinking and the nostrils tingling.

Day-light-long. Now purple dusk. Dull embers
flare fitfully. And my rapt mind remembers
old foliage burned in many sad Septembers.

Letter to Hugh MacDiarmid, 1940

A MhicDhiarmaid, ye wish me and the lave
could come awa up to Whalsay to see ye,
Hay and Davie and Sorley MacLean
and the ither bit sparks i the tail o your comet.
I jalouse it wald be an unco conclave.
Ach anis tha mi coma an Abairdheathain,
this *cnocan*'s owre blate to rin to Mahomet.
Dod, I kenna but what I'ld be feart to be wi ye.
Feart? Why feart? Ye needna wunder
gin ye ken hou a rummle o far awa thunder   10
gies ye whiles an awfu stert.
Your words, your words in black cauld prent
pit me aye in a reid lowe, and the sclent
o your thochts sets me aff on a fearfu gait
o my ain. But nae mine alane. It's a common Fate,
ξυγγενὴς ἀνάγκα, that chaps at my hert
when I read what ye scryve. The Voice o Scotland,
la voix du sang, de mon sang, rairs fae your mou
γηγενεῖ φυσήματι like a lava spew
fae the yirth's guts. The Voice o Scotland,   20
i the lave the thin echo of a half-forgot land,
or the dumb-deid whisper of an absolutely-not-land,
speaks loud and clear in you, καπυρὸν στόμα Μοισᾶν
Ἐσσὶ Καληδονίασ μοῦνοθ καπυρὸν στόμα Μοισᾶν.

Is thon no bonny nou? A compliment fae Theokritos.
"Ye alane are a dry mou o the Scottish Muses."
A loud clear mou, that is. Like your ain quotation
for Deòrsa and Somhairle, (that's Hay and MacLean), –
"*fead chruinn chruaidh Chaoilte.*" Round hard whistle,
καπυρὸν στόμα. *Vive l'entente helleno-celtique.*   30
But I'm nae shair about the *Drunk Man and the Thistle*,
nae καπυρὸν στόμα, nae 'dry mou' thon. The Scottis nation
is nae sae fond o thon Μηδὲν ἄγαν as the ancient Greek.
Puir deevils, they'd nae whisky. When a Scotsman boozes
siccan a polyphloisboisterous language he uses.
Quel 𝕸𝖎𝖘𝖈𝖍𝖒𝖆𝖘𝖈𝖍 di luath-bheulachd. Lugeret Democritus.

Wheesht nou, and I'll tell ye. I heard her speak,
Scotland our mither, through you aamaist alane.

    Here's a story t'ye nou. The mornan at fowr
    I was bydan on a train at the Waverley station,   40
    at Embro, ye ken, eftir lea'an a *soiree*
    wi Davie and Hay, maist talkan o yersel.
    My lane i the dumbdeid I'd made a tour
    o thon fossil capital of an extinct nation.
    Tuim skeleton streets, the lyft murrey,
    the air frore as the Gaelic Hell.
    Deid? Or juist dozent? I thocht to mysel.
    Can oniething reeze them? I thocht to mysel.

    Sae I won to the Waverley waitan-room,
    and sat doun there in a cauldruif gloom,   50
    a wae blae licht and a hantle o stinks,
    wi twa dizzen sodgers around on the binks,
    Chamberlain's conscripts, Joan Tamson's bairnies,
    in ski'an breeks the colour that shairn is,
    and Inglish sailors in navy blue,
    snoran and swytan to gar ye grue.

    I gaed and sat at the muckle table
    whaur a seaman was sleepan, the sort they caa Able,
    (by contrast, nae doubt, wi the naval bosses
    that sit in Wite'all communicatan losses.)   60

    I sat doun there on a chair I found
    and set to readan your *Scots Unbound*,
    (a present o whilk I weel remember
    giean to Deòrsa ae day in December
    fowr year syne. And I'd aislie show it
    set him on to becoman a poet.
    Thon's a thing wi rime but nae reason,
    the makan o Hay in a winter season.)

I the dreich mirk aye the fowk swytit and snored,
and I got aye mair dozent and cauld and bored,   70

when the sailor chiel on the table began warsslan and mutteran
smoorit sabs, as in a yirth-mair, and I heard him stutteran,
The Germans is coman, the Germans is coman.

He warsslit a while wi his feet drumman
on the timmer table, and a whyte faem rinnan
out at his mou, and his face grinnan
wi a frichtenan girn as wan as linen.

I was aye gantan at him there, till a clock beguid to chime,
and he up and speirt at me, *Sy, mytie, wassa time?*

I ettlit sair to tell him, but, Dod, I juist leuch, 80
I gantit aye and leuch, tho I kent weel eneuch.
For a thocht had fillt my heid at thon unco sicht
o the hag-rid sailor, and I ken weel it's richt.

Scotland's been sleepan, that's what's the maitter,
and nou she's in a yirth-mair, the puir dozent cratur.
But she'll wauk ae day, she'll wauk ae day. I ken by mysel.
She's warsslan nou, she's waukan nou, at the chappan o the bell.
The Deil a bell! Whatna bell? Ye're the bell yoursel.

The bell, the bell, that muckle bell, that's chappan aa the while,
it's the bell sall reeze the fowk, the bell o Whalsay isle.   90
Wha's chappan neist time, wha's chappan nou?
Ye've been chappan aa the time wi a muckle-clappert mou.

She'll wauk ae day, she'll wauk ae day. I ken by mysel...
The muckle mou o Whalsay'll be thinkan, *What the hell,
What the hell's he mean wi thon "ken by masel"* ?

Och weel, I'll tell ye. It was juist τοὐμὸν ὄνειαρ ἐμοί
my ain dream to me, when ae day for a ploy
I began to *feuilleter*, 𝔡𝔲𝔯𝔠𝔥𝔟𝔩𝔞𝔢𝔱𝔱𝔢𝔯𝔫, your buiks in a shoppie,—
the *Drunk Man* it was, — and I coft a copy,
and was kind o dumbfoundert a wee as gin I'd been drinkan 100
to see in prent a chiel thinkan as I'd been thinkan,
to hear at last the authentic voice o Scotland,
la voix du sang, de mon sang,

and nae the muffin-mouit mummle o Saxonie and Jutland
that had threepit at me sae lang.

The national subconscious that my Psyche is part o spak
psychosympathetically throu your prentit splairgean,
and doun intil unplumbed deeps my Thumos plungeit back
like a backet intil a well, syne again emergean
brimfou o a life unkent afore. And my saul, that thrillt   110
as in a *viole d'amour* to the *voix du sang*, was fillt
wi a fouth o energie and music and licht o its ain.
In a gless that was derk afore I began to see mysel plain.
My saul warsslit to waukan at sound o your mou, –
Pushkin's Душе настало пробужление
And saw the "*Eidolon o oor fallen race,
           shinin in full renascent grace.*"

Scotland spak to me aamaist alane throu you,–
sinsyne throu Muir, Gibbon, Soutar, - and nou
Somhairle and Deòrsa. But och, – tho I wadna offend ye,–   120
the voice rairan fae your megaphone mou, –
ye ken it yersel, – it's nae the richt sound yet.
It's naebut a kind o subliminal mutteran,
like thon daimonical stutteran I heard frae the sailor
warsslan in his yirth-mair – aa your διάῤῥοια λόγων,
Icelandic and Scots and German and whiles Greek,
Provençal, Chinese, and the lave that ye speak, –
aa your galvanic energie fizzan and sputteran;
I wadna offend ye, I dinna mean you're a failur,
but we maun aye twirl a wee at the whigmaleeries o a radio set 130
till we get loud and clear the richt authentic tone.

And what'll that be, the richt authentic tone
o Scotland's voice? Ye've tellt us yoursel –
"*fead chruinn chruaidh Chaoilte.*" Hard and round,
Caoilte's whistle, – that wheeple-whauples the nou,
whiles, in recorder-notes, like Hay or MacLean,
amang the grand διά πασῶν amphilalous Scotland
plays awa at on the muckle organ that's you.
Ae day, – sune be it! – thon whistle sall sound
a dirlan siren in ilk dozent toun,   140

the Ur-Gaelic *voix du sang* cryan again, –
Hay's *"gach fear a bhith fearail dha fhein,"* –
to reeze the Scottish fowk in city and glen,
reeze them to swink and drink and aiblans think, –
until this Not-land, cretinized-sot-land,
land fit for heroes, be a land fit for men.

Uime sin, MhicDhiarmaid, I'll say with MacGhillEathain,
soraidh leat. Tho I dinna speak wi the tung
my forebears spak, – *mòr mo naire,* – I's remain,
wi you for Alba,   150
    Douglas Young

This verse-letter was offered by me to the Editor not for its intrinsic merits but as a literary-historical document of the Scottish Renaissance of which Hugh MacDiarmid is the begetter or misbegetter. Wishes that it should be published have been expressed by George Hay, Sorley MacLean, Willie Soutar, Sydney Smith, and others. The occasion of its composition (which was accomplished in a couple of hours on 6th May, 1940, at Old Aberdeen) was the receipt of a letter from Hugh MacDiarmid, inviting me and others to visit him at Whalsay in the Shetlands, and enclosing a poem 'On Receiving the First Scottish Gaelic Poems of George Campbell Hay and Somhairle MacGhillEathain'. But there had long been in my mind the notion of executing a parody of the polyglot amorphous outpourings with which the great Hugh had been experimenting increasingly within the last decade, and examples of which had greatly stimulated my attention on their publication in his quarterly *The Voice of Scotland* during 1938 and 1939. Actually my production, as Somhairle MacGhillEathain at once remarked, did not turn out a parody at all. And, in fact, it may be worth mentioning that I had myself quite of my own accord developed a tendency to polyglot versification, some time before I took any heed of MacDiarmid's later poetry. My experiments were doubtless prompted partly by my student occupation of Latin and Greek verse-turning, but mainly, I think, sprang from my frustration in English, a frustration felt also by persons of English blood who attempt to use the modern language for poetry. MacDiarmid is in no need of my humble reinforcement, for he can trade critical punches with any biped or quadruped, but I should like here to record my opinion that these recent polyglot developments, which have bewildered so many admirers of his early lyrics, are not simply *panache*, but are spontaneous manifestations, inevitable, necessary, and, if not exemplary, at least stimulating.

(l. 3) George Campbell Hay and George Elder Davie, 'George the poet and George the philosopher,' as Somhairle says W.B. Yeats would have called them if he had met them in one of the limestone lordly houses.'
(ll. 59-60) The letter was composed at the time when the extent of the Norwegian fiasco was being communicated to the public.
(ll. 65-66) For the literary historian of the future I should mention that George Hay was already an accomplished poet by 1932, but the acquaintance with MacDiarmid's work, formed in December, 1936, stirred him up to performances of novel and striking varieties.
(l. 116-117) A quotation from MacDiarmid's poem, see *Lucky poet,* p.358
(l. 119) By way of supplements to the galvanic influence of MacDiarmid, I was much stimulated in the process of rediscovering Scottish culture by the conversation of Edwin Muir, the novel *Sunset Song* of Lewis Grassic Gibbon, and the writings, and later by the conversation, of Willie Soutar. But this list is not exhaustive.
(l. 133) In the earlier part of this Letter I stated that the Voice of Scotland spoke 'loud and clear' in MacDiarmid. At this stage I compare his utterance to the "atmospherics" of a wireless, Scotland's Voice speaking loudly but helluva confusedly, and go on to state that 'the richt authentic tone' can only be Gaelic, a view in which Captain D.J. Munro heartily concurs. However, I now take leave to say that the insistence on the Gaelic, the whole Gaelic and nothing but the Gaelic is too exclusive. I have become an adherent of Major Sleigh's doctrine that 'Whatever a Scotsman speaks is Scots,' even if it is Latin or Hindustani (my own first speech) – a doctrine to which MacDiarmid by implication subscribes in his anthology called *The Golden Treasury of Scottish Poetry*.
(l. 141) By the word 'Ur-Gaelic' I do not mean the Gaelic of Ur of the Chaldees, though it would not surprise me to find MacDiarmid claiming that those worthies were Gaelophone Culdees from the Urr in Galloway (not failing to note that the word signifies 'water' in the Basque language). Ur here is the German word meaning 'aboriginally ancient, Ogygian'. I suspect MacDiarmid coined '*Ur*-Gaelic' himself and used it in *The Voice of Scotland* whence I adopted it.

lave: rest *unco:* unusual *blate:* timid, shy *whiles:* sometimes *sclent:* inclination, leaning *chaps:* knocks *scryve:* write *dumb-deid:* dead of night *my lane:* by myself *tuim:* empty *lyft:* sky *dozent:* sleepy *cauldruif:* chilly *hantle:* a fair amount, much *gar ye grue:* make you shudder *syne:* back *mirk:* darkness *chiel:* fellow *warsslan:* struggling, wrestling *smoorit:* smothered *beguid:* began *speir:* ask *ettlit:* tried *neist:* next *dumbfoundert:* amazed *threepit:* urgently reiterated *fouth:* abundance *dirlan:* vibrating *aiblans:* perhaps

Sonnet for a Phone-Call

20th August 1940, in time of general apprehension of a German invasion of England

That pleasant voice nearly sawed me asunder.
   A man I knew at Oxford spoke on the phone,
   telling me gossip of some men we'd known
at New Coll., once. Those days seem buried under
layers of thick history now. *D'you know, I wonder,*
   what's come of Hugh? Old Christopher was thrown
   into the show in France, and nearly blown
to smithereens...of course, a fearful blunder.

   That English man's eager confident tone
     shook me a lot. I thought how I alone,   10
of all that friendly crew at the Old College,
   am unimpassioned. Scotland's doom is not
   momently hazardous, and I'm a Scot, –
whatever comfort comes from that self-knowledge.

And yet I think they'd understand my attitude,
not write me down a monster of ingratitude,
   after the full and joyous life I led,
four years, at England's oldest university.
   New College ever, with admirable perversity,
     put up a tablet to its German dead,   20
and may forgive a non-belligerent Scot,
who is, by Scottish lights, a patriot.

To a Friend on a Campaign

Ye're aff and awa, meikle the dreid
   lest the faemen shoot ye.
Ye've taen the warld under your heid
on cauldruif muir and lanely glack,
   and it's dreich without ye.
I'll aye think lang while ye be back.

Merry we hae been thegither,
   mair delyte and lear
frae ye I've had than onie ither
chiel that ever I hae kent.   10
   Nane has come sae near
my ain ingyne's orra sclent.

Ye first outhoundit me to sclim
   our Scottish Helikon,
and shared my ilka ploy and whim
in Gaelic poetry and in Scots,
   forbye kept me on
the anely course for patriots.

I ken that gin I dinna see
   yoursel onie mair   20
the lave o my life canna be
crouse as it has been sae lang,
   blyth and free o care,
like the owrecome o an auld sang.

---

meikle: great *faemen:* enemies *cauldruif:* chilly *glack:* pass *lear:* wisdom, experience *chiel:* fellow *ingyne:* mind *orra:* odd *sclent:* leanings, inclinations *outhoundit:* incited *sclim:* climb *forbye:* besides *anely:* only *lave:* rest, remainder *crouse:* merry

For Alasdair

Standan here on a fogg-yirdit stane,
drappan the bricht flees on the broun spate,
I'm thinkan o ye, liggan thonder your lane,
i the het Libyan sand, cauld and quate.
        The spate rins drumlie and broun,
        whummlan aathing doun.

The fowk about Inverness and Auld Aberdeen
aye likeit ye weel, for a wyce and a bonny man.
Ye were gleg at the Greekan o't, and unco keen
at gowf and the lave. Nou deid i the Libyan sand.   10
        The spate rins drumlie and broun,
        whummlan aathing doun.

Hauldan the Germans awa frae the Suez Canal,
ye dee'd. Suld this be Scotland's pride, or shame?
Siccar it is, your gallant kindly saul
maun lea thon land and tak the laigh road hame.
        The spate rins drumlie and broun,
        whummlan aathing doun.

(l. 16) *the laigh road*: by which the dead travel, very speedily – 'Ye'll tak the high road and I'll tak the low road, and I'll be in Scotland afore ye.'

fogg-yirdit: moss-covered *spate:* flood, swell *liggan:* lying *your lane:* by yourself *quate:* quiet *drumlie:* muddy *wyce:* intelligent *gleg:* sharp, intelligent *unco:* unusual, excessive *lave:* rest, remainder *siccar:* surely

For a Scotsman Slain

In England's hour o need
he quit his greitan bride,
wi youthfu virr and pride
gaed aff and focht and dee'd.

Sick wi despair and grame
tuim day follows day.
Aa we do or say
canna bring him hame.

virr: vigour   *grame:* rage   *tuim:* empty

Dulce et Decorum...

D' ye see thon muckle black angel o Cupar,
a buirdly queyn wi muckle black wings,
standan thonder on a pedestal aside the Fluithers,
to commemorate the laddies and their wasteit lives?

Dod, the sicht o't fair pits ye in a stupor.
They micht hae spent their pennies on a hantle ither things,
thae profiteeran fermers and lairdies, and the mithers
greitan for their sons, and the widdawt wives.

They're geyan orra fowk the buddies o Fife,
mair keen to pit out siller on daith nor on life.　　　　　10

   (l. 3) The Fluithers is a park on the east of Cupar-Fife, so called because sometimes flooded by the Eden.

  buirdly queyn: stately damsel　　*hantle:* a fair amount, much　　*geyan:* considerably　　*orra:* odd　　*buddies:* bourgeoise　　*siller:* money

Carmen In Patriam Suam

Melodiae aptum Abelardie "O quanta qualia sunt illa sabbata"

S   Scotia, patria mea carissima,
       terrarum omnium terra dulcissima,
       de novo liberam te restituere
       laetabor, hoc ego totus in opere.

C   Clara per secula tua progenies,
       patrum nobilium filii nobiles,
       nunquam sunt foediter passi servitium.
       Libertas optimum omnibus premium.

O   Omnibus Calgaci, semper Valesii
       cantetur gloria, Bruxisque splendidi.   10
       Romanos invicem, Saxonas vicimus,
       invicta natio unica fuimus.

T   Tot claris proavis nostri homunculi,
       proh aetas degener, pravi miserrimi.
       Scotorum cordibus quando prefervidum
       ardebit pristinum illud ingenium?

I   Interim nostrum est mentes erigere,
       et totis patriam votis appetere;
       ad regnum Scotiam spreta Britannia
       post longa regredi tandem exilia.   20

A   Ampla potentia, plena fecunditas
       liberam te manent, summa felicitas.
       Libertas sit tibi, paxque perpetua,
       dilecta patria, usque per secula.

For the Old Highlands

That old lonely lovely way of living
in Highland places, – twenty years a-growing,
twenty years flowering, twenty years declining, –
father to son, mother to daughter giving
ripe tradition; peaceful bounty flowing;
one harmony all tones of life combining, –
old wise ways, passed like the dust blowing.

That harmony of folk and land is shattered, –
the yearly rhythm of things, the social graces,
peat-fire and music, candle-light and kindness.   10
Now they are gone it seems they never mattered,
much, to the world, those proud and violent races,
clansmen, and chiefs whose passioned greed and blindness
made desolate these lovely lonely places.

Winter Homily on the Calton Hill

These chill pillars of fluted stone
shine back the lustre of the leaden sky,
stiff columns clustered on a dolerite hill
in solemn order, an unperfected vision
dimly gleaming. Not at random thrown
like old Greek temples that abandoned lie
with earthquake-riven drums. Rigid and chill
this still-born ruin stands for our derision.

A fine fantasy of the Whig literati
to build a modern Athens in our frore islands,   10
those elegant oligarchs of the Regency period,
Philhellenic nabobs and the Scots nobility.
As soon expect to meet a bearded Gujerati
stravaiging in a kilt throu the uttermost Highlands,
or in Princess' Street gardens a coy and blushing Nereid.
Athens proved incapable of such mobility.

Is the thing meaningless, as it is astonishing,
a senseless fantasy, out of time and place?
Apeing foreign fashions is always derisible,
and mimicry, for Plato, was the soul's unmaking.   20
The ruin is symbolic, a symbol admonishing
Scottish posterity. Seekers after grace
must not imitate the outward and visible.
The culture of Athens was a nation's awaking.

Simplon Tunnel

The bens are nae ayebydan. Frost and sun,
   rain and the winds fret doun the proudest hicht.
   See thonder Monte Rosa's massy micht,
whas spelderan snaws skinkle tae mak ye blin'.
Its thretteen thousand feet that rise abuin
   the Val d' Anzasca like a touer o licht.
   sall aa ligg laigh and level. Time sall dicht
the hale warld epple-round or aa be duin.
But Nature's forces wark owre slaw for Man,
   whas life is brief, whilk gars him mak mair speed.   10
     He terraces his roadweys up the glens,
  wins out their ores for steel, brings til ae heid
    their water-pouer, and tunnels throu the bens.
Sall warld-wide peace owretax his hairns tae plan?

spelderan: sprawling *skinkle:* sparkle *ligg:* lie *dicht:* put in order
duin: finished *gars:* makes *hairns:* brains

Epilogue to Theokritos

I dinna ken the sense o ma trauchlan
owresettan thochts frae a by-gane leid
nou that amang the ruins of Europe
me and my students micht sune be deid.

Is it time tint threepan Theokritos
at the King's College in Aberdeen
to thir twa lasses and seeven callants
wi their scrabblan pens and their bricht een?

Whiles they're gleg and whiles dozent,
I crack my jokes to mak them gay,   10
but I dout a wheen o us'll sune be lauchan
wi ither fowk's chafts, as the Greeks say.

What matter a syncopate second aorist
or a variant lection in manuscript C,
Arsinoe's tableau or Simaitha's havers,
when Daith bydes on us momentlie?

Instans tyrannus... But och, why fash
for the waesome war, that doesna inspire us,
nae me oniewey, wi onie rowth o pleasure?
As weel warssle wi the Antinoe papyrus.   20

The first stanza is a metapoiesis of Sorley MacLean's 'Dàin do Eimhir' LV.

trauchlan: struggle, toil *owresettan:* translating *leid:* language *tint:* lost *threepan:* arguing, engaging in controversy *callants:* boys *whiles:* sometimes *gleg:* sharp, intelligent *dozent:* sleepy *a wheen:* a few *lauchan:* laughing *chafts:* jaws (cf. 'laugh on the other side of one's face') *rowth:* abundance *warssle:* wrestle

Sang by the Sea

Nae bore o blue i the lither lyft,
nae gair o blue i the dullyart sea;
eerie and dreich the cluds drift,
dreich and eerie the swaws shift,
and me dowf as a chiel can be.

C'wa, lass, and turn your een on me,
the wints o your een that are bonny blue,
lauchan wi a leam like sun on the sea
fraemang your face's sunbrunt blee,
the twa lauchan starnies I loe.   10

bore: patch, gap *lither:* undulating with dim clouds *lyft:* sky *gair:* patch *dullyart:* dull *swaws:* waves *dowf:* dull, weary *chiel:* man, fellow *wints:* pupils *lauchan:* laughing *leam:* gleam *blee:* complexion *starnies:* stars *loe:* love

Whiles

It's nae juist canny, whiles, readan Plato
or onie ither buik
a young man's een see twa ither een
wi a glamarie luik,
sae's he canna tak tent
what auld Plato meant
for thir een and their glent.

An orra thing tae, at Ochrida or onie place
whaur there's a loch
whiles ye see i the faem o the swaw   10
a shouther or hough,
sae's ye'd aamaist swear
a lass sooms there
i thon gesserant gair.

Ye ken it's by-ordinar, at Sveti Naüm
or in onie skug
whaur fullyerie reeshles, whiles a voice
rouns i your lug
couthy and saft
wi an auntran waft   20
sae's ye think ye're daft.

whiles: sometimes *glamarie:* magic *glent:* gleam *orra:* odd *swaw:* wave *hough:* thigh *sooms:* floats *gesserant gair:* sparkling patch *skug:* sheltered place *fullyerie:* foliage *reeshles:* rustles *rouns:* whispers *lug:* ear *auntran:* occasional

Sabbath i the Mearns

The geans are fleuran whyte i the green Howe o the Mearns;
wastlan winds are blawan owre the Mownth's cauld glacks,
whaur the whaups wheep round their nesties amang the fog and ferns;
and the ferm-touns stand gray and lown, ilk wi its yalla stacks.
The kirk is skailan, and the fowk in Sabbath stand o blacks
are doucely haudan hame til their denners wi the bairns,
the young anes daffan and auld neebours haean cracks.

Thon's bien and canty livan for auld-farrant fermer-fowk
wha wark their lives out on the land, the bonnie Laigh o Mearns.
They pleu and harra, saw and reap, clatt neeps and tattie-howk,   10
and dinna muckle fash theirsels wi ither fowks' concerns.
There's whiles a chyld that's unco wild, but sune the wildest learns
gin ye're nae a mensefu fermer-chiel ye's be naething but a gowk,
and the auld weys are siccar, auld and siccar like the sterns.

They werena aye like thon, this auld Albannach race,
whas stanes stand heich upo the Mownth whaur the wild whaup caas.
Focht for libertie wi Wallace, luikit tyrants i the face,
stuid a siege wi leal Ogilvie for Scotland's king and laws,
i the Whigs' Vaut o Dunnottar testifeed for Freedom's cause.
Is there onie Hope to equal the Memories o this place?   20
The last Yerl Marischal's deid, faan doun his castle waas.

(l. 18) Sir George Ogilvie of Barras held Dunnottar Castle, with Charles II's regalia inside, against the Cromwellian General Monck.

geans: wild cherry trees   *glacks:* passes   *whaups:* curlew   *ferm-touns:* farm-buildings   *lown:* quiet   *skailan:* dispersing   *doucely:* soberly   *daffan:* joking   *canty:* cheerful   *auld-farrant:* sage   *clatt:* hoe   *whiles:* sometimes   *unco:* unusual, excessive   *mensefu:* moderate, well-behaved   *siccar:* sure   *sterns:* stars   *leal:* faithful

Confluence

Yonder a black flood pouring among green beeches,
the deep Don moving in dark lustrous reaches.

At my feet the fresh roaring, the white streaming
of the mill-lade waters tossing and creaming,
from the grey granite mill tumultuously dashing,
in uproarious riot shouting and flashing.

Silently they glide, smoother now, by the springing grasses,
their young turbulence hushes, their brilliance passes,
till quietly, evenly, whispering, sliding on,
they melt as a milky mist in the swart swirling Don.   10

W.B. Yeats

(On reading his *Last Poems and Last Plays*)

An auld man in an auld touer,
a wan warlock wi words o pouer,
with ane maist perfit Art
smurlan his tuim hert.

You were no eagle of the intellect;
as patriot scarce worthy our respect;
aesthete of aesthetes, over-finicky
for men's red-blooded sensuality.
As for your sometimes vaunted aristocracy, –
a pretty pose, an innocent hypocrisy.   10
But for swift swoop and soaring sweep of words
homage be paid in Parliament of Bards
"do 'n iolaire iomaluath," Eagle of Words.

smurlan: devouring imperceptibly   *tuim:* empty

(l. 13) *'do 'n iolaire iomaluath,'* to the multi-swift eagle (a phrase from Sorley MacLean's lyric 'An t-Aigeach' in the long opinionative rant interspersed with lyrics called 'An Cuilithionn'.)

Russian Thought

Some folk seem to be cold inside,
and the fires of their life dwindled,
smothered by greed and fear and pride.

But hope is long and the world is wide.
Dead souls may be re-kindled.

The Roots of Love

Love grows in the heart
as a pine's roots grope through stones.
See them grapple and wrap
and split the strata apart.
The sunlight plays on the bole,
the wind in the branches moans;
there's a stir and a thrill in the sap,
a stir and a thrill in the soul.

May Nocturne

A thrush screams in the night,
for a cat has invaded her nest.
Screams and is silent with fright.
And my heart too is distressed
as I think of that quivering breast
in the dark shrub under the wall,
and the cruel claws.

A Love

It came unsought for, undesired,
and left me unregretted.
A day or two my soul was fired,
but dwindling soon that flame expired,
and my dirige was "Let it".
I'd sooner lie calm and cool.
Why trouble to boil a stagnant pool?

For Willie Soutar — October 1943.

Twenty year beddit, and nou
   the mort-claith.
This suld gar ilk ane grue,
   sic a daith.

Was his life warth livan? Ay,
   siccar it was.
He was eident, he was blye
   in Scotland's cause.

Liggan quate, his hairns were thrang
   for Libertie,
his pen wove thegither sang
   and musardrie.

In the time of tyrants he
   testified truth,
and sae our yirth bydes aye free,
   saut wi fresh youth.

Sic smeddum, kindliness, and wit,
   hope and faith,
   nou that his corp is by wi it,
   outlive daith.

For Willie Soutar, October 1943

Twenty year beddit, and nou
   the mort-claith.
This suld gar ilk ane grue,
   sic a daith.

Was his life warth livan? Ay,
   siccar it was.
He was eident, he was blye
   in Scotland's cause.

Liggan quate, his hairns were thrang
   for Libertie,
his pen wove thegither sang
   and musardrie.

In the time of tyrants he
   testified truth,
and sae our yirth bydes aye free,
   saut wi fresh youth.

Sic smeddum, kindliness, and wit,
   hope and faith,
nou that his corp is by wi it,
   outlive daith.

---

mort-claith: funeral pall *gar:* make *grue:* shudder *siccar:* surely
eident: busy *blye:* cheerful *quate:* quiet *hairns:* brains *thrang:* busy, crowded *musardrie:* meditation *yirth:* earth, soil *smeddum:* courage
corp: body, corpse

D. til H.

I canna woo ye, lass, sae stark
   as I'd be blyth tae woo ye.
I'm unco thrang wi ither wark,
   but when I've time I loe ye.
Ye ken lang syne my normal nature's
   nae infatuate.
I'm owre taen up wi monie maitters,
   fecklie affairs o state.
But ye maun tak what I can spare,
   ae quarter o my hairt,   10
and giff ye think the offer fair
   I'm siccar ye'll be sairt.
Ae pairt belongs my auld mither,
   our countrie's cause has taen
ae muckle quarter aa thegither,
   a wee bit neuk's my ain.
But yet thir fowr pairts mak ae hale,
   and our fowr luves suld mell,
or rin quadriga-like a trail
   couthilie parallel.   20
Ye loe your fowk as I loe mine,
   our countrie equallie,
and thir twa quarters maun combine
   tae mak ae moietie.
Ye hain a wee neuk til yoursel,
   I've feck a rown for you.
Forbye self-likean I dow tell
   ye loe me fond and true.
Aince we hae struck the balance fair
   we's gang our gate throu life,   30
an aesome complementit pair
   a Scottish man and wife.

stark: strong   *unco:* unusually   *thrang:* busy   *loe:* love   *siccar:* sure   *feck:* plenty   *forbye:* besides

For a Wife in Jizzen

Lassie, can ye say
   whaur ye ha been,
whaur ye ha come frae,
   whatna ferlies seen?

Eftir the bluid and swyte,
   the warsslin o yestreen,
ye ligg forfochten, whyte,
   prouder nor onie queen.

Albeid ye hardly see me
   I read it i your een,   10
sae saft blue and dreamy,
   mindan whaur ye've been.

Anerly wives ken
   the ruits o joy and tene,
      the march o daith and birth,
         the tryst o luve and strife
i the howedumbdeidsunsheen,
   fire, air, water, yirth
      mellan to mak new life,
lauchan and greetan, feiman and serene.   20

Dern frae aa men
   the ferlies ye ha seen.

---

jizzen: childbed   *ferlies:* marvels   *warsslin:* wrestling, struggle   *ligg:* lie   *forfochten:* exhausted by struggle   *anerly:* only   *ruits:* roots   *tene:* sorrow   *march:* boundary   *howedumbdeidsunsheen:* sunshine at dead of night   *mellan:* encountering   *lauchan:* laughing   *greetan:* crying   *feiman:* tumultuous   *dern:* hidden, secret

Obair-Bhrothaig

Thar bheanntan na h-Eachdraidh
   thig guth neo-bhàsmhor,
guth ar sinnsearan fearail,
   guth Alba an àrdan,
chuireas gaisge anns an t-sluagh
   tha fo bhreòiteachd an daorsa,
is gu 'n èirich an cruadal
   Alba na saorsa.

There echoes down the centuries
   that Arbroath Declaration,
a call that animates and frees
   the spirit of our Nation,
asserting Scottish Liberties
   against all domination.
Such old heroic memories
   can aid our Liberation.

For D. D-H

Black on whyte i the paper, *Dauvit's deid*,
far frae his hame a man o an auld Scots breed,
but was his fecht that Scotland suld be freed?

He led a squadron fechtan throu the luift
frae Kent and Malta, smeddumfu, skeely, swift,
mellan wi Daith as ane wald tak a gift.

Elbruz and Matterhorn nae mair he'll spiel,
hills o Tirol and Alba kent sae weel,
nor souch owre *canntaireachd* nor dance a reel.

He ettled lang and weel til understand   10
and loe the common fowk o ilka land,
but laithed the murder-mongers either hand.

Hame and wife and bairns and hope o fame
pit past, he focht and dee'd in Freedom's name.
But gif the Scots default on Scotland's claim
sic daiths as his mak moniefauld our shame.

luift: sky *smeddumfu:* spirited *skeely:* skilful *mellan wi:* encountering
spiel: climb *Alba:* Gaelic name of Scotland *souch owre:* sing over
without voicing, hum *canntaireachd:* a syllabic system of noting the
Classical music of the great Scots bagpipe ('Ceòl Mòr' or 'pibroch') *ettled:*
tried, studied *loe:* love *laithed:* loathed *either hand:* on each side *pit
past:* put away *mak moniefauld:* multiply

Requiem

The swaws o the firth whammle and freeze til a wyce daith,
syne lown and douce tyne their micht in a flather o fraith,
but monie waters canna droun luve and faith.

Monie waters wi aa their sound, and the warld's stour,
ramstam rair o the cities, and siller's pityless pouer,
can clort, can brak, can whammle the body's bruckil fleur.

But the ruit bydes stieve i the yird, the luift carries the seed,
a braird o bairns renews the true and aefauld breed,
and memorie lives and grows when aa that can dee is deid.

swaws: waves *whammle:* overwhelm *syne:* then *lown:* quiet *douce:* gentle *tyne:* lose *flather:* foamy pouring *fraith:* froth *stour:* dust *ramstam:* headlong *siller:* money *clort:* dirty *bruckil:* brittle *ruit:* root *stieve:* firm *yird:* earth *luift:* air *braird:* crop, growth *aefauld:* simple, pure

Fermer's Deein

He turns awa frae life,
   frae the sun and the sterns,
wi hardly a word for his wife,
   or a curse for his bairns,
forfochten wi rowth o strife
   and man's puir concerns.

He's tyauvt wi kye and corn
   and scarce thocht why,
aamaist sin he was born.
   Nou Daith stilps by,   10
ohn hope, faith, fear, or scorn,
   fegs, he's blye.

sterns: stars *forfochten:* worn out fighting *rowth:* abundance *tyauvt:* worked hard, been embarrassed *kye:* cattle *stilps:* stalks with long strides *ohn:* without *blye:* cheerful, blithe

Sainless

I hae stuid an hour o the lown midsimmer nicht
til twal o the knock i the leelang glamarie-licht
by the cherry-tree at the midden, luikan aa round.
There's never a steer owreby at the ferm-toun,
the reek gangs straucht i the luift, that's lither and gray,
wi an auntran gair o gowd i the North by the Tay.
The whyte muin owre Drumcarro, the Lomond shawan
purpie i the West, and a lane whaup caaan.

The ither birds are duin, but thon whaup's aye busy,
wi the dirlan bubble-note that maks ye dizzy,   10
the daft cratur's in luve, tho it's late i the year,
aa round Lucklaw he's fleean wi an unco steer.
There's a wheen stots owre i the park by the mansion-hous,
skemblan about whiles, dozent and douce,
and a rabbit nibbles amang our raspberry canes
for aa our wire and our traps and the lave o our pains.

But the feck o the hour I hae gowpit owre the dyke,
taen up wi a sicht thonder that I dinna like,
a day-auld cowt liggan doun i the gress
and the Clydesdale mear standan there motionless.   20
The hale hour she has made never a steer,
but stuid wi her heid forrit, rigid wi fear,
it's a wonder onie beast can haud sae still.
The fermer douts the cowt has the joint-ill,
that canna be sained. Ye'd speir gin his mither kens?
Ay, beasts hae their tragedies as sair as men's.

lown: quiet *knock:* clock *leelang:* livelong *glamarie-licht:* magic light
midden: dungheap *steer:* stir, disturbance *owreby:* over yonder *ferm-toun:* farm-buildings *reek:* smoke *luift:* sky *lither:* softly undulating with clouds *auntran:* occasional *gair:* patch *duin:* finished *whaup:* curlew *dirlan:* vibrating *unco:* unusual, excessive *a wheen:* a few
stots: bullocks *skemblan:* shambling *whiles:* sometimes *dozent:* sleepy
douce: sedate, gentle *for aa:* in spite of all *lave:* rest *feck:* most part
gowpit: gaped *dyke:* wall *taen up:* preoccupied *cowt:* colt *liggan:* lying *douts:* suspects *sained:* healed *speir:* ask

Ice-Flumes Owregie Their Lades

For Archie Lamont

   Gangan my lane amang the caulkstane alps
that glower abune the Oetztal in Tirol
   I wan awa heich up amang the scalps
o snawy mountains whaur the wind blew cauld
   owre the reoch scarnoch and sparse jenepere,
wi soldanellas smoort aneath the snaw,
   and purpie crocus whaur the grund was clear,
rinnan tae fleur in their brief simmer thaw,
and auntran gairs o reid alproses, sweir tae blaw.

   And syne I cam up til a braid ice-flume,   10
spelderan doun frae aff the Wildspitz shouther,
   a frozen sea, crustit wi rigid spume,
owredichtit whiles wi sherp and skinklan pouther
   frae a licht yowden-drift o snaw or hail,
clortit by avalanche debris, gaigit deep
   wi oorie reoch crevasses, whaur the pale
draps o sun-heatit ice ooze doun and dreep
intil the friction-bed, whaur drumlie horrors sleep.

   They say ice-flumes maun aa owregie their lades,
and corps o men win out ae day tae licht.   20
   Warsslan remorseless doun reluctant grades
the canny flumes hain their cauld victims ticht.
   But no for aye. Thretty or fowrty year
a corse may ligg afore his weirdit tide
   and yet keep tryst. Whiles they re-appear
gey carnwath-like the wey the glaciers glide,
whiles an intact young man confronts a crineit bride.

   A Lausanne pastor wi 's Greek lexicon
vanished awa amang the Diablerets,
   syne eftir twenty year the Zanfleuron   30
owregya the baith o them til the licht o day,
   still at the Greekin o't. Twa Tirolese,

faaen doun a gaig, ate what they had til eat,
   scryveit their fowk at hame, and syne at ease
stertit piquet. Baith had the self-same seat
saxteen year eftir, but their game was nae complete.

   In Norroway in Seeventeen Ninety Twa
frae fifty year liggin aneath the ice
   a herd appeared and syne beguid tae thaw
and gaed about as souple, swack, and wyce   40
   as when he fell frae sicht i thon crevasse.
Sae sall it be wi Scotland. She was free,
   throu aa the warld weel kent, a sonsy lass,
whill whummlet in Historie's flume. But sune we'll see
her livan bouk back i the licht. Juist byde a wee.

(l. 24) Professor Forbes o St Andrews was the first prophet anent glaciers' deliveries. In 1858 he foretauld the re-appearance about 1860 o the corps o the 3 spielers lost i the Bossons flume o Mont Blanc in 1820. They were fand in instalments frae 1861 til 1865, 9000 feet frae whaur they had the mishanter, as calculate by Forbes.

(l. 26) In 1914 Sydney King disappearit in Mount Cook, Nyou Zealand, and in 1939 cam out three inches thick.

(l. 27) At Grindelwald a Mr Webster was engulphit on his hinnymune and 21 year eftir gien back til his bydan widdaw.

(l. 28) In 1917 Pastor Schneider gaed aff amang the Diablerets, in 1938 he was dischargit by the Zanfleuron glacier and the fowk kent him by his wordbuik.

(l. 32) In 1919 Peter Freuchen and anither chiel fell intil a crevasse in Tirol, and in 1935 were fand perfitly intact, ilk ane haudan a partlie playit haund o cairts.

(l. 37) This and the airer curious informations I deriveit frae an article in *Chamber's Journal* for August 1942, by Mr Frank Illingworth.

Gin it had been mair circumstantial my verses wald been mair circumstantial tae.

ice-flumes: glaciers *owregie:* give up *lades:* loads *gangan:* going *my lane:* by myself *caulkstane:* limestone *glower:* frown *reoch:* rough *scarnoch:* scree *jenepere:* juniper *smoort:* smothered *auntran gairs:* occasional patches *alproses:* rhododendrons *sweir:* unwilling *blaw:* bloom *syne:* then *spelderan:* sprawling *owredichtit:* wiped over *whiles:* sometimes *skinklan:* glittering *yowden-drift:* down-driving storm *clortit:* filthied *gaigit:* fissured *oorie:* dank *drumlie:* turbidly filthy *corps:* bodies, corpses *warsslan:* moving slowly, struggling *hain:* keep *corse:* animated corpse *weirdit:* fated *tyde:* tide *gey carnwath-like:* exceedingly distorted *crineit:* shrivelled *owregya:* gave up *scryveit:* wrote *beguid:* began *swack:* strong *wyce:* intelligent *sonsy*: well-conditioned, thriving *whill:* until *bouk:* bulk, body

Hielant Colloguy

What can ye shaw me here, i this land o the Scots?
   Breckans and maithie yowes and virrless stots,
   tuim untentit crofts whaur aathing rots.

Is there nae richt fouth o growth by the side o the loch?
   Drains faaen in, parks fuggit and moch,
   wuids clortit wi fozy stumps o birk and sauch.

Whatna larachs are thir wi the nettles atour?
   The hames o a race lang syne had virr and pouer,
   but nou they belang a London capitalist boor.

Whaur are the fowk and the bestial suld be here?   10
   A by-gane Marquis soopit the countrie clear
   a yearhunder syne to gie rowm to the grouse and the deer.

And the drover-lad and the lass wi the milkin-pail?
   They're awa wi the cou and the pleu, the yill and the kail.
   Whaur the Sassenach comes the Hielant fowk maun skail.

But the toun at the heid – it luiks like a place o rank?
   Ou ay, wi a schule, twa hotels, three kirks, and a bank,
   a Masons' Lodge, and a castle let til a Yank.

Are there nae Scots fowk think lang til their ain track?
   An auntran ane i the Gorbals, Detroit, Iraq,   20
   Lagos, or Leeds. But ae day we'll aa win back.

maithie: maggoty *yowes:* ewes *virrless stots:* emasculated bullocks
tuim untentit crofts: empty uncared-for crofts *fouth:* abundance *fuggit:* mossy *moch:* damp *clortit:* filthied *fozy:* putrid *atour:* around *sauch:* willow, poplar *larachs:* ruined foundations *thir:* these *lang syne:* long past, long ago *virr:* animal vigour *soopit:* swept *yearhunder:* century *rowm:* space *yill:* ale *skail:* disperse, leave *think lang til:* yearn for *auntran:* occasional

Last Lauch

The Minister said it wad dee,
   the cypress buss I plantit.
But the buss grew til a tree,
   naething dauntit.

Hit's growan stark and heich,
   derk and straucht and sinister,
kirkyairdie-like and dreich.
   But whaur's the Minister?

lauch: laugh *stark:* strong *heich:* high

A Cameronian Cat

There was a Cameronian cat,
   a-seekin for its prey.
went ben the hoose and catcht a mous
   upo the Sabbath day.

The Elders, they were horrifeed,
...and they were vexit sair:
sae straucht they tuik that wicked cat
   afore the Meenistair.

The Meenistair was sairlie grieved,
   and much displeased did say:
'Oh, bad, pervertit pussy-cat,
   tae brak the Sabbath day !'

'The Sabbath's been, frae days o yore,
   an Insti-tuti-on:'
sae straughtway tak this wicked cat
   tae Executi-on !'

A Ballad o Saughton Jail

Five year owre the sea at the war,
   cam hame and fand his wife
muckin about wi ither men,
   and stickit her wi a knife.

He canna wale is time tae dee.
   The Law maun fix that date.
The sodger lad frae Kennaquhair
   maunna anticipate.

No like a daith i the hospital,
   or daith in a shipwraik,   10
or daith in a bluidy battle,
   this hangin by the neck.

He'll never be his lane again,
   aa his nichts and days.
Twa warders watch his movements,
   coman in relays.

Fornent the coalshed liggs a yaird
   whar twicet a day he's seen,
walkan dullie round and round
   afore their watchfu een.   20

The kind Deputy Chaplain
   comes wi a moist ee.
"Keep your hert up nou, ma son."
   "I'll try it, sir", says he.

I the chaipel swindlers, bigamists,
   pykepooches, gangsters, thieves,
stand up and sing in unison
   what nane o them believes: —

"Can we, whose souls are lighted
  with wisdom from on high,   30
can we to men benighted
  the lamp of life deny?"

The Governer's embarrassed,
  but he maun keep his rules.
The warders aa obey them.
  Justice needs her tools.

They wriest a bit about the job,
  but when it comes their wey
they hae tae mak the best o hit,
  and draw their extra pay.   40

---

stickit: stabbed   *his lane:* by himself, alone   *liggs:* lies

Thochts Anent Bluid and Roses

For Robin Black

'I do believe now that independence would be a material gain, but that is not sufficient justification for Nationalism. A Nationalism founded on reason is a monster, and like all monsters sterile. Self-interest neither gives us the moral right to demand freedom nor the moral force that stultifies all opposition. Only on faith and sacrifice can a working, a practicable Nationalism be founded. Pearse and Connolly saw that, and the Ireland of today is founded on their graves. Scotland has not yet seen it, and is not even fit for freedom.'

James Allan Air

The wee whyte rose o Scotland that braks the hairt
wants bluid, wants bluid, guid bluid, gin we wald sair it.
Afore the freedom o Scotland be won
fouth o bluid maun rin i the cundie,
meikle bluid fraith on the grund.
Sune come the day our Scottish youth
sall tent aince mair this manifest truth.

The fushionless North British that jundie,
hogshouther and strive frae Monday to Monday,
trauchlan aye to plenish their ain bit larder,   10
are gey far ahint in nationalist ardour,
and kenna hou smeddum and aspiration
maun gae to rebigg the Scottish Nation.

The wee whyte rose o Scotland that braks the hairt
wants bluid, reid bluid. Wha nou sall dare it
to pit it to the touch or tine it aa?
That Scotland stand free Scots maun faa.
Yeats, Burns, Montrose, that's three
kent hou to mak a richt rose-tree.

Meikle bluid maun wat the stour,   20
mony a corp turn to manure,
to pit a flourish on the whyte rose-fleur.

sair: serve, preserve *fouth:* flood *cundie:* conduit, gutter *meikle:* a large amount *fraith:* froth *fushionless:* spiritless *jundie:* agitate *hogshouther:* jostle *trauchlan:* slaving *smeddum:* courage *stour:* dust *corp:* body

Thomas Joseph Williams

Nineteen year auld he dee'd for Ireland's cause,
   the unitie and freedom o his nation,
that Irish fowk suld live by Irish laws.
     Gin he were Polish, Czech, or Serb, or Norse,
     the British Press wald adulate the corse
that nou they murder. Clartie hoodie craws
   pike a deid falcon, and vituperation
    may smoor a true-bred patriot's noble desperation.

Nineteen year auld, the British gart him hing,
   a leal sodger o the I.R.A.   10
Fechtan for Ireland's richts he daured his fling
    and shot a policeman. The lave o his fiers
    maun tine in jail the best o their young years.
What wurdie tribute can a Scotsman bring
   tae patriot Irishmen, when sic as they
   canna be found in Scotland, seek as lang's ye may?

Nineteen year auld he owregya fifty year
   that suld been his, the best o his life tae be:
owregya his hopes o gaitheran guids and gear
    tae mak a happy hame tae weans and wife,   20
    'true pathos and sublime human life.'
Owregya aa thir, and saw his dutie clear
   tae dae his bittock, gif need were tae dee,
   and wi his fiers tae mak his ain fowk trulie free.

Aiblins the methods of the I.R.A.
   are brutal, ineffective, and uncouth.
Their amateurish detonations may
    slauchter the innocent and turn til hate
    fowk that wald sympathize wi Ireland's state.
Yet, spite o this, I wald mak bauld to say   30
   their Irish ructions offer us a fouth
   o lear that suld be tentit by our Scottish youth.

Hitler and Churchill send a thousand planes
   til influence the hostile population.
And they hae feck o tanks and armoured trains,
    and battleships and pushionous gas nae doubt.

      The Irishmen maun be content tae shoot.
But tuim metallic potency attains
  nae permanence agin a resolute nation
    o men that seek their ain wi richt determination.   40

Material means are aa a symbol merely,
  a gesture springan frae the herts o men.
Gin men be found that loe their countrie dearly,
    like thae that rose at Easter wi *Sinn Féin*,
      they sall find means tae come by what's their ain.
An ardent will that sees its objects clearly
  can bruik aathing that liggs within its ken,
    revolver, dirk, torpedo, wireless, bomb, or pen.

And action may be negative, as Gandhi
  has shown by passive non-cooperation,   50
a wapin aisy til be learnt and handy,
    for ilka wurdie man maun siccar ken
      what is his place amang the warld o men.
Monkeys, nae men, will aye be playan the dandie,
  nou this, nou thon, wi fashion's variation.
    A true man hains his proper integration.

Sae is it that a proper Irish man
  ettlesna til be British like the lave.
Yearhunders lang the British lain a ban
    on aathing Irish, music, claes and leid,   60
      and socht tae change the ancient Irish breed.
Brak up the stable system o the clan,
  usurped the land and frae the wale o't drave
    the freest o the free and bravest o the brave.

Yearhunders lang, in ilka generation,
  Irishmen, few or monie, rose again
tae rule theirsels, a free and separate nation.
    Whiles daft, whiles brutal tho their gestures seem
      Honour inspired them and O'Rahilly's dream,
thon weel-loed vision gies their animation   70
  til ilka fowk's self-waleit foremaist men, –
    a vision that the dozent Scots yet scarcely ken.

The Irish race breeds hero eftir hero,
  auld Ireland's freedom never wants defence.
But Scotland's umquhile fame has crined tae zero.
    The thristle brairdsna nou, but in its steid
    moch paddock-stolls and fozy buff-baas spreid.
Scotland is guideit by a kind o pierrot,
  Westminster Winston, fou o fause pretence,
  leadan a troupe that want baith honesty and sense.   80

The Irish fecht gangs on. Ours hasna stertit.
  The Scottish nation ligg in apathie,
  nae mindan what we've tint or hou we smertit
    yearhunders lang under Great British rule,
    fushionless, smoort in infamie and dule.
But gif ae day the Scots suld be convertit
  tae fecht, as ithers fecht, for libertie,
  that sall be Scotland's tribute to patriot Irishrie.

(l. 69) O'Rahilly's dream stands for the poem 'Gile na gile' by Egan O'Rahilly (c. 1710), one of the best aisling (vision) poems, where the poet sees Ireland as a beautiful woman, bereft of her husband and subjected to a boor i.e. England, alias Great Britain.

corse: body *clartie:* filthy *hoodie craws:* hooded crows *pike:* peck *smoor:* smother *gart him hing:* make him hang *leal:* loyal *lave:* rest *fiers:* comrades *owregya:* gave up *aiblins:* perhaps *bauld:* bold *fouth:* abundance *lear:* instruction, learning *tentit:* heeded *feck:* plenty *pushionous:* poisonous *tuim:* empty *loe:* love *bruik:* use *liggs:* lies *siccar:* surely *ettlesna:* does not try *yearhunder:* century *leid:* language *wale:* choicest *whiles:* sometimes *ilka fowk:* every people *self-waleit:* self chosen *foremaist men:* leaders *dozent:* sleepy *umquhile:* former *crined:* shrunk *brairdsna:* does not sprout *moch:* damp *paddock-stools:* toadstools *fozy:* putrid *buff-baas:* puffballs *guideit:* governed *tint:* lost *fushionless:* spiritless *dule:* misery

Du Bellay in Fife

Blyth that stravaigs the warld braid and fair,
   his Odyssey, his gowden fleece conquesst,
   and syne wins hame, wi lear and insicht blest,
to bruik the lave o his life wi his ain fowk there.
When sall I see again reek sclim the air,
   wae's me! frae thon wee toun whaur I wald rest?
   What time o year my kailyaird triglie drest
that maks my province, ay, and meikle mair?

Better I like the hous my forbears biggit
than Roman palaces, heich and proudlie riggit,   10
   fine sheep-cropt gerss nor marbles dour and vogie,
the Moutray burn than Tiber's classic tide,
reoch Lucklawhill than Palatino's pride,
   than ocean's saut the clover-parks o Logie.

---

stravaigs: wanders *conquesst:* attained *syne:* then *lear:* wisdom, experience *bruik:* enjoy *lave:* remainder *reek:* smoke *sclim:* climb *triglie:* trimly *drest:* tended *meikle:* much *riggit:* roofed *dour:* harsh *vogie:* brilliant, showy *reoch:* rough

Til the *Andantino* frae Gluck's *Orpheus*

Wha wald hae thocht that gowden hair
could wi its cranglin sae ensnare
een that hae seen its fair beautie's spate rowean doun?
Hou suld it be that twa blue een
aye glent at me wi starny sheen
tho I suld steek baith mine whether eenan or noon?
Naething as saft suld ever be
sae hard as is your ee on me.
Delicatelie kaimit gowden hair
suldna bind about my hairt sae sair.   10
Radiant fair, ye kenna hou ye wound.
Smile nou upo your faithfu chiel,
aiblins yoursel micht ae day feel
hou sair despair ryves leal hairts wi steel-cruel stound.

Gowden as hinny, pure and clear,
smoothly suffusean aa your cheer,
leams your cheeks' blee saftlie sheenan, even and fou.
Shouthers ye hae like mountain snaw
whaur throu the nicht the munerays faa
skinklan sae brilliant bricht starnies aa fade frae view. 20
Deil tak your hinny-gowden blee,
mair wud nor onie bee tae pree.
Snaw nor hail was never half sae cauld
as your shouther i the plaidie's fauld.
Frozen beautie winna thaw tae loe.
Yet I sall be sae bauld as state
ae day ye s' be infatuate.
Crueltie trulie maun thole its fate that is due.

cranglin: winding *spate:* flood, swell *rowean:* rolling *starny:* starry *steek:* shut *eenan:* evening *kaimit:* combed *chiel:* fellow *aiblins:* perhaps *ryves:* tears, rends, impairs *leal:* faithful, loyal *stound:* pain *hinny:* honey *cheer:* face *leams:* shines *blee:* complexion *skinklan:* glittering *starnies:* little stars *wud:* mad, resentful *pree:* sample, (pree a mou:* kiss) *fauld:* fold *bauld:* bold

Reconciliation

There's a steer amang the shadaws
   thrawn by a lowean thocht,
dern weeferty-wafferty shadaws
   flichteriff and aflocht.
A cauldruif savendie thirls them
   wi its grame whytehetlie wrocht,
while the mochy shadaws crine
   and the lowe dwynes to nocht.

steer: stir *thrawn:* thrown *lowean:* burning *dern:* obscure *weeferty-wafferty:* unstable and tenuous *flichteriff:* fugitive *aflocht:* high-flying *cauldruif:* chilly *savendie:* intellect *thirls:* pierces *grame:* passion *whytehetlie:* white-hot *wrocht:* wrought *while:* until *mochy:* dank *crine:* shrivel, disappear *lowe:* fire *dwynes:* dwindles

Luve

   Gie aa, and aa comes back
     wi mair nor aa.
   Hain ocht, and ye'll hae nocht,
     aa flees awa.

hain ocht: keep anything   *hae nocht:* have nothing

On an Auld Map o Scotland

For J.B. Salmond

A seventeenth-century Dutchman made it,
   thon map o Scotland that hings on the waa,
wi its paper runklit and the colours fadeit,
   nae siccar guide til a traveller avaa.

Loch Hew in Assynshire wi Mines o Iron,
   Hilles o Allabaster in easter Rosse,
frigates on the swaws, ilk abbey wi a spire on,
   ilk burgh pentit reid wi a steeple and a cross.

The Orkney isles are aa tapsalteerie,
   the Shetland isles are nae tae be seen.   10
Nae a road, and seldom a toun tae cheer ye,
   but mountains and muirlands and lochs atween.

Amstelodami, apud Joannem Janssonium.
   Ilka gangrel Scot that ever cam
siccar wald hae made a sair pandemonium
   in Jan Jansson's luckenbuith in Amsterdam.

A dheairg amadain, c' a' bheil Inbhiraora?
   Thon's naething like the *frith o the Forth*.
I dinna see Loch Ericht, nor yet Glengarry.
   Ye hae pitten Formartine *owre faur i the North*.   20

Sic a map they carried in their marchin and their campin,
   Cavalier and Roundheid, til Auldearn and Philiphaugh,
wi *Scotia regnum* and the reid lyon rampan.
   Runklit and fadeit, let it hing upo the waa.

---

runklit: wrinkled *siccar:* sure *avaa:* at all *swaws:* waves *tapsalteerie:* upside down *gangrel:* vagrant *luckenbuith:* shop *owre faur:* too far

Sleep saft and sound
  till the dawn o the day:
Weel are ye happit
  and weary wi play:
Lea ither fowk that
  wald sleep gin they may:
Sleep saft and sound
  till the dawn o the day.

Rattons may rin
  throu the waas o the hous;
Be na ye feart
  for the cheep o the mouse;
Keep a calm souch, my bab,
  cannie and douce,
Sae we may rise again
  cantie and crouse.

Wheesht, lambie, wheesht,
  or your faither will swear;
Ye've had your milk nou
  and he's had his beer;
Doors are aa steekit
  and bed-time is here;
Why suld ye fash
      the hale hous
        wi a steer?

Words and Music by Douglas Young.
Designed by George Bain.

Bairn-Music

For Miss F. Marian McNeill

Sleep saft and sound
  till the dawn o the day:
Weel are ye happit
  and weary wi play:
Lea ither fowk that
  wad sleep gin they may:
Sleep saft and sound
  till the dawn o the day.

Rattons may rin
  throu the waas o the hous;   10
Be na ye feart
  for the cheep o the mouse;
Keep a calm souch, my bab,
  cannie and douce,
Sae we may rise again
  cantie and crouse.

Wheesht, lambie, wheest,
  or your faither'll sweir;
Ye've had your milk nou
  and he's had his beer;   20
Doors are aa steekit
  and bed-time is here;
Why suld ye fash
  the hale hous wi a steer?

    happit: wrapped *souch:* murmur, sleep, trance *douce:* gentle, sedate
cantie: cheerful *crouse:* merry *steekit:* shut *steer:* stir, disturbance

On A North British Devolutionary

They libbit William Wallace,
  he gart them bleed.
They dinna libb MacFoozle,
  they dinna need.

libbit: gelded, castrated   *gart:* made

Duncan the Joiner

A ballant o the second sicht

I tell ye a tale o a simmer nicht
   and a ferly that befell
i the mountainous isle o Barra
   amang the Atlantic swell.

The fowk were sittan at *cèilidh*
   in Duncan the joiner's hous,
the young anes flytan and daffan,
   and auld cronies crackan crouse.

Nou Duncan the joiner, the man himsel,
   was a thrawn man, and a queer;   10
he'd a wey wi 'm whiles and a glunsh in his ee
   that wald pit ye under fear.

Thon ae nicht as he sat his lane
   he leuch lang lauchters three,
syne quickly scryveit a braid letter,
   and the saut tear blint his ee.

Syne he cam back to the body o the kirk
   and gya the bit letter til a callant,
a braw young lad, whas name I dinna ken,
   but it's nae needit nou i ma ballant.   20

Laddie, quo he, and the fowk tuik tent,
   it's ye sall post this letter.
It'll bring ye a thing that'll dae ye your time,
   and you'll nae speir eftir a better.

At the mid mirk hour we haud awa hame,
   thon laddie, and myself wi 'm,
and he posts the letter i the reid pillar-box,
   for I was there to see 'm.

The neist ae day, the neist ae day,
   the neist but barely three,   30
he rade on a sheltie, a reoch course beast,
   owre a precipice intil the sea.

And when the fowk pit by their wark
   and ran to sort them out,
whilk was the laddie and whilk was the cuddie
   they sairlie were in dout.

The neist ae day, the neist ae day,
   the neist but barely ane,
frae the undertaker in Glesca toun
   a kist cam owre the main.   40

A braw timmer kist o the elm tree,
   pitten on wi fallals rarely.
They hae scheucht the laddie intil the kist
   and yirdit him hoolie and fairlie.

The laddie had postit the letter that ordert
   his ain kist to be sent to Barra.
To mak siccar I'll timmer't ye up i the Latin:
   Quisdam quaedam futura clara.
Nou I'll lallanise that sae ye'll ken it richt:
There's some fowk whiles has SECOND SICHT.   50

(l. 48) *Quisdam quaedam*: to some people some future things are clear

ferly: marvel   *cèilidh:* conversation with musical and other items
flytan: disputing   *daffan:* joking   *cronies:* boon-companions   *crackan:* conversing   *crouse:* cheerfully   *thrawn:* perverse   *whiles:* sometimes
glunsh: morose look   *his lane:* by himself   *lauchters:* laughs
syne: then   *scryveit:* wrote   *braid:* broad   *body o the kirk:* middle of the gathering   *gya:* gave   *callant:* boy   *speir:* ask   *mirk:* dark   *neist:* next
sheltie: small horse   *reoch:* rough   *course:* coarse   *cuddie:* gypsy word for a donkey, thence generally any small or inferior animal of the equine sort
kist: coffin   *scheucht:* stowed   *yirdit:* covered   *hoolie:* cautiously   *siccar:* sure   *timmer 't ye:* arrange it for you   *lallanise:* translate into what Robert Burns called 'plain braid Lallans', alias 'Braid Scots'

The Ballant o the Laird's Bath

In Switzerland lang syne befell
   a deed o great renoun,
i the Whyte Buik o Sarnen
   was trulie scryveit doun.
Alzellen's Laird rade out his lane
   ae simmer mornan early;
midmaist the wuids of Uri
   he sune gat wandert fairlie.
He's socht the wey baith aist and wast,
   but canna win back hame;   10
the shelt grows mair disjeskit aye,
   the Laird mair wud wi grame.
Near lowsin-time he cam at last,
   aa clortit owre wi stour,
til a bonnie bit hous in a gair o park,
   and breenged intil the bouer.
"Guidwife", quo he, "gae fetch to me
   a tassie o caller wine,
and thraw a fat hen's craig about.
   Alzellen's Laird maun dine.   20
But saft... I pray thee pardon, dame,
   I suldna been sae reoch,
nou that I see your bonnie blee,
   your weel-faur'd breist and hough.
Anither thochtie I hae thocht.
   Fair dame, I'ld speir at thee,
mak het a chaudron o clear watter
   and syne come bath wi me."
The douce guidwife was michtilie fleggit
   at sic an orra demand,   30
the mair that she kent Alzellen's Laird
   was a sair man to withstand.
Nocht answeran him she brocht the wine,
   pit on the pat to boil,
syne threw a pullet's craig about,
   and prayed a prayer the while:
"O Mary, mither o charitie,

>   ressave me frae this shame;
> haud back the Laird frae his intent
>   whill my guidman wins hame." 40
> She's plied the Laird wi monie a tass
>   o the sweet Riesling wine,
> and staad his wame wi dentie meats
>   fit for King Charlemagne.
> Syne she's duin aff his braw sword-belt,
>   wi gentie mien and douce,
> his cordinant shuin and the lave o his claes,
>   and taen them ben the hous.
> He's lowpit intil the warm watter,
>   crouse as the Deil was he; 50
> then bydan on that dame's return
>   he sings fou lustilie.
> Thon randy ballant echoes loud
>   amang the wuids of Uri,
> the guidman's heard it frae the byre,
>   and hame cam he in a furie.
> He's breenged inby wi birsslan baird,
>   swingan his cleaver-axe;
> he's chappit the naukit Laird in twa,
>   and syne in eichty-sax. 60
> The wan watter i the bress chaudron
>   rins reid wi bree o bluid.
> Let that be a lesson to Lairds and the lave
>   nae to get tint in a wuid!

lang syne: long ago *scryveit:* written *his lane:* by himself *shelt:* pony *disjeskit:* fatigued *wud wi grame:* mad with rage *lowsin-time:* end of working day *clortit:* filthied *stour:* dust *gair:* patch *breenged:* rushed *bouer:* women's apartments *caller:* fresh *thraw:* twist *craig:* neck *reoch:* rough *blee:* complexion *weel-faur'd:* well-favoured *hough:* thigh *speir:* ask *fleggit:* startled *orra:* odd *pat:* pot *whill:* until *staad:* stuffed *wame:* belly *duin:* finished *gentie:* elegent, delicate *douce:* sedately *cordinant:* of Cordova leather *lave:* rest, remainder *ben:* inside *lowpit:* leapt *crouse:* merry *tint:* lost

Jessie o Balronald

A Mid-Victorian Romanys

The waas o the muckle haa in Portree
   flattered wi tartans gay,
the candle shene frae the chandeliers
   skinklit as bricht as day.

The knabrie o Skye and the neebour isles
   forgaithert there at the baa;
it's Jessie Macdonald, the lass o Balronald,
   was the fleur amang them aa.

Quhan she cam by and in at the door,
   quhaur bonnie leddies were thrang,   10
dumbfoundert they stuid and spak nae word,
   but luikit at her hard and lang.

Auld chaperone kimmers heeld their clash,
   wi their lorgnettes intil their nieves,
a gesserant stane on ilk whyte finger,
   and bangles round their sleeves.

Ilk gallant lichtliet the lass o his hert,
   tho lang and sair he'd socht her;
his een flew aff and his hert eftir
   to Balronald's luvelie dochter.   20

Then by and cam young Mogstat's laird,
   a bauld and buirdly chiel;
nae siller had he, but a braw philabeg,
   and the ladyes loed him weel.

With ae bauld blenk o his black een
   it's she's beglamoured fairlie;
and ae saft glent o her blue een
   infatuates him sairlie.

He's lowtit laigh and kisst her hand
   and speirt at her to dance;   30
they waltzed awa, and sae began
   monie a strange mischance.

Ye maun ken that auld Balronald the laird
   had nae great tocher to gie;
there cam a rich Sassenach (Couper by name)
   and speirt her cannilie.

Young Jessie was sweir, and the laird was sweir,
   but the siller wan them owre;
it's Couper sall wed her and bed her baith,
   for aa Mogstat may glower.   40

There cam a wild and wintry nicht
   wi a cauld wind straucht frae Hell,
(the Gaelic Hell is cauldruif, ye ken),
   and it blattert lang and snell.

Thon nicht afore her bridal day
   young Jessie was dowie and sad,
playan the piano in her faither's spence,
   hapt wi a silken plaid.

She sang the sang *Mo Robairneach Gaolach*,
   and lang she thocht til her jo,   50
that was owre the Minch in haarie Skye
   ayont the wild swaws' flow.

Mogstat has gaithert three trusty fiers,
   brayn-wud wi luve and grame.
Gin a spindle-shankit Sassenach buddie
   suld bed her I'd think it shame.

They hae taen a birlinn wi saxteen men,
   saxteen that waldna flinch;
they're droukit wi weet o the saut and the sleet
   outowre the gurly Minch.   60

To Harris they wan i the howe-dumb-deid,
   til auld Balronald's haa;
they've breenged inby and fleggit the fowk
   and rave burd Jessie awa.

Aa day they flee outowre the spase
   and win to the Kyle i the mirk,
syne rade the road til Inverness,
   and were weddit there i the kirk;

Nou Maister Couper and auld Balronald,
   wow but they were wud;   70
they were feart to sail the stormy Minch,
   and bydeit on a slud.

I the midst o the meantime the bruit gaed round
   aa owre the Hebrides
that young Mogstat and his wife were awa
   doun til the Antipodes.

Gin ye follow me owre the mapamound
   ayont the braid Equator
by fiery Cancer and Capricorn baith
   I'll tell ye what happent later.   80

They woned richt crouse in a timmer hous
   on what they caa a *station*,
but the young Austrylyuns were sune beglamourit
   wi thon unco infatuation.

Jessie was leal and loed her man,
   and goamedna onie ither;
she'd eneuch to dae wi the gairden and hous,
   and was sune to be a mither.

But her gowden hair and her ransie blee
   and her een sae blue and saft   90
were owre muckle for a neebour fermer,
   and fairlie sent him daft.

I the gloaman he cam wi a trusty fere
   quhan Mogstat was caaan the yowes;
he's taen the lady her lane,
   and he's aff outowre the hills and howes.

Mogstat has lowsit his bluidhound keen,
   and gallops far and fast
i the eerie munelicht throu the *bush*,
   and he wins at them at last.   100

The lady raid midmaist the three,
   he shoots baith left and richt;
and there aside the twa het corps
   he's kisst her i the wan munelicht.

---

flattered: fluttered *knabrie:* gentry *thrang:* crowded *dumbfoundert:* amazed *clash:* gossip *nieves:* fists *gesserant:* sparkling *lichtliet:* spurned *bauld:* bold *buirdly:* stalwart *chiel:* man, fellow *siller:* money *philabeg:* kilt *loed:* loved *blenk:* glance *glent:* gleam *lowtit:* bowed *speirt:* asked *tocher:* dowry *sweir:* unwilling *glower:* frown *cauldruif:* chilly *blattert:* blew boisterously *snell:* cold *dowie:* dispirited *spence:* drawing-room *hapt:* wrapped *lang she thocht til:* much she wearied for *jo:* sweetheart *haarie:* misty *swaws:* waves *fiers:* comrades *brayn-wud:* raging mad *grame:* passion *spindle-shankit:* spindle-legged *buddie:* bourgeois *birlinn:* galley *droukit:* drenched *gurly:* stormy *howe-dumb-deid:* dead of night *breenged:* rushed *fleggit:* startled *rave:* tore *burd:* maiden *spase:* open sea *mirk:* darkness *syne:* then *slud:* calm interval *bruit:* rumour *mapamound:* map of the world, earth's surface *woned:* lived *crouse:* merrily *unco:* excessive *leal:* faithful *goamedna:* did not heed *ransie:* red, sanguine *blee:* complexion *gloaman:* twilight *fere:* companion *caaan:* driving *yowes:* ewes *her lane:* by herself *howes:* valleys *lowsit:* set loose *corps:* bodies

Kintra Couplin

This poem, of which a manuscript has recently been found in a mouldering mansion beyond the Forth, appears to be the original of George Buchanan's Latin epigram, *In Rusticum*.

When he beguid tae chap the wuid
   for winter firin, beech and aik,
Jock Tamson aye was heard tae cry
   Hup! Hup! at ilka dingan straik.
His wife cam by, and speirt him why
   he cried *Hup! Hup!* at ilka hit.
"It helps the wark, and maks me stark
   tae caa the wadge richt up the split."
The neist ae nicht she grupt him ticht.
   "C'wa, Jock, *Hup! Hup!*, and speed the pleu in."   10
"Och, havers, Annie. Juist caa cannie.
   I'm no for splittin. I'm for screwin."

Kintra: country   *beguid:* began   *dingan:* heavy   *straik:* blow, stroke
speirt: asked   *neist:* next

Aisling na h-Alba

For R.E. Muirhead

How shall we adore and adorn thee, Scotland, our mother and bride,
when we, thy lovers, are thy masters, in patriot zeal and pride?
Sorely have they defaced thee, the boors that have held thee in thrall,
entombed thee in slums of cities with squalor and smoke for a pall,
defiled thee with hideous churches and shops upon every side,
smothered thee foully in ragweed and bracken over all.

The day of our future shall come, when we shall ourselves decide.
Sweet springing pastures we'll give thee, and crops upon every side,
fair buildings and fairer people and life fairly planned,
temples of art and science and music on every hand.   10
Such be our masterful zeal and such our patriot pride,
so adoring and adorning our bountiful motherland.

Pious Ejaculation in Aberdeen

We ken we maun hae our ain seuch,
but we dinna ken faur it'll end.

The winnin o siller's nae eneuch,
   drinkin and clappin and sic-like trullerie.
For as muckle's ye may ye canna pretend
   that your life is nae an unco dullerie.
Hopean naething, naething believan,
   menseless and joyless, shaddaws o men...
to live as the feck o fowk are livan
   in Scotland the nou is never eneuch.   10
    We dinna ken faur it'll end,
    but we ken we maun hae our ain seuch.

---

seuch: quest *siller:* money *unco:* excessive *menseless:* without dignity or sense of values *feck:* most part

Eternitie

Whan ye can see a yirdit suin
   wi sichtless een
syne ye'll ken your day is duin
   and ye hae been.

yirdit: buried *syne:* then *duin:* finished

Vishnu

I am the thinker and the thocht,
  the slayer and the slain:
I was, I sall be, but can nocht
  become what I remain.

Duncan the Joiner and the Laird of Jura

The Laird o Jura raised a troop
   o territorial sodgers.
Aa owre the isle he soopit them up,
juist like chookies intil a coop,
   but Duncan's sons were dodgers.

The Laird gaed aff to Dunk himself,
   but Dunkie beguid to scare him
wi a second-sicht tale he had to tell
that in three years' time they'd aa be in hell,
   but for ane that'd tine an arm.   10

In three years' time it aa cam true,
   the waefu proposition.
The Laird's son's slauchter wald gar ye grue,
but Duncan's sons were as guid as new.
   Thon's Hielant superstition!

soopit: swept *beguid:* began *gar:* make *grue:* shudder

Rabbie in Plastics

The Immortal Memory: A Metrical Toast to Robert Burns

There was a lad was born in Kyle,
and still we think it warth our while,
in Greenock, Mandalay, Carlisle,
   New York, and Gaimrie,
to celebrate in formal style
   his daithless memory.

His faither was a Norland chiel,
Yerl Marischal's kin, upricht and leal;
in Charlie's cause he drew the steel
   i the Fowrty-Five;   10
syne 'neath the Whigs' triumphant heel
   he couldna thrive.

His mither's forebears had gainstuid
the warst o Claver's despot muid,
a crouse coorse fowk o Carrick bluid,
   raucle randy,
loed troggin frae the gaugers hid
   and stowps o brandy.

Young Rab was bred on crofts and fairms,
acquent wi aa the season's charms;   20
grew wicht wi pleuman's shanks and arms,
   gawcie and gash;
but kent the cares o annual terms
   and factors' snash.

Wark was a warstle, but the boy
had pleasure frae an auntran ploy:
frae buiks he socht wi eident joy
   wisdom and lair;
nae kiaugh and thrangetie could destroy
   his zeal for mair.   30

His dad respectit education
to raise his bairnies' social station,
and ettled eftir Anglification
   in scrift and voice;
threeped Suddron for their edification
   wi tentie choice.

But Rab was a wanrestfu loon,
and wi his uncle Samuel Broun
fell in wi randie gangrels doun
   about Kirkoswald;   40
syne danced and boozed and daffed around,
   like Auchinleck Boswell.

Tarbowton suin and Irrwin kent
the ramstam Bard's experiment
wi fine MacKenzie sentiment
   and Shenstone's art;
syne Fergusson gae anither sclent
   til his Scottish hert.

His Musie's pouer still embryonic
noo fand in love a potent tonic.   50
Clash o his anters yet is chronic,
   they fash and sate us.
No aa Rab's loves were juist Platonic:
   nae mair were Plato's.

Be thankit for thae bonnie lassies
that gart young Rabbie spiel Parnassus.
His loves cam frae aa kinds and classes,
   a variorum.
In fouth o love-sangs he surpasses
   aa poets afore him.   60

And syne his anters' consequence
brocht in anither influence,
his fecht agains the fause pretence
   o Mauchline Session,
that lichtlied him for want o mense
   and fornication.

This kittled up the Bard belyve:
in raucle Lallans he baud scryve
reuch rantan satires, fowr or five,
   agains hypocrisy: 70
his smeddumfu ingyne gart thrive
   aefald democracy.

A rebel frae the Auld Licht rule,
frae State and Kirk o nyaff and fule,
a rebel frae the Inglish schuil,
   by this reversal
he made his braid Scots tung a tool
   that's universal.

Burns gars dounhauden craturs ken
their independent richts again,   80
gars peoples tak a turn and mend
   frae tyrants' throttling,
maks masses individual men,
   and Scotland Scotland.

The lad was born in Alloway,
his spreit still lowes wi kindly ray:
in Greenock, Carlisle, Mandalay,
   New York, and Gaimrie,
Scots and the lave suld drink this day
   his daithless memory.   90

Notes for 'Sassenachs, Lord Provost of Glasgow and siclike':
(l. 10) *Fowrty-Five*: 1745 Rising
(l.14) *Clavers*: John Graham of Claverhouse, Viscount Dundee
(l. 15) *Carrick*: South Ayrshire
(l. 42) *Auchinleck Boswell*: James Boswell of Auchinleck
(l. 43) *Tarbowton*: where Burns attended a dance class
(l. 43) *Irwin (Irvine)*: the seaport where Burns studied flax-keckling
(l. 45) *Mackenzie*: author of "The Men of Feeling", two copies of which Burns wore out with reading
(l. 46) *Shenstone*: a much publicised English poetaster imitated by Burns
(l. 47) *Fergusson*: the Scots poet whose work inspired Burns to turn from English to Lallans for poetry and on whose grave he erected a headstone.
(l. 73) *Auld Licht*: a narrow, Calvinist sect

Norland: North country   *chiel:* fellow   *leal:* loyal   *gainstuid:* withstood   *crouse:* cheery, proud   *coorse:* coarse   *raucle:* raucous, sturdy   *troggin:* merchandise   *gaugers:* Excise officers   *stowps:* large mugs   *wicht:* stout   *shanks:* legs   *gawcie:* massive and breezy   *gash:* intelligent and talkative   *snash:* abuse   *warstle:* struggle   *auntran:* occasional   *ploy:* frolic   *eident:* diligent   *lair:* learning   *kiaugh:* anxiety   *thrangetie:* having too much to do   *ettled eftir:* aimed at   *scrift:* writing   *threeped:* constantly spoke   *Suddron:* the English of South England   *tentie:* attentive   *wanrestfu:* restless   *loon:* lad   *randie:* debauched and quarrelsome   *gangrels:* vagabonds   *boozed:* imbibed copiously and frequently   *daffed:* sported   *sclent:* slant, direction   *clash:* talk   *anters:* adventures   *gart:* made   *spiel:* climb   *fouth:* abundance   *lichtlied:* slighted   *mense:* good behaviour   *kittled:* tickled   *belyve:* presently   *Lallans:* Burns term for the old literary language employed by the Scots Makars, Court, Parliament, and most of the people in the Lowlands.   *baud scryve:* behoved to write   *reuch:* rough   *rantan:* noisily, jocular   *smeddumfu:* bold and vigorous   *ingyne:* genius   *aefauld:* pure, single-minded   *nyaff:* puny and tiresome person   *dounhauden:* subjected   *spreit:* spirit   *lowes:* burns   *the lave:* the rest

Snaw Thochts

Gangan hamewith throu the snaw
   along the loanie up the brae,
I mindna on the storms that blaw
owre the sea frae far awa,
   but the ingle-lowe whar the bairnies play

Endlins won hame, forfochten sair,
   I finn the cantie bieldit scene,
auld grannie on her elbuck chair
kaiman Clara's gowden hair,
   the babbie sleepan douce and bien.   10

Syne I think on the snaws that flee
   and hameless fowk but hous or hauld,
in China, Russia, Germanie,
wi blitz and blizzard dri 'en tae dee,
   and human charitie gane cauld.

---

gangan: going *loanie:* lane, track *ingle-lowe:* fireplace *forfochten:* exhausted by struggle *cantie:* cheerful *bieldit:* sheltered *kaiman:* combing *douce:* sober, sedate *syne:* then *but:* without *hauld:* refuge, shelter

Thow Thochts

Gairs o green gerss again i the policies,
the frost gies owre its grup o the buddan trees,
ilk bird biggs eident and blyth singan flees.

A couthier sun unsteeks the aconite,
nesh snawdraps keek in bourachs chitteran white,
gowd gawcie crocus lowp wi gleg delyte.

Thon warst o winters has devaald, and here
rowes in belyve the springtime o the year.
Ruits that luikt deid renew their annual steer.

Sae maun it be wi Scotland. Sune or syne   10
this thowlessness maun thow frae her ingyne,
sae rowth o growth sall braird and flourish fine.

gairs: patches *biggs:* builds *eident:* diligent *unsteeks:* opens *nesh:* delicate *keek:* peep *chitteran:* shivering *gawcie:* massive and breezy *lowp:* leap *gleg:* sharp *rowes:* rolls *belyve:* presently *ruits:* roots *steer:* stir, riot *thowlessness:* indolence *ingyne:* mind *rowth:* abundance *braird:* crop, yield

THOW THOCHTS

Bairs o green gerss again i the policies,
the frost gies owre its grup o the buddin trees,
ilk bird biggs eident and blyth singin flees.

A couthier sun unsteeks the aconite,
nesh snawdraps keek in bourachs chitterin white,
gowd gawcie crocus lowp wi gleg delyte.

Thon warst o winters has devaald, and here
rowes in belyve the springtime o the year.
Ruits that luiked deid renew their annual steer.

Sae maun it be wi Scotland. Sune or syne
this thowlessness maun thow frae her ingyne,
sae rowth o growth sall braird and flourish fine.

                    Douglas Young

THOW THOCHTS

Gairs o green gxm gerss again i the policies,
the frost gies owre its grup o the buddin trees,
ilk bird biggs eident and blyth singin flees.

A couthier sun unsteeks the aconite,
nesh snawdraps keek in bourachs chitterin white,
gowd gawcie crocus lowp wi gleg delyte.

Thon warst o winters has devaald, and here
rowes in belyve the springtime o the year.
Ruits that luiked deid renew their annual steer.

Sae maun it be wi Scotland. Sune or syne
this thowlessness maun thow frae her ingyne,
sae rowth o growth sall braird and flourish fine.

                                        Douglas Young

27th March 1947

The Shepherd's Dochter

Written on the occasion described in Fife in 1947

Lay her and lea her here i the gantan grund,
   the blithest, bonniest lass o the countryside,
   crined in a timber sark, hapt wi the pride
o hothouse flouers, the dearest that could be fund.

Her faither and brithers stand, as suddentlie stunned
   wi the wecht o dule; douce neebours side by side
   wriest and fidge, sclent-luikan, sweirt tae bide
while the Minister's duin and his threep gane wi the wind.

The murners skail, thankful tae lea thon place
   whar the blithest, bonniest lass liggs i the mouls,   10
   Lent lilies lowp and cypresses stand stieve,
Time tae gae back tae the darg, machines and tools
   and beasts and seeds, the things men uis tae live,
and lea the puir lass there in her state o Grace.

gantan: yawning *crined:* shrunk *timber sark:* wooden shirt, coffin *hapt:* wrapped *wecht:* weight *dule:* grief *douce:* sober, sedate *wreist:* strain *fidge:* fidget *sclent-luikan:* looking sideways *sweirt:* reluctant *while:* until *duin:* finished *threep:* harangue *skail:* scatter *liggs:* lies *mouls:* clods *lowp:* leap *stieve:* stiff *darg:* day's work

For Edwin & Willa, Bannockburn Day 1947

Far is the flicht frae Prague to canny Fife
Owre the reoch o desperate Germanie,
Reoch as the years bygane since last we three
Enjoyed St Andrews' lown and leisured life.
Dae ye mind o Friday breakfasts and the strife
We aften had afore we culd agree
In auntran blads o verse owerset by me,
Never afore essayed by man or wife?
& twa-three sennichts syne by Lammastide
We met at PEN. Blyth was I at your mood   10
Inspired by livin wi a risen nation,
Livin wi ilka facultie renewed.
Lang life be yours, and lifelang inspiration,
Ambassadors o kindness, Scotland's pride!

reoch: rough   *lown:* quiet   *auntran:* occasional   *blads:* pages, sheets

Naomi Mitchison

Naomi Mitchison, but umquhile Haldane
Ardent, weel-leirit, eident authoress
O monie a buik anent puir fowks' distress,
Massacred Helots, Viennese downtrodden,
Idyllic Gaeldom connached at Culloden,
Maelstrom o Rome in Gaul, ilk pitiless
Imperialism's successive strife and stress
Throu lang yearhunders ragean het and scaldan,
Campioun o aa puir fowk, the fowk at hame
Hae need o ye the maist, douce Scots that want   10
Ingyne and smeddum for self-government,
Smoored wi auld blethers, staad wi caucus cant.
Owre aa the land gar our true word be kent,
Never gie owre assertin Scotland's claim.

umquhile: former *eident:* diligent *connached:* destroyed *yearhunders:* centuries *douce:* sober *ingyne:* mind *smeddum:* courage *smoored:* smothered, covered *staad:* overflowing *gar:* make

Young Kilkerran

Ye are my theme nou, tremble, young Kilkerran,
Outspoken critic o the Plastic Muse,
Uphaulder o reactionary views,
Nicegabbit, nescient, unco sweir to learn,
Green gardener that canna weel discern
Kailyaird frae mountain heather, and eschews
Immortal Phoebus in his tartan trews,
Live Lallan words to you are fremt and dern.
King Alexander Third and Wallace Wight
Engaged your scholartise to mair effect; 10
Research at hame amang your ain fowk's letters
Restored Dunnichen frae owre lang neglect.
Archplastophobe, devall! Your plastic betters
Needna your naggin, for we ken we're richt!

unco: strangely *sweir:* unwilling *dern:* obscure

Maurice Lindsay

Maurice, musician, makar, moniefauld
Anthologies you plan and execute,
Urbane, warmhertit, catholic, astute,
Radiant o hope, wi sweirties unappalled,
In spite o kiaughs and comitees untauld
Castan your nets for renascental loot,
Editor, critic, eident to recruit
Leal Scots for our Kulturkampf, slee and bauld,
I scryve this thrawn acrostich raw on raw
No cataloguan aa the credit due,   10
Dear Maurice, to your zest for tune and rhyme
Scotland's Renaissance awes a feck to you,
Anither Allan Ramsay come in time.
Your wark's weel ruitit, as its fruct sall shaw.

makar: poet   *moniefauld:* multiple   *kiaughs:* anxieties   *eident:* diligent
leal: loyal   *bauld:* bold   *scryve:* write   *thrawn:* perverse   *feck:* most part
ruitit: rooted   *fruct:* fruit

Hugh MacDiarmid

Hou sall a makar makarize your name
Uisdean MhicDhiarmaid, Christopher Murray Grieve?
Greatest o Makars, as the young believe,
Heraud o Scotland's swith renascent fame,
Megaphone that dunnered wide wi clangorous grame
Aa owre the realm wi raucle words to deave
Complacent cuifs and gar half-deid Scots live,
Drastic assertor o our nation's claim,
Isna it time ye practised what ye preach,
Archipoets plasticissime?   10
Renew your neo-Lallans organ-peals,
Μακαρων τὸ πρὶν δὴ τρίσμακάρτατε.
Iconoclast even o your ain ideals,
Dinna get drouned amang your wrecks o speech!

makar: poet *swith:* quickly, rapidly *dunnered:* reverbated *grame:* passion, rage *raucle:* raucous, sturdy *gar:* make

London, 1948

Earth hath not many things to show less fair
   than this far-sprawling city. Blatantly
   the wen of Britain festers, foul to see,
with noisome fumes staining the island air.

Worldwide Finance fixed here its vampire lair,
   as once in Rome, Carthage, Nineveh.
   Behold the debris of Plutocracy,
where German bombs laid Roman ruins bare.

And yet the folk are better than their town,
   adaptable, enduring, cheerful, witty.   10
     And much their need to be. The sands are shifting
   on which was built the Empire's parasite city.
     Let them beware their politicians drifting.
Paralysis can get the best men down.

Ane Acrostich Sonnet in the auld Scots for the Queen's Grace in Embro, on Bannockburn Day 1953

Queemly the Queen fares furth; the pipers play;
Undeemous fowk throngs up the Royal Mile;
Embro salutes in leal auld-farrant style
Elizabeth, "Second to Nane" they say.
Nou comes the Honours Three, in braw display
Effeirandlie brocht furth in proud defile;
Lords bear them nou, that dernit lay lang while,
In symbol of auld Scotland's dowf decay.
Zenith and nadir, fluid and ebb we see
Alternate in mankind's unsiccar fate,   10
But Scotland sall live free gin Scots be leal.
Eftir the Queen's example, dedicate
To serve her fowk, let Scots serve Scotland's weill.
Here's Scotland's Queen, wi aa the Honours Three.

queemly: in serene state *undeemous:* countless *leal:* loyal *auld-farrant:* old-fashioned *effeirandlie:* in due order *dernit:* hidden *dowf:* listless *unsiccar:* insecure

Maister John Knox's First Blast o the Trumpet again the Yerl o Balcarres

My Lord Balcarres, tak tent til your ways.
Quhat means this shameless shaw o braw auld claes?
Ye wad win siller for your neibour kirks.
Ye ettle weel. But are thir godlie warks?
Tae brak the Sabbath wi a fashion-shaw, –
John Calvin wadna likeit this avaa.
Ye wile the fowk in buses frae aa airts
tae gowp at silk-clad gentry playan cairts.
The Deevil's Buiks in wyce Lord Menmuir's hous!
"Ends justifie means," – a Jesuit's excuse! 10
Ahab and Jezebel gaed gawdie dressed,
but no the Twal Apostles, I protest.
Sic volage geegaws Marion Melgund bure,
the bluidie Cardinal Dauvit Beaton's hure.
Mary and Rizzio loed sic vanitie,
and then arch-traitress, Catherine Medici.
My ain three godlie wives, weel-faured o face,
were nae sic trash, but lived in hopes o Grace.
Trumperie frae China, Italy and Paris
suld hae nae rowm in godlie, douce Balcarres. 20
But whatna monstrous sicht, – a "bathing Belle"!
Haud back, guid sirs, – there gants the yett o Hell!

    In May 1954 Lord and Lady Crawford and Balcarres opened their house in Fife with a display of historical costumes in aid of local churches. On seeing the final costume in the series, a Victorian Bathing Belle, an extraordinary vision of the Reformer Knox presented itself to the eyes of the bard.
    (l. 9) John Lindsay, Lord Menmuir, Secretary of State, and Chancellor of the University of St Andrews, acquired Balcarres, and was father of Sir David, known as the Alchemist, 1st Lord Lindsay of Balcarres, father of the 1st Earl of Balcarres.
    (l. 13) Marion Ogilvy, daughter of John, 2nd Lord of Airlie, enjoyed the favour of David Beaton, Abbot of Arbroath, later Cardinal, and was styled Lady Melgund; their daughter, Margaret, had 4,000 merks of tocher on marrying the Master of Crawford. Cardinal Beaton later cursed the Lindsays; the line of his son-in-law, the 10th Earl of Crawford, died out;

and the premier earldom of Scotland eventually passed (1808) to the 6th Earl of Balcarres, descended, through Lord Menmuir, from the 9th Earl of Crawford.

siller: money *ettle:* try *avaa:* at all *wile:* lure, entice *gowp:* gape *wyce:* intelligent *loed:* loved *douce:* sober, gentle *gants:* yawns

A Ballad of the Plockton Hay-Drier

(to be pronounced in West Highland English)

"Using the rain to dry the hay" –
   why, surely, this is queer.
The man that fancies that is fey,
   worse than the Brahan Seer.

It's queer, but you can see it done
   beside the Loch Carron shore.
The driest, sweetest hay is won,
   however hard it pour.

Tom Johnston's busy Lowland brain
   devises cunning ways   10
to make the heavy Highland rain
   an industry that pays.

Now concrete lochs the storms impound;
   they pour down tunnels steep;
electric light and power abound
   the more the heavens weep.

Upon the twisting line to Kyle,
   where Plockton station lies,
the Cuillins in majestic file
   astound the tourist's eyes.   20

But Torquil Nicolson has planned
   a new, more wondrous, sight.
Behold the braw hay-drier stand,
   hued and proportioned right.

Academicians used to limn
   the spikes of Sgurr nan Gillean
beyond the foothills' violet dim
   in sunset's wild vermilion.

Now aesthetes from the Café Royal
   have found a finer theme;   30
the Cuillin background serves as foil
   for Torquil's colour-scheme.

Words fail me to convey each hue,
   each subtlety artistic;
but, pending that enchanting view,
   you'll hear a brief statistic.

A twenty-eight by fourteen feet
   rectangle, seven feet high,
with two days' draught and timely heat
   near two tons hay can dry.   40

So now from June till Martinmastide,
   however hard it pour,
the crofters of Lochcarronside
   their winter feed can store.

More cattle soon will greet our sight,
   more beef, veal, milk, cream, cheese.
Highland and Lowland wits unite
   to win Scots wealth and ease.

Soon harnessed tides may dry, some think,
   seaweed for food as well;   50
and *Celtic Algal Magmas Inc.*
   our dollar trade may swell.

Three cheers for Tom and Torquil then,
   and Highland restoration,
and all the enterprising men
   that serve the Scottish nation.

Garlic in Colinton Dell

For Moray McLaren

Thirty years on: now I tread the same garlic
   on the beech-towered slopes of the Colinton dell:
the tongue of memory seeks a faint far lick
   of that poignant pervasive original smell.

On soaring or sweeping boughs the silky
   soft small beech leaves swell and unfold:
bluebell waves are spattered with milky
   garlic; and who is that fifteen-year-old?

Thirty years on: from afar and asunder
   I gaze on that beardless boy with the bike.   10
Time halts for a moment of intimate wonder
   at the flicker-pattern of like and unlike.

The garlic is potent and now it's evoking
   memories that throng through the lichened boles:
a wee shop by the brig, and illicit smoking,
   and those beezing tuppeny sausage-rolls.

The Fleurs of Embro

The fleurs of Embro sae blythlie leaman
   frae aa the windaes in ilka street,
a blink o springtime in wintry weather,
   they cheer the people in rime and weet.

The curly hyacinth, the purple crocus,
   lent lily buskan her gowden croun,
steer hertsome memories amang the auld fowk
   and howpfu ettlins in lass and loon.

A seekan wind blaws frae aistland Europe
   and smoors the new braird wi icy braith,   10
but hamelie skuggit the fleurs of Embro
   proclaim the simmer and grow in faith.

leaman: radiant   *buskan:* readying   *steer:* stirs   *ettlins:* attempts   *loon:* lad   *smoors:* covers, smothers   *braird:* growth, crop

Van Gogh – *The Starry Night*

(Museum of Modern Art, New York)

Van Gogh paints night with her milky ways.
But how? His gilded stars spin round.
His cypress trees writhe from the ground,
flaunting flames in a black-green blaze.

His cornered moon has her horns askew;
his mountain horizon surges and gushes.
His Milky Way too wrestles and rushes,
like an anaconda in a sea of blue.

Yet amid his tortured star-whirled riot
Van Gogh asserts one element of quiet.   10
From farm lamplight and olive-grove green
a grey church-spire stands up serene.

Passing Poet

Crail Harbour

Ay, shair eneuch, that's Crail ye're seein nou,
the royal and ancient burgh, famed for partans,
wi rowth o pleisur boats the tourists loe.
Its snell Aist wind wad freeze the teuchest Spartans.
Observe the herbour waas Dutch weemen biggit,
Auld crawstept hooses, sclate- or pantile-riggit,
wi braeface gairdens fou o fleurs and kails.
A couthie neuk, hybrid frae *Crawl* and *Trail*.

partans: crabs   *rowth:* abundance   *loe:* love   *snell:* cold   *riggit:* roofed

St Andrews Castle

See here the castel whaur they killed the Cardinal.
The douce Sant Andrews fowk were fair bumbazeit
tae see his Scarlet Eminence's corp
hung like a clout whaur nae lang syne he'd gazeit
upo the burnin o the martyr Wishart.
The auld grey toun sees nae sic ongauns nou.
The modern scarlet gouns the castel sees
belang to students coman tae swot or woo.
They hae pitten electric licht i the Bottle Dungeon;
a caravan city spelders alang the braes;   10
a Sassenach novelist says "This Varsity's chic."
Siccar there's monie a differ frae my young days.
What's cheenged the least is thon Royal and Ancient Howff,
the International Parliament o Gowf.

douce: gentle   *corp:* body   *spelders:* sprawls   *siccar:* surely

Photo from Pitlour Towards East Lomond

They're bonnie bens the Lomonds, Aist and Wast.
I like to see them rise ayont the Howe,
i the 'hint o hairst, whan corn is cut and stackit,
and on the trees the leafs begin tae lowe.
They mind me sair o lang bygane Septembers
on my uncle's ferm on the Riggan, wi its wide view,
whaur I'd lend a hand at the hairst, or gae oot wi a shotgun,
and aye i the Wast we would see the Lomond blue.
Forbye I like tae see a weelkept steadin,
and the muckle trees o the policies roond aboot it,　　　10
and a guid job made o the Howe's braid rowthie acres.
It's a richt braw Kingdom, Fife, and wha's tae dout it?

hairst: autumn　*lowe:* burn (turn red)　*forbye:* besides　*rowthie:* plentiful, abundant

Falkland Palace (floodlit photo)

There's nae place whaur ye can feel the Auld Alliance,
and see it, sae close as at Falkland Palace here,
a French chateau bieldit ablow the Lomonds,
whaur ghaists o historie thrang frae far and near.
The Pictish Yerls o Fife had here their castel,
the race o Macduff, that had the foremaist richt
at the King's crounin at Scone. Syne the Stewarts
biggit it new, wi braw Renaissance slicht.
There's a chalmer thonder whaur James Fift lay deein.
"It cam wi a lass. It'll gang wi a lass," said he.　　　10
But it didna gang wi his ain lass, bonnie Mary.
Queen Anne was the last o the Stewart dynastie.
Lang years the braw auld hoose stuid sair neglectit,
till the Crichton-Stuarts tuik the wark in hand,
and now the National Trust keeps aathing brawlie.
Sic pride and zeal are needit throu the hale land.

bieldit: sheltered　*ablow:* below　*thrang:* crowd　*slicht:* style　*chalmer:* room　*brawlie:* magnificently

Dunfermline Abbey

Dunfermline toun heard auld Sir Patrick Spens
get sailin orders frae an auld King o Scots,
i the intervals o drinkin the bluidreid wine.
Oor Auld Alliance wi France purveyit the tots.
Syne there's the makar Robert Henryson.
He "tuik ane drink his spreitis tae confort,"
and screivit the fable o the toun and kintra mice.
But Andrew Carnegie was a chiel o a different sort.
He lichtlied wine and poesie, and sailed the Atlantic,
ingaithered millions o dollars, and gae them awa.   10
He wrocht for peace, and spent his siller for culture, –
the Scots Universities tae. Wasna that braw?
It's a right royal burgh, Dunfermline. A Queen frae Hungarie,
Sant Margaret, inspireit thir Abbey waas,
whaur ligg the banes o Scotland's best king ever.
Duis onie ettle tae serve the Bruce's cause?

makar: poet *screivit:* wrote *chiel:* fellow *lichtlied:* spurned *siller:* money *ligg:* lie *ettle:* try

St Andrews Castle

The waves' unwearied washing on the walls
   whose random ruins into greensward glide;
   towers on the promontory above the tide;
   calm havens where unnumbered sea-brids ride.
Though fallen low the grandeur of its halls
   I love this castle in its shattered pride.

Grey arch of sky, grey leagues of ocean-swell,
   green sweeps of turf and shining links of sand
   where mirrored sunset lingers; rising grand
   Sidlaws and Grampians; that long pebbled strand   10
below the Kinkell braes: I knew not well
   until I left how much I love this land.

2: Political and Social Comment in Verse Form by Douglas Young

Scotlann, Awauk

(to be sung by the Scottish people at the storming of the new Calton jail)

Scotlann, awauk, be again a nation,
   win back thy walth an thy libertie.
Shak aff the chains o the dominatioun
   o Lunnon toun an the bourgeoisie.
Tak in thy haunds thine ain salvatioun,
   rich, proud, an free, rich, proud, an free.

The maisters' greed hauds doun the masses,
   but they are few, no few are ye;
the Lunnon boss your wealth amasses;
   he profiteers frae your miserie.   10
Scotsmen, unite, a' creeds an classes,
   an be aince mair rich, proud, an free.

Five million fowk, frae the desolatioun
   o Lallan slum an Hielant muir,
tae rule yoursels is the ae foundatioun
   o walth for a'. Why are ye puir?
Your haunds an brains can rebigg the natioun.
   Scotlann's your hope. Your hope is sure.

Scotland's Complaynt to his Mistress Industry

Tae the tune, "Hoo can ye gang, lassie?"

Scotland: O hoo can ye gang, lassie, hoo can ye gang?
O hoo can ye gang for tae leave me?
By drifting tae the South ye are daen me muckle wrang.
and nae benefits comeback tae relieve me.

Industry: O ye're a feckless mannikie. That's why I'se gang.
Ye winna mak a stir for tae loe me.
The Lunnon lads are rich, but I'se nae byde there for lang,
gin ye wad but tak tent for tae woo me.

Scotland: O fusionless I've been, siccar, fusionless I've been.
But noo I've a mind for tae reeze me. 10
I'se guide my gowd an gear an I'se busk ye lik a queen,
an ye sall haste ye back for tae please me.

Industry: O that's my ain laddie noo. Brawly said an weel.
Ye'se gang your ain gate lik a free man.
An I'se gang wi you again, for I loe a mensefu chiel,
an the baith o' us 'll win prosperitie, mon.

Baith: Then here's tae us baith, kimmers. Here's tae us twa.
thegither We'se be kenspeckle fowk whan we're mairrit.
We'se hae peace an libertie an walth an ease for a',
an the bairnies a' sall jine for tae share it. 20

loe: love *siccar:* sure *busk:* dress *mensefu:* well-mannered *chiel:* fellow
kimmers: friends, lovers, relations

Scotsmen, Wake Up!

Scotsmen, wake up, and face the facts. In spite of these "appeasement" pacts they'll soon decoy you off to war. And what will you be fighting for?

Two million Scots are underfed, a Tory secretary has said. It may be that the Cameroons are not unmitigated boons. Dictators and their chamberlains are not too well endowed with brains; a "gentlemen's disagreement" may land us all in war one day. Is it a Scotsman's sacred duty to die that France may have Jibuti? Surely you'd be a lot of loonies to fight for Corsica or Tunis.

To have your head blown off, what joy, defending Nizza or Savoy. To shed your long-descended blood for Tanganyika…are ye wud? What difference will it make to you, kicking your heels at the old "buroo", whether or no Port Mahon be run by the Italian or the Hun? I do declare that it absurd is to wrap a kilt around your hurdies and fix a bayonet and syne let blatter at the Siegfried Line. It won't be glory or romance "kicking the Fuehrer in the pants."

Your enemies are nearer home, the London boss is not in Rome. This British Empire may be nice for profiteers who fix the price at which the armaments are made that guarantee their routes of trade. Our quarter million unemployed can surely not be overjoyed at thinking that the Union Jack flies in St Kitt's and Sarawak. Their total Empire trade is near eight hundred million pounds a year, but for their great re-armament six hundred million pounds are spent. Expensive? Ay, but wait a second. Your blood and anguish were not reckoned. Ah, but of course your blood and tears don't interest the profiteers.

On March, the 24th last year Mr Chamberlain made it clear if any scoundrel should attack Portugal, Egypt, or Iraq, or Angola, or Mozambique, he would not turn the other cheek; the Tory gang would raise a shout that we must lay the bully out. The London boss will tell you that he is fervent democrat; "fighting the Axis you will be fighting for true democracy." "You hoary hypocrite, come off it. You profiteers make war for profit. When we have got it you will see us fighting for democracy."

So, canny Scotsmen, do not run to shoot the Dago or the Hun. Realise that it is no go to die for Palestine or Togo. The conflict we can localise; non-intervention would be wise. Our turn for self-determination; we will not fight another nation. Leave war and hate to knaves and sots; let's have appeasement for the Scots. Join up for Scots neutrality: Home Rule is true democracy. God willing, we again shall see Scotland achieve her destiny.

Pious Canticle

Home Rule be ours and we shall see
Scotland achieve her destiny.
Planned economy and peace
shall make prosperity increase.
A nation that has lost its way
shall see again the light of day.

Now we see a dismal queue
lining up for the buroo;
mill and furnace idle stand,
bracken covers half the land;
everywhere we look we find
idle hand and idle mind.

But when we have got Home Rule
our empty bellies shall be full;
well-farmed land shall give us health,
mill and furnace pour out wealth.
Science in industry shall be
the source of true prosperity.

Every art and grace of life
shall flourish from Argyll to Fife;
culture and ease on every hand
from Berwickshire to Sutherland.
The world shall come to us to school
when we have won again Home Rule.

The French are surrounded

The French are surrounded on every frontier,
outnumbered and helpless on front and on rear;
their airforce and navy know they can't win,
their pro-fascist rulers are sure to give in.

The Russians are strong, but they're gey far awa, man;
I doot that they canna help England ava, man.
Then of course the English are snobbish, and so
think Soviet Bolshies are not nice to know.

Roosevelt and the Yankees are verra near frantic
for war with the Nazis, across the Atlantic.   10
But if there was fighting at London or Dover
they'd never get started until it was over.

The English have got what Beaverbrook intended;
Isolation, but it won't be splendid.
They'll soon be asking with unusual deference
what is Herr Hitler's Imperial Preference.

Will Cameroon appease him, or does he seek a
larger territory, like Tanganyika?
"Will you have Barbados or just Jaipur, or – ?"
"Gib mir Indien." "Jawohl, lieber Führer."   20

The far flung khaki empire now
shrinks to three acres and a Gau.
Thanks to Brummagem's brightest brain
the English are going to be down the drain.

Prognostication, April 1939

The English are going to be down the drain,
thanks to their Mr Chamberlain.
I'll tell you a wonderful bit of news,
if they go to war they'll certainly lose.

They abandoned the Czechs, they let down Spain,
now they are going to be down the drain.
By deserting their friends to appease the dictators
they've ruined themselves, the fusionless craturs.

And now they're promising guarantees
to Poland, Romania, Turkey and Greece.
If I were a Pole, Turk, Rouman, or Greek,
I'd think such security sadly to seek,
remembering how England (and France) guaranteed
the Austrian Republic (wee nations, tak heed).

The English navy may rule the waves,
and Britons will never, never be slaves;
but the air's more important, the Germans rule that,
they can bomb down London as flat as your hat.

"The bomber will always get through," honest Stanley
(that's Baldwin) kept saying in speeches most manly.
Of course, he's a Tory, but if I were you,
I'd wonder for one if his statement were true.

Remember, although we are never omniscient,
the German bombers are very efficient,
and numerous too. Dear me, what a fright
the Cockneys will get if they try to show fight.

Chain Stores

Owned by the Lunnon boss they stann,
in ilka street a' ower the lann,
multiple shops that tak oor trade,
                     tae oor sad loss,
Speir ye till wham the profit's paid.
                     The Lunnon boss,
he feeds on's lik a caterpillar.
Marks and Spencers get oor siller,
Burton an Boot an mony anither
                     exploit us a',   10
while oor ain trades juist dwine an wither
                     lik ice in thaw.
Woolie's pay divvies at cent per cent;
It's nae in Scotland the siller's spent.
The Lunnon parasites live off it,
                     luxurious eaters.
Scotland's puirtith is Lunnon's profit.
                     Deil tak the creatures.
Ere time be tint, Scotsmen, tak tent.
Join up for Scots Self-Government.   20
Protect your trade against sic plaisters
                     o' fowk lik these.
Scotsmen, awauk, be your ain maisters,
                     wi walth an ease.

speir: ask *siller:* money *dwine:* waste away *puirtith:* poverty *tint:* lost *plaisters:* fools

Timor belli ne nos conturbet

Noucht upon erde hier stands siccar.
Dictators threaten and democrats bicker,
Stalin is slick, but Hitler is slicker.
Timor belli ne nos conturbet.

There winna be war, wars bring revolution.
Neville advises a peaceful solution.
The Duce will make a great contribution.
Timor belli ne nos conturbet.

But havena we made a Polish alliance?
Are'na we bidding the bullies defiance? 10
Thon's only a trick of the Municheer science.
Timor belli ne nos conturbet.

Bamboozling the Churchills, electioneering,
are necessary tactics of Municheering.
War-scares are helpful to profiteering.
Timor belli ne nos conturbet.

The armament-magnates run the nation.
God bless Krupp and his ramifications,
And keep the plebs in their proper stations.
Timor belli ne nos conturbet. 20

It's Easy Sperin'

The English at last have gaen tae war,
but they dinna ken whit they're fechtin' for.
The reasons they gie are sae far frae clear,
ye canna believe they're at a' sincere.
Frae Maister Ch-mb-r-l-n's broadcast letter
tae the German people it's naethin' better
nor a stairheid flytin'. Gin ye maun speir,
N-v-l-e says Ad-lf's a xxx leear.

"Freedom for Poland, Home Rule for Czecho-
Slovakia," baith the Front Benches re-echo.   10
Let the English Justice adjust her scales,
an weigh oot some freedom for Scotland and Wales.

"Freedom, Democracy, Anti-aggression,
the Christian religion, release from oppression,
the equal right of every nation
to rule itself our civilisation..."
The Parliament gentry chant the sang,
an' the hale press echoes it loud an' lang.
It's a' verra fine, an' we quite agree –
there's a lot we could dae, gin we were free.   20

The Indians tae, they want some Democracy,
they want tae be rid o' the English bureaucracy;
but the English bosses winna gie
Home Rule tae the ceevilized Bengalee.
Gin ye speir at a Hindu or Arab or Boer,
he'll tell ye that Hitler's a puir amachoor;
compared wi' the English the Germans are tame
at playin' a skeely imperialist game.

Sae here's tae Freedom, Home Rule, and Democracy,
damnation tae Hitler an Tory plutocracy.   30
Up the Pole, an' the Czech, an' the Bengalee,
an' a'body else wha wants tae be free.

flytin: disputing *speir:* ask *skeely:* skilful

Crusade

The refugee royalties
   Wilhelmina and Haakon
beyond the sheltering seas
   indomitably talk on.
Benesh and Beck & Co.
   encourage their nations' resistance
not in the face of the foe
   but from a convenient distance.
Otto and Trotsky and Zog,
   Pierlot, Strasser, the Negus,   10
roll each his particular log
   in ways that they think will intrigue us.
Their propaganda streams
   over the vast Atlantic
from the world's safer extremes,
   becoming extremely frantic.
Importunate and sonorous,
   the European plutocracy
regale the yanks with a chorus
   of democratic hypocrisy.   20
Crusading at Nazi foes
   they'll battle across the savannahs,
till the New World overflows
   with Bernhards and Julianas.
The next one to traverse the seas,
   leaving his folk in the lurch, 'll
find quite a bunch of grandees,
   (democ)rats one and all, like...
   Reynaud.

Mr E. Brown's Highland Tour, or Muckle Cry and Little Oo

Do Dingwall farmers curse and frown?
   Are there complaints from the Braes o Balquidder?
The Right Honourable Ernest Brown
   will "earnestly and sympathetically consider."
"The Scotsman" chronicles this Cockney's tour
among our Highland lochs and hills.
"Earnest," "sympathetic," will he secure
some remedy for Scotland's ills?
We don't believe it. Our alien mentor,
   this Sassenach Secretary of State,   10
will "earnestly" out-Stentor Stentor,
   "sympathetically" vociferate.
The Highland lairds, those "Britons" staunch,
   may flock together and rejoice,
beholding his Right Honourable paunch
   sympathised with by his "earnest" voice.
The bankrupt farmer, the distressful crofter,
   could tolerate a belly less immense,
welcome pronouncements somewhat finer,
   if only they contained more sense.   20
This largest loudest stooge so far
   will prove as useless as the rest.
Viewing our glens from his dining-car
   he'll leave our Highlands still distressed.

The Bold Sloganeer

SPASMODICAL SUPPLEMENT FOR ENGLISH READERS. (FREE ADVICE)

Our prospects may be fearful,
but let us all keep cheerful.
Though forced on the defensive,
let none of us be pensive.

Every two or three days
Churchill will coin us a phrase,
(the art of which he's a master),
like "cataract of disaster".

"The springs of England's action
have undergone compression." —
regrettable contraction,
but an elegant expression.

The German air-force presses
from Narvik round to Brest,
creating nightly messes
north, south, east and west.

Shall British hearts grow frantic
if convoys meet their fate
upon the broad Atlantic
where U-boats lie in wait?

The Blitz gets more intensive,
but the war's as good as won
with Churchill's GREAT OFFENSIVE
of 1941.

The great Britannic Shogun
will search the dictionary through
to find a cheering slogan
for 1942.

Though dark the days before us,
black as black can be,
we'll sing a triumph chorus
for 1943.

No war of mere attrition
the future holds in store,
but a brilliant expedition
in 1944.

This black-out may be hateful,
but it's grand to be alive,
looking forward to the fateful
campaign of '45.

Among our toppling cities,
in showers of hurtling bricks,
we'll chant the merriest ditties
of 1946.

Thrilled stiff with stirring stories
by Cooper or by Bevin,
we prepare for greater glories
in 1947.

What though the Teuton bluster,
the Dago vent his hate,
our forces we shall muster
by 1948.

Our progress, slow but steady,
goes all along the line.
That old England of theirs might even perhaps be very nearly ready
somewhere round about — yes, I really don't see why not —
1999.

Moral Problem

Nou it's Peru and Ecuador
owregie the peace and gang to war.
What wald it matter to me and you
gin Ecuador suld beat Peru?
Whilk are maun Scotsmen fecht for nou,
when neither's wurdie fechtan for?

owregie: give up

The Umpteenth Forefront

A rumour flees round frae the verra Heidquarters
  o a Scottish Brigade that when they attack
the West o Europe ae third o the starters
  'll be Scots sodgers, the kind they caa "crack".
    Ae third o the U.K. troops to be Scots,
    and the ither twa-thirds a wheen orra lots.

The tyauv o the job maun gang tae the Jocks,
  they get the first place in ilka attack,
the Germans 'll gie them a fair share o knocks,
  and mair frae the British gin onie win back.   10
    The Press cheers them on agin General Rommel
    as the Ministers threept to the slaughter by Cromwell.

Foremaist in war, in peace left ahint,
  an auld tale that, and it's aye been the same.
Ye'd think they were dozent, daft, deif, dumb and blint,
  gin ye luik on the rackets they thole when at hame.
    It's plain and strauchtforrit the war agin Hitler,
    but the fecht for Scotland's a bluidy sicht kittler.

The Gadarene swine were possessed wi a deil,
  the Scots are bumbazed wi the Press and the Wireless, 20
wi Flick, Schule, and Kirk, till they dinna ken weel
  the richt facts o their life, hateless and desireless.
    It raxes their hairns to think for theirsels,
    sae the British devise them a series o hells.

The British decide what's richt and what's wrang,
  they mak aa the plans and the Scots doucelie thole them,
the Brits deave the Scots wi lees loud and lang,
  conscript them and tax them, coerce and cajole them.
    They fleece them like sheep and caa them like stots,
    but aiblins they'll find THE CAAD YINS ARE SCOTS. 30

a wheen: a few *orra:* spare, extra *threept:* endlessly reiterated *dozent:* sleepy *thole:* endure *hairns:* brains *doucelie:* sedately *aiblins:* perhaps

To the Hymn Tune "Veni Immanuel"

O come, o come Emmanuel,
give light to us that now in darkness dwell.
Explain to us in words brief and clear
when shall the boons of Socialism appear.

> Rejoice who can. Emmanuel
> is Minister of Power and Fuel.

Two million workers stroll about and sneeze
while bureaucrats de-coal the factories.
You told us, Mannie, you had a plan.
Now show us how it's working, if you can.   10

> Own up; come clean: Emmanuel,
> You've bungled it, the truth's the tale to tell.

The nation owns the coal mines now, and you
are there to do what we tell you to do.
When we're supplied at home and the works
the surplus you may trade to Swedes and Turks.

> Til then refrain, Emmanuel,
> from shipping coal across the ocean's swell.

Poor Christian voters could not have foretold
your new Jerusalem would be so cold.   20
Bureaucracy has squandered our stocks,
and doctrinaires are steering for the rocks.

> O go; o go: Emmanuel.
> And may your colleagues all resign as well.

Lady Grant

The Lady Grant
sets her eyebrows aslant,
   when Scotland is mentioned
   she's so well-intentioned,
but she won't really help, for she can't.

Lady Grant of Monymusk
finds Scots hecklers rather brusque.
   When she asks for their votes,
   they ask: "Faur's our oats?
Scotland's been left wi a husk."   10

There was a slee lawyer caad Hughes
wha cam to the North wi his views.
   His particular ramp
   was a Scots Labour camp
wi the lave o the fowk in buroos.

Only a Fool LIKES London Rule.

Stop the hoary Tory rot.
Vote for Walker, the honest Scot.

Fiscal and Advocate

Arthur Johnston, M.D., Curses on two pettifogging lawyers
    (Delitiae Poetarum Scotorum, ed. 1637, I, 498)

Fiscal and Advocate, you're monsters baith.
Breeders o pleas and fees, I wiss your daith.
May fuddries frae the luift soop ye awa,
or the sea droun ye wi a whummlan swaw.
May some plague-pushion gar your thrapples lowe,
or corbies ryve ye, dansan in a tow.
May the suin raist ye, broken on a wheel,
may the whup flay ye, flypit weal by weal.
Your meat withhauden, teeth howkt out, may you
guts up yoursels and aa your legal crew.   10
Compare your crimes and pains, the crimes' summation
exceeds fire, sea, plague, tow, wheel, whup, starvation.
           a.d. Iii Non. Oct. MCMXLVII, Edinburgi

luift: sky *soop:* sweep *swaw:* wave *pushion:* poison *gar:* make
thrapples: throats *lowe:* burn *corbies:* crows *ryve:* rend, tear *tow:* line *flypit:* torn off

The Glesca Muckers
An Againflytin tae George Todd's "The Embro Makars" (*Voice of Scotland*, Dec 1948)

A barefaced trousered keelie,
whas verse is hardly skeely,
flytes Embro Makars' bairds and philabegs.
But gin ye luik around
the poets o that toun
ye'll see hou Geordie Todd is aff his eggs.

Time was when Diarmid's Hugh,
the Makars' Sacred Coo,
wad gae about wi hairy chin and shanks.
But he's a Langholm loon, 10
and hit's a hairy toun,
weel kent for tinks and intellectual cranks.

It's verra true that twa
kenspeckle Makars shaw
auld Scotland's kilts and whiskers waffan rife, –
the Lindsay licht and gay,
that wones on Hillheid brae,
and Douglas Young that comes frae canny Fife.

But mark the Embro-born
poets, they dinna scorn 20
the safety razor and the bourgeois trouser:
Garioch, the eident prenter;
MacCaig, the image-stenter;
and slee MacNib, the multilingual bruiser.

The muckers frae the Clyde
maun shaw mair cause for pride
nor juist tae shauv the phyz and wear the breeks.
Let's keep the Movement free
frae local jalousie
and taylor-made or parlour-Bolshie cliques. 30

flytin(g): scolding , specif. a contest between poets in mutual abuse *skeely*: skilful *makars*: poets *philabeg*: kilt *loon*: lad *waffan*: waving, wagging *rife*: abundant, plentiful *wones*: dwells *eident*: diligent

Anthem for the Primrose League

(to the tune: "Onward, Christian Soldiers")

Hold tight, Tory diehards
  of the Primrose League:
soon we'll be in power,
  quite without fatigue.
Labour's front is splitting
  Attlee's reign is o'er;
soon we'll see the clock back
  where it was before.

> Hold tight, Tory diehards
>   of the Primrose League:
> soon we'll be in power
>   through a Left intrigue.

Lionhearted limpets
  cling by their teeth's skin
to each juicy office
  Tories should be in:
but Nye Bevan's faction
  splits the Marxist mob.
Hail, true blue Reaction!
  For each nob a job!

> Hold tight, Tory diehards
>   of the Primrose League:
> soon we'll be in power
>   through a Left intrigue.

We need no adventures,
  plans or policies:
artificial dentures
  rend our enemies.
Socialist controls now
  soon will disappear:
none will check our scramble,
  free to profiteer.

> Hold tight, Tory diehards
>   of the Primrose League:
> soon we'll be in power
>   through a Left intrigue.

Labour's Call to Rally

Steady, Labour comrades;
   splits will cause our rout:
we're the Thinking Party;
   let us think things out.

Ministers resigning need not cause dismay:
free and frank discussion is the Labour way.
Democratic planning by the rank-and-file
thrives on disputation tempered by a smile.
Socialists can argue, free from spite and hate:
rival spokesmen serve to organise debate.   10
Each side may be partly wrong and partly right,
comradely exchanges bring the truth to light.
Let us see both sides and see the problems whole.

Steady Labour comrades;
   splits will cause our rout:
we're the Thinking Party;
   let us think things out.

Translations

Translations from Gaelic
Frae the Gaelic o Sorley MacLean

Dàin do Eimhir XXVIII
The Ghaists

Lassie, gin ye'd made me your lad
aiblins ma sangs wald never had
thon toom desartit eternitie
and their weirdit perpetuitie.
Frae far awa their keenan's be,
frae dowf shores, luve, ayont the sea,
thinkan lang, outcryan for ye.
They'll sclim the bords o mountains heich
o monie bairn-times, greitan dreich,
for luve o ye thinkan lang, 10
roosan your beautie aye in sang.
They'll pad the causeys naukitlie
o Historie and Poesie;
on heich sma hill-tracks they 's be seen
o herts, stendan eternallie;
i the dumb-deid they 's haud conveen
wi makars, hapt in cleidans shene;
i the candle-licht they 's wauk the deid,
brakan o dey 's nae smoor their gleid.
Around the yirdan-kist they'll stand, 20
whaur the clay liggs, moch and wan,
deid luve o ilk eerie makar-chiel.
Ayont the graff they'll tak their stand,
wi nae blee o bluid, and their chafts dun.

Rose-like the mountain-taps they'll spiel
at the risan-up o the makars' sun.

aiblins: perhaps *toom desartit:* empty deserted *weirdit:* fated *keenan:* keening *dowf:* dull, weary *sclim:* climb *roosan:* praising *causeys:* streets *naukitlie:* nakedly *stendan:* striding *dumb-deid:* dead of night *makars:* poets *hapt:* wrapped *cleidans:* clothing *shene:* shining, gleaming *smoor:* smother *gleid:* brilliant light *liggs:* lies *moch:* damp, moist *makar-chiel:* poet-fellow *graff:* grave *blee:* colour, tint *chafts:* jaws *dun:* sallow, grey *spiel:* climb

Dàin do Eimhir XXXIII
The weird o makars

The weird o makars is as muckle warth
as the weird o ither fowk on the yirth.
Donncha Ban 's fortun ne'er rin furth,
but Weelum Ross was staad wi a fouth
o dule, consumption, and daith.

weird: lot, fate *makars:* poets *warth:* worth, value *staad:* overflowing
fouth: abundance *dule:* grief

Dàin do Eimhir XXXIV
When I am talkan o the face and natur...

When I am talkan o the face and natur
and the whyte spreit o ma whyte dear cratur,
ye'd aiblins say I'd never seen
the muckle mire wi ma blind een,
thon hideous flow, reid and broun,
whaur the bourgeoisie slounge and droun.

But I hae seen frae the Cuillin's hicht
baith shitten puirtith and glory licht;
I've seen the sun's gowden glitter
and the black moss o soss and skitter.   10
I ken the ingyne's wersh smert
mair nor the gleg delyte o the hert.

spreit: spirit *aiblins:* perhaps *shitten:* defiled with excrement *puirtith:* poverty *soss:* soggy mess of food *skitter:* thin excrement, diarrhoea *ingyne:* mind *wersh:* bitter *gleg:* sharp, quick

Dàin do Eimhir XLII
Were we thegither, me and you...

Were we thegither, me and you,
on Talisker shore, whaur the great whyte mou
gants atween the hard chafts twa,
Reid Needle and the Staney Skaw,
I'd stand thonder aside the sea
renewan i ma saul ma luve o ye,
the while the spase upfillt the bay
o Talisker for aye and a day.
Thonder I'd stand on the beld scree
till Preshal lowtit his stane-horse bree.   10

And were we thegither, you and me,
in Mull on the shore o Calgarie,
atween Scotland and isle Tiree,
atween the warld and eternitie,
bydan till Doomsday at leisure
draff by draff the sand I'd measure.
And owre in Uist on Hosta beach,
thon toom desartit lanely reach,
drainan the muckle spase dry
dreg by dreg I'd byde for aye.   20

Were we on Moidart's shore sae whyte,
thou unco ferly o new delyte,
I'd bigg thegither in luve for ye
draff on dreg the sand and the sea.
At Stensholl Staffin on the chad,
gif owre 's the chuckie-stanes were caad
by a rastless eerie swaw upthrawd,
I'd mak a stark dyke suld keep frae ye
fremmit smurlan eternitie.

chafts: jaws *spase:* open sea *beld:* bald, grassless *lowtit:* bowed *bree:* brow, face *unco:* unusual *ferly:* marvel *chad:* shingle *swaw:* wave *stark:* strong *fremmit:* alien, foreign *smurlan:* devouring imperceptibly

Dàin do Eimhir XLIII
Were't no for ye

Were't no for ye the Cuillin wald be
a sherp machicolate blue waa
girdan in wi its merch-dyke
my ramstam hert's ilka thraw.

Were't no for ye the Talisker sand
that liggs compactit, whyte and swack,
wald be to my hopes an endless carse
whaur the arrow Desire ne'er turned back.

Were't no for ye the jaws o the spase
i their swawan grame baith and their dwalm   10
wald upfraith my ingyne's ilka sweek
pittan in on a michty calm.

My savendie wald be as lang
and as braid 's the muir, braikit and broun,
but ye pit doun on them a rule
abune ma ain hert's stound.

The tree o strings was blawan bonnie
owre far awa on a growthy cairn,
amang its fullyerie your face,
my reason, and the semblance o a stern.   20

---

machicolate: indented, serrated (like battlements)   *merch-dyke:* march-wall, boundary-wall   *ramstam:* rash   *thraw:* opposition, twist   *liggs:* lies   *swack:* abundant   *jaws:* waves   *spase:* open sea   *swawan:* wave-crest   *grame*: rage, passion   *dwalm:* fainting fit, swoon   *upfraith*: send up in froth   *ingyne:* mind   *sweek:* talent   *savendie:* intellect, understanding   *braikit:* parti-coloured, speckled or striped   *stound:* pain   *blawan:* blooming   *growthy cairn:* luxurious summit   *fullyerie:* foliage   *stern:* star

Dàin do Eimhir LI
I the connachan time

I the connachan time o the sterns
ma savendie spak til ma hert:
"It's ye are buskan the beautie
that'll be til your ain smert.
Wi a spate frae the luft ae day
there's come on ye dule and wae."

Brubbit and lane, my spreit
liggit, bruckil and frush,
trummlan at the muckle bysen
o thon cauld sherp flush.   10
Wi the daithlie skreigh atour it
the bauld green braird was smoorit.

I'd ken the sense o the warsslan
that's in the naukit drounan
and the mene o the jurmummlan
that's in the wud swaws' soundan,
did ye no raise your bree
that whummles the sense in me.

connach: destroy *sterns:* stars (i.e. ideals) *savendie:* intellect, understanding *buskan:* preparing *spate:* flood, swell *luft:* sky *dule:* grief *brubbit:* bruised *lane:* alone *spreit:* spirit *bruckil:* brittle (of a hard thing) *frush:* brittle (of a soft thing) *bysen:* prodigy *flush:* piece of boggy ground *atour:* around *bauld:* bold *braird:* young growth *smoorit:* smothered *warsslan:* torment *mene:* intention *jurmummlan:* mutilation *wud:* mad *swaw:* wave *bree:* brow, face *whummles:* overwhelms

Dàin do Eimhir LIII
I fashna masel for the grand revolution...

I fashna masel for the grand revolution
that 'll redd up the puirtith o the human race,
nou I've seen the pictur o aa nobilitie
wrocht out i the glister o a bonnie face.

redd up: clear up *puirtith:* poverty *wrocht:* wrought

Dàin do Eimhir LIV
Ye were the dawn

Ye were the dawn on the hills o the Cuillin,
the bousum day on the Clarach arisan,
the sun on his elbucks i the gowden flume,
the whyte rose-fleur that braks the horizon.

Gesserant sails on a skinklan frith,
gowd-yalla luft and blue o the sea...
the fresh mornan in your heid o hair
and your clear face wi its bonnie blee.

Gowdie, my gowdie o dawn and the derk
your loesome gentrice, your brou sae rare...   10
albeid wi the dullyart stang o dule
the breist o youth's been thirlit sair.

bousum: genial, bounteous *flume:* stream *blee:* colour, tint *gesserant:* gleaming *luft:* sky *blee:* colour, tint *gowdie:* jewel *gentrice:* gentle character *dullyart:* dull *stang:* sting *dule:* grief *thirlit:* pierced

Dàin do Eimhir LV
I dinna ken the sense o ma trauchlan...

I dinna ken the sense o ma trauchlan,
pittan thochts in a deean leid,
nou that the hale whuredom o Europe
lowps up in a brulyie o sturt and dreid.

Och, but a million o years is gien us,
a wee bittock o the waesome space,
the commonty's tholemudness and smeddum,
and the rare ferly o a bonnie face.

trauchlan: struggle, toil *leid:* language *lowps:* leaps *brulyie:* close confused conflict *sturt:* strife *tholemudness:* patience *smeddum:* courage *ferly:* marvel

Dàin do Eimhir LVII

A face aye hauntan me,
day and nicht untwynablie,
   the triumphant face o a lass
clamant eternallie.

It threeps awa to my hairt;
that Desire maun never part
   frae the thing desireit, albeid
it can neither win nor sair 't;
that Beauty is siccar enow
tho monie a blemish grow,
   the day that's gane is free
as the morn's morn sall be;
thiss moment bydes secure
albeid anither hour
   wi rebel cry for change
renay its Sovran pouer;
sin that it's nou alive
its form and bein sall thrive
   for aye, nae alteration
its aefaldness sall ryve;
a thing outwaleit i the prime
by the een's desire bydes throu Time,
   as thochts that win eternal shape
frae novel phrase or rhyme.

Baith Patricks' arts arena mair blessit
   and graceit nor it, and aiblins less,
but smooth music canna express it,
   or chisellit stane its luveliness;
albeid ye canna represent
its form or hue wi brod or paint
   til eftir-bairntimes without
corruptan blemishment.

Face, face, will thou tine, tine thy micht,
the ferly-potency o thy sicht?
   The couthy blyth generous hairt
smerts as thy beauty grips it ticht.

Gin stane or brod canna tak
your semblance, what suld music mak,
   or rhyme, sin wey there isna to pit
thiss minute in a wee sma pack?

Gin nae man kens the kittle craft
to kep thiss hour 's transient waft
   and haud it amang the sands o change
wi an anchor's chaft,
afore it lifts the new sails
for the trip to whaur memorie fails,
   afore the een tine the canvas
as their vision pales?

Ah, hauntan face thou, aye wi me,
fair face that speaks eloquentlie,
   will thou gyng wi thiss present time,
gyng and speirna your auld plea?

Quhan the thesaurs o ilka memorie crine
that wald loe ye or bring ye whiles in mind,
   tuim and forgotten, your auld delytesome
aefaldness wald thou tine?

I wald speir for your luveliness
nae ither everybydandness
   but what suld hain it hoolie and fairlie
hale as nou it is.

I suldna speir oniething new
forbye what I've seen i your ain brou,
   I suldna speir music's potency,
multivocal to fowk that loe.

A braw pentit brod wald gie
but ae brief blenk to memorie
   gin an it hainit a third o your charms
thesaurit in its blee.

And sae, thou moment and thou face,
ilk by ither haud your place,   70
   for aye, or aiblins at the hour's finish
micht be backslitherin frae Grace.

Thou Moment o Time, quhan flees awa
your sovrantie like haars that blaw,
   to whilk new-kindlit perceivin
sall your neist journey shaw?

Moment o Time, and the relicts that gang,
the lave o oursels that stends alang
   eftir your feet, what course o steerin
brings us renoun in tale or sang?   80

Whatt there waz o us, and what iz noo,
gin an their permanence were true,
   frae distant shores sae far frae hame
hou micht the tale o them win throu?

What ee culd kep their sicht a-flocht?
Human lug wald hear them nocht,
   journeyan their weary lane
ayont the ingyne's langest thocht.

What and quhaur's the fowrth dimension
culd bring sic fairheid to the apprehension   90
   o the ee, the savendie, or onie sense,
frae owre the bottomless immense?

What sense ayont the senses micht
perceive thon luveliness sae bricht
   when unperceivit by onie lug,
tung or finger, smell or sicht,

and when it isna fauldit ben
the livan memorie o men
   or wi the rinnan thochts that aye
renew the prizes that they hain?   100

Gif fand there be na for apprehension
onie ither sense, or yet dimension,
   what form or bein sall your grace
hae i the merches o Time and Space?

Hauntan face thou, aye wi me,
ferly that speaks eloquentlie,
   hae ye onie merch-dyke forbye the yirth,
is there onie hyne in Time for ye?

Paian o human form, amang
the universe, sae braid and lang,   110
   can nae dimension gie ye haleness
mair nor Music, Art, or Sang?

Tho the Reid Army o Mankind
fechts to daith i the Ukraine
   it isna hits hero-deed
liggs neist this hairt o mine;
but a face aye hauntan me,
day and nicht untwynablie,
   the triumphant face o a lass
clamant eternallie.   120

ilk wey: everywhere *clamant:* urgent, calling for redress *threeps:* urgently reiterates *sair:* serve, preserve *siccar:* surely *renay:* deny *aefaldness:* simplicity, integrity *ryve:* rend, impair *outwaleit:* chosen *aiblins:* perhaps *brod:* board *tine:* lose *ferly-potency:* magical power *kittle:* intricate, hard to manage *kep:* catch *chaft:* jaw *crine:* shrink *loe:* love *whiles:* sometimes *tuim:* empty *everybydandness:* permanence, perpetuity *hain:* keep *hoolie:* cautiously *forbye:* besides *blenk:* glimpse *thesaurit:* treasured *blee:* colour *haars:* mists *neist:* next *lave:* remainder *stends:* stalks *gin an:* even if *a-flocht:* flying *lug:* ear *their lane:* by themselves *ingyne:* intellect *fairheid:* beauty *savendie:* understanding *fauldit:* folded *ben:* inside *merches:* bounds *ferly:* marvel *merch-dyke:* boundary-wall *hyne:* haven *liggs:* lies

Dàin Eile XVII
Wald ye be atween a lassie's houghs

Wald ye be atween a lassie's houghs
wi your mou on her breists sae fair and sauchin,
and the Reid Army warsslan to daith,
jurmummlit and forfochen?

houghs: thighs *sauchin:* supple, tender *warsslan:* tormented
jurmummlit: mutilated *forfochen:* exhausted by fighting

Hielant Woman

Hae ye seen her, ye unco Jew,
ye that they caa Ae Son o God?
Thon trauchlit woman i the far vine-yaird,
saw ye the likes o her on your road?

A creelfu o corn upo her spaul,
swyte on her brou, saut swyte on her cheek,
a yirthen pat on the tap o her heid,
her laigh-bouit heid, dwaiblie and sick.

Ye haena seen her, ye son o the vricht,
wi "King o Glory" fowk roose ye weel,   10
on the staney westland machars thonder
swytan under her wechtit creel.

This spring o the year is by and gane
and twenty springs afore it spent,
sin she's hikeit creels o cauld wrack
for her bairns' meat and the laird's rent.

Twenty hairsts hae dwineit awa,
she's tint her simmer's gowden grace,
while the sair trauchle o the black wark
pleud its rigg on her clear face.   20

Her puir saul is eternallie tint,
as threeps aye your kindly Kirk;
and endless wark has brocht her corp
to the graff's peace, lown and derk.

Her time gaed by like black sleek
throu an auld thaikit hous-rig seepan;
she bruikit aye sair black wark,
and gray the nicht is her lang sleepan.

unco: great, strange *trauchlit:* toiling *spaul:* shoulder *yirthen:* earthy *vricht:* carpenter *pat:* pot *dwaiblie:* feeble *wechtit:* heavy *wrack:* seaweed *hairsts:* autumns, harvests *dwineit:* wasted away, dwindled *tint:* lost *corp:* body *threeps:* endlessly reiterates *graff:* grave *lown:* quiet *thaikit:* thatched *bruikit:* inherited, possessed

My een are nae on Calvary

My een are nae on Calvary
or the Bethlehem they praise,
but on shitten back-lands in Glesga toun
whaur growan life decays,
and a stairheid room in an Embro land,
a chalmer o puirtith and skaith,
whaur monie a shilpet bairnikie
gaes smoorit doun til daith.

chalmer: room *puirtith:* poverty *skaith:* hurt *smoorit:* gradually extinguished, smothered

Gealach Ùr:

A Communist Sicht o the New Mune

I'll pit a haundle on the heuk o the mune
and my hard thoumb like a hammer abune
on the bruckil gowd, and even throu;
sic blasphemie God wald gar me rue.

A bluid-reid gumphion syne it's be,
lang-thocht-til Hope's ain blasounrie,
Mankind's enseinyie rampan grand,
a new licht kindleit owre the land.

heuk: sickle *bruckil:* brittle *gar:* make *gumphion:* funeral banner
syne: then *enseinyie:* ensign, flag *rampan*: romping boisterously

Reothairt

While eftir while, and me broken,
   my thocht faas on you i your youth,
and a tide sall flow, unkent, unspoken,
   wi a thousand sails on the sea's fouth.

The waesome shore derns wi a smooran
   flood owre its craigs and dreich sea-wraick;
ohn brakin the spase smites, pouran
   at my feet wi a saft happan straik.

Hou suldna the spring-flood byde
   that was blyther to me nor to birds o the day,   10
and I tint its seil as the ebb-tide
   crines drap on drap in dule and wae?

fouth: abundance, flood *derns:* is hidden *smooran:* smothering *owre its craigs:* over its rocks *dreich sea-wraick:* miserable sea-weed *ohn brakin:* without breaking *spase:* open sea *happan straik:* wrapping stroke *blyther:* more welcome *tint:* lost *seil:* blessing *crines:* shrinks *dule:* grief

Frae the Gaelic o George Campbell Hay

Thonder they ligg

"Thonder they ligg on the grund o the sea,
nae the hyne whaur they wald be."
Siccan a thing has happenit me
sin my son's been gane. When he was wee
I dannlit the bairn like a whelpikie
and he leuch i ma airms richt cantilie.
It's the auld weird nou I maun dree.

The luft grows derk, the sun gangs laigh,
atour the skerries the sea-maws skreigh,
the rowtan kye come schauchlan doun,   10
the laddies rant out-throu the toun;
but here I rock at the fire ma lane,
mindan o him I had that's gane.

I see your jacket on the heuk,
but the hous is lown in ilka neuk,
never a sound or a word i the room,
nae sclaffan o buits on the threshart-stane,
the bed cauld and the chalmer toom.

Gin it's the sych that traivels far
ye'll hear my sychan whaur ye are,   20
sleepan i the wrack, jundied aye,
wi ugsome ferlies sooman by,
the ghaistlie monsters o the sea.

"Wheesht, woman, wheesht, and deavena me.
My wae's the mair to see ye greet.
The ship brak doun under our feet,
life gaed aff, and memorie wi 't.
London slew me, weary faa 't,
connacht the een that never saw it.
Aiblins I was acquent wi you,   30
the saut has reingeit my memorie nou.
Here I stravaig i the merchless faem,

yestreen Donald was my name.
The wecht o your wae liggs sair on me.
Woman, wheesht, whae'er ye be."

Sair the price maun be dounpitten
by the island-fowk for the greatness o Britain.

ligg: lie *hyne:* haven *weird:* fate *dree:* endure *luft:* sky *atour:* around *kye:* cattle *my lane:* by myself *heuk:* hook *lown:* quiet *chalmer:* room *sych:* sigh *wrack:* seaweed *jundied:* rocked, jostled *ferlies:* marvels *sooman:* floating *connach:* destroy *aiblins:* perhaps *reinge:* scour *stravaig:* wander *merchless:* unbounded *wecht:* weight

Guestless Howff

Wae for the lanelie kirkyaird fowk,
   ilk ane in his lair, pit past for aye,
maister o a hous whaur nane chaps,
   nane ettles tae speir gin he's inby.

Sun risesna, nor starn thonder,
   cloud nor shouer nor wind move,
bluein o day comesna nor derkenin,
   peace nor tulzie, grame nor luve.

chaps: knocks   *ettles:* tries   *speir:* ask   *starn:* star   *tulzie:* tumult
grame: wrath

Lass wi the Keekin-Gless

Luve I never was acquent wi,
   kentna sic a thing existit,
but nou it's cranglan round my feet,
   wae's me! atour my heid it's twistit.

Thon ane that wiled me 's a doolzie lass,
   glentan cannie she lowts her bree,
but her flichteriff hert stravaigs awa
   like a hard squall on the swaw o the sea.

She's ne'er a braal o pitie to shew,
   she never goams my miserie,   10
straikan her lint-whyte hair wi a kaim,
   tho for sake o her I'm like tae dee.

Lass wi the keekin-gless, and your bree whyte as the wax,
   ye glent i my face, but I kenna the mene o the hert i your breist.
Tho saftlie your een byde on me, your thochts dinna follow their tracks.
Keep your glink tae yoursel, and gie me my hert again, BEAST!

keekin-gless: mirror *cranglan:* winding *atour:* around *wiled:* lured, enticed *doolzie:* frolicsome *glentan:* glancing *lowts:* lowers *bree:* brow *flichteriff:* fickle *stravaigs:* wanders *swaw:* wave *braal:* fragment *goams:* heeds *lint:* flax *kaim:* comb *glent:* glance *mene:* intention *glink:* occasional or sidelong glance *gie again:* restore

Frae the Scots Gaelic o William Livingstone

Eirinn ag Gul. Ireland Greitan

Uttermost isle of Europe,
loveliest land under sky,
often I saw your coastline
beyond ocean's bellowing cry.

With the south-east blowing gently
and in heaven no mist or cloud
the Gaels in the Rhinns of Islay
admired your beauty aloud.

Your pastures grassy and goodly,
Magh Aoidh, smooth Lag an Rotha,   10
your wooded dells where the winged
singers sheltering go.

Pure springs bubbling freshly,
strong herds thronging your glens,
woods, hills, and meadow-scenery,
and you green from end to end.

In boyhood's innocent morning
I heard talk of ancient days
by the hearths of Clan Donald in Islay
before exiling of the Gaels.   20

We thought they were true, as bairnies,
the tales that the old folk had;
we believed you were always merry,
as we'd heard, exulting and glad.

Today as of old I descry still
your sky-line over the swell
from Islay's southern wave-beach,
but your state is mournful to tell.

Sad tale of eviction, oppression,
dearth, injustice, woe;   30
and no way of abating your burden,
since you struck your own strength the blow.

Where is the three Hughs' ardour, --
the valiant O'Donnell, O'Neill,
Maguire among foemen steadfast
to death, not yielding on his feet?

And where is the breed of the brave ones
at Dun-a-bheire shunned not fight,
like a moorland torrent charging
with targe-rims speckled bright?   40

The rocks reply with an echo
to the yell of the battle-sound;
breathless the foxes are tumbled,
their blood purling on the ground.

(l. 38) *Dun-a-bheire*: Berehaven

Frae the Erse, Eichteenth Yearhunder

Do Threasgair an Saol

The warld whummlit them aa, the wind soopit them aff,
Alexander and Caesar and aa their fowk, like chaff,
Tara's yirdit in gerss, and the larach o Troy ye can see,
and the English thersels ae day aiblins they'll hae to dee.

soopit: swept *yirdit:* covered *larach:* ruined foundation *aiblins:* perhaps

Frae the Gaelic.

An t-Iarla Diurach – *by a MacLaine Lady of Lochbuie to a Campbell of Jura.*

(to Mr Francis George Scott's version of the tune)

Although, my love, you always betrayed me,
though you were breaking your promise-making,
yet I for ever shall tell your praise,
although, my love, you always betrayed me.

Still I lie here under sorrow,
'tis the chief's love is my torture;
and from my eyes tears flow down in torrents,
my heart is torn with love's keenest pain.

I was by you in my dreaming
there in Jura of the steep bens,   10
your kisses tender like cress of streamlet.
But gone the dreaming, the wound remains.

Still the moon will shed her lustre
and the sky light up with sunshine.
But East or West I heed not their journeys,
I die with love for the island laird.

Come, O love, and close my eye-lids
in the chest I'll never rise from.
My dust be tomb-dust of Jura island,
my rest and quiet is but the grave.   20

From the traditional Gaelic

Raasay Lament – "*Cumha Mhic 'ille Chaluim*"

(to the tune for the words in *The Songs of the Hebrides,* II.)

I ever seated at the sea-ford,
   none to greet or salute me.
Never song I've sung of joy
   since the Friday of my ruin.
Sheelorovaho, sheelohorovaho, sheeloro, sheelorovahoronyaily.

From that day of the drowning,
   lost the boat and the hero,
Gille Calum, Iain Mor,
   the young lord, my tale is grievous.

Strong were ever thy shoulders,   10
   though the ocean subdued them.
No man yet of Adam's clan
   would lay hand on thee but rued it.

Lowly to-night is thy pillow,
   cold billows thy tomb-stone,
graveyard of the shore at ebb
   is the bed of my adored one.

Many a white-coifed lady
   would bewail at thy keening,
noble maidens young and fine   20
   be untimely under weeping.
Sheelorovaho, sheelohorovaho, sheeloro, sheelorovahoronyaily.

Frae the Lallans o Burns

"Caa the Yowes"

Βοιωτιστί.

Βόσκε τὰς ἦγας τού νουν ἂν κολώνας,
δηῦτε πότ τὰν ἀνθεμόεντ' ερίκαν·
ἦγας εν κρωνὸν σουνέλα ρίοντα,
    νούμφα ποθεινά.

Σίγα δ' αὐδὰν ϝεσπερίαν κιχείλας
τάνδε πὲρ βάσσας ἀΐοισα Θίσβας
ἦγας ἐν σταθμὼς ταχέως ἔλα μοι,
    νούμφα ποθεινά.

Πάρ δε Περμεισσοῦ ἀνίωμες ὄχθαν,
τάνδ' ἐν ἠγίρων σκιόεσσαν οὔλαν,
εἶ ριῖ δίνης οὐπὸ τὰν σελάναν
    παμφανοώσης.

Ἄστού νουν μέττα Ὠγούγιον σιωπᾷ
νουκτὶ Θίσβας, εἶ Χάριτες σελάνᾳ
τῦ χόρυ χήρονθι τά τ' ἄνθε' ἀδρᾷ
    στίλβι ἐέρσα.

Μεὶ φόβου τεῖν Λαμίας ποκ' ἔντων
μειδὲ Μορμόος τοὺ γὰρ Ἀφροδίτᾳ
φιλτάτα θιοῖσί τ' ἀδᾶος ἔσσῃ,
    νούμφα ποθεινά.

Ἀλλὰ καλά γ' ἔσσα, κόριλλ' εραννά,
στείθιος κάρδιαν κεκλόφωσ' ἔχις τού·
τεθνάνη 'στω, μείδ' ἀπολιμπάνην τίν,
    νούμφα ποθεινά.

"Ae Fond Kiss"

    Δωριστί.

Ὕστατον ἀμὲ φίλαμα μένει, χωρισμὸς ἔπεστι.
  ἓν τόδε Χαῖρε λέγω, κὠδέποκ' αὖτις ἐρῶ.
δάκρυα δ' ἐκ βαθέος στέρνω προρίοντα προπίνων
  τᾷ στάσει ἰυγμῶν καὶ στοναχᾶν μάχομαι.

Ἀλλὰ Τύχαν τίς ἐρεῖ δυσδαίμονα καὶ πολύκλαυστον
  Ἐλπίδος ὄφρα κ'ἔχῃ τὸ σθένος ἀστέροσῴς;
σμικρόταταν δ' οὐ πώ ποκ' ἐν ὠρανῷ ἔδρακον αἴγλαν,
  ἄχθος αμαυρὸν ἀεὶ κρύπτει ἀμαχανίας.

Οὐ τὸν πολλὸν ἔρωτα, τὸν ἄφρονα τόνδ', ὀνοτάζω.
  Ἁλιοδώραν γὰρ πᾶς κεν ἰδὼν ἐμάνη.
εὐθὺς ἰδὼν ἐμάνη τε καὶ ἐς βαθὺν ἄλατ' ἔρωτα,
  τάν τε φιλεῖ μώναν τάν τε φιλάσει ἀεί.

Αἰ 'πεφιλάμεθα νῶ γα πόθῳ μὴ τὼς μανιώδει,
  αἰ 'μεμανάμεθα μὴ τυφλοτάτᾳ φιλίᾳ,
αἰ μὴ πώ ποχ' ὁμοῦ 'γεγενάμεθα, μή ποκα χωρίς,
  οὐ κα νῦν ἄμφω τόσσον ἀθυμέομες.

Ἀλλά κορᾶν τὺ καλᾶν καλλίστα χαῖρε καὶ ἔμπας,
  χαῖρε τὺ τὸν λοιπόν, φίλτατον ὄμμα, βίον.
Αἰὲς πᾶσα χάρις καὶ ἀγάλματα πάντα παρείη
  χάρματα θ' Ἁσυχίας δῶρά τε τας Κύπριδος.

Ὕστατον ἦς τὸ φίλαμα τόδ' ἀμίν, μέσφα δ' ἐς αἰές
  ἕρπωμες χωρὶς δάκρυσι καὶ στοναχαῖς.

Classical Translations

Frae the Aiolic o Psappho

Thon time we aa wonned

Thon time we aa wonned thegither,
she was shair o ye then, and worshippt ye neist;
she loed your singan abune aa ither.

Braw amang Lydian leddies nou
she gaes, like the rose-fingert mune
wi aa the starns about her brou,

eftir the sun's doungangan. The leam
streiks out on the monie-fleurit hauchs
and kelters owre the saut sea's stream.

Doun draps the dauch in a bonnie shouer,   10
roses blaw rowthie, and saft chervil,
and the hinnie-sawrit clover-fleur.

Stravaigan aften her lane she'll gae,
thinkan lang til her gentie Atthis,
forfant in spreit, and her hert wae.

wonned: dwelt *neist:* next *loed:* loved *starns:* stars *leam:* gleam
kelters: tips *dauch:* dew *blaw:* bloom *rowthie:* plentiful, abundantly
hinnie-sawrit: honey-smelling *stravaigan:* wandering *her lane:* by
herself *thinkan lang til:* yearning for *gentie:* elegent, delicate *forfant:*
faint, enfeebled

Til Anaktoria

Maik o the gods he seems to me,
thon man that sits in front o ye,
and hears your talkan couthilie near,
sae saftlie and clear,

your luvelie lauchan. My hert stounds
rowsan i ma breist when your lauch sounds,
and gif I glent at ye sittan there
I canna speak mair.

Ma tung freezes i ma mou, a nesh
lowe rins chitteran throu ma flesh;   10
nae sicht i ma een; wi their ain thunner
ma lugs dunner.

Swyte reems doun me; frae heid to fuit
a trummlan grups me, sae's I sit
greener nor gerss, in sic a dwalm
I kenna wha I am.

maik: mate *lauchan:* laughing *stounds:* pains *glent:* glance *nesh:* delicate *chitteran:* shivering *lugs:* ears *dunner:* reverbate

Frae the Aiolic o Psappho

Aa that was lowsit by the bricht day's mou
   the gloaman mirk caas hame thegither:
caas hame the yowes, caas hame the cou,
   caas hame the bairnie til his mither.

lowsit: set loose *day's mou:* dawn (Gaelic 'Beul an latha') *gloaman:* twilight *mirk:* darkness *aas:* drives *yowes:* ewes

   ...

Minnie, I canna caa my wheel,
or spin the oo or twyne the tweel.
It's luve o a laddie whammles me.
Ech, the wanchancie glamarie.

minnie: mother *caa:* drive *oo:* wool *tweel:* cloth *whammles:* overwhelms *wanchancie:* uncanny *glamarie:* glamour, magic

   ...

The mune has gane doun
and the Pleiads abune:
midnicht is by-gane,
and I'm beddit my lane.

my lane: by myself

   ...

Caller rain frae abune
reeshles amang the epple-trees:
the leaves are soughan wi the breeze,
and sleep faas drappan doun.

caller: fresh *reeshles:* rustles *soughan:* murmuring

   ...

The starns around the bonnie mune
   dern ilk its skinklan ee
when she i the dull o the nicht sheens full
   owre aa the yirth and the sea.

starns: stars   *dern:* hidden   *skinklan:* glittering

   ...

Deid sall ye ligg, and ne'er a memorie
sall onie hain, or ae regret for ye,
sin that ye haena roses o Pierie.
In Hades' howff a gangrel ghaist ye'll flee,
amang derk ghaists stravaigan sichtlesslie

ligg: lie   *roses o Pierie:* the Muses' flowers   *howff:* resort, (used especially of churchyards and public houses)   *gangrel:* vagrant   *stravaigan:* wandering

Mox tu morte jaces. remanent oblivia longa
   nec desiderium tempus in omne tui.
nam rosa nulla tibi Aoniae. comitaberis Orci
   Manibus obscuris caeca misella vaga.

Frae the Greek

The partan tellt the ether
  his strang grip hookit:
*A fier maun be straucht
  and nae think cruikit.*

(N.B. – *Anerly deid snakes are straucht*)

partan: crab *ether:* snake *fier:* comrade *anerly:* only

Frae the Greek o Theognis o Megara

Fowr Epigrams

I've been a gangrel bodie, I've been to Sicilie,
and owre til Euboia wi the vines upon its howe,
bonnie Sparta on Eurotas whaur the rashes grow.
And aa the fowk in ilka place were guid to me.
But I'd nae rowth o pleasure for aa that I micht see.
Och, I'd suner be at hame in ma ain countrie.

They pledge me nae mair in wine, for nou anither,
far waur nor me, courts ma dentie lassie.
In cauld watter they curse me, her faither and mither.
Aye greetan for me she rins to fill the tassie
at the well, whaur yince wi ma airm about her back
I kisst her halse, and saftlie her mou spak.

Yill's ma guid frien, but ae thing that's agee, –
when I get fechtan-fou and meet wi ma enemie.
But gin it flees to ma heid and winna byde i ma wame,
och, then I gie owre the yill and gae awa hame.

Drinkan, I heedna puirtith that eats the hert,
or the clash o ill-deedie men that wad mak me smert;
but I'm wae for ma luvely virr that desarts me nou,
and I greet for auld age coman, that gars me grue.

gangrel: vagrant *howe:* valley *rowth:* abundance *waur:* worse *yince:* once *halse:* neck, throat *yill:* ale *agee:* in a disordered state, off the straight *wame:* belly *puirtith:* poverty *clash:* gossip *virr:* vigour *gars:* makes *grue:* shudder

...

The lyon dinesna aye on flesch, strang tho he be
whiles the proud beast is staad in sair perplexitie.

whiles: sometimes *staad:* overflowing, crammed, brimming

Frae Homer's Iliad, VI, 392-496.

Hektor's Twynan frae Andromacha

Syne when he cam to the Skaian yetts as he gaed throu the burgh,
whaur he beguid to gae under the port on his wey to the howe-lann,
there his weel-tochert wife Andromacha cam til him rinnan,
King Eetion's dochter that was, girt-hertit and namely,
auld Eetion's sel, that wonned in weel-wuidit Plakos,
under Ben Plakos in Thebe, Cilician fowk was his people;
his ae dochter it was that was merrit on Hektor the bress-graithit.

Thon time she cam to meet him. A hous-queyn followit eftir,
haudan the bairn til her breist, juist a wee bit tapetless bairnie,
Hektor's bairn that he loed, that was bonny as ane o the starnies. 10
Hektor wad caa him Skamandrios aye, but Astyanax maistlie
aabody nemmt him. Alane it was Hektor was sauvan the citie.

Lauchanlie then he luikt at his bairn, luikt lauchan, but spakna;
stannan aside him the wifie Andromacha grat, and wi greitan
gruppit his hann and caad him by name and spak til him, sabban:

"Fey that ye are, yer micht'll be daith til ye. Niver yer bairnie
tak ye thocht til ava, or yer wifikie, me that'll sune be
widdawt o ye. The Achaians aiblins'll sune hae ye slauchtert,
aa rinnan on ye at yince. An me, gif e'er I suld tine ye,
better for me to gae under the yirth. For niver anither   20
solace I'll ken, quhan ye sall dree yer weird that is weirdit.
Naething but dule. Nae faither I hae, or leddie my mither.
Na, na. Lang syne faither was slauchtert by godlike Achilles,
him that herriet the thraipfu broch o the fowk o Cilicie,
Thebe o heich-biggit ports, an Eetion's sel he dounharlit.
Ruvena the graith o him tho, but respectit him out o his honour,
brunt his corp on a pyre wi his wappens bonnilie roun him,
biggit a cairn til him tae. The nymphs that wone i the hielants
plantit ellums aroon it, the dochters o Zeus wi the aigis.

"Ay, an at hame thon time I had seeven brether aboot me.   30
Och, but the hale o them gaed thon ilk ae day doun til Hades.
Aa in ae tulyie he slew, the feeryfit godlike Achilles,
there wi their schauchlan kye an the yowes wi the kenspeckle flesches.

Mither forbye, that was queen, owre thonder by weel-wuidit Plakos,
her he brocht here thon time wi the lave o the gear that he herriet,
syne lat her gae awa hame for a ransoun fairlie past countan.
Doun in her faither's haa it was archeress Artemis strack her.

"Hektor, ye nou alane are my faither and matronlie mither,
ye are my brither alane, forbye the braw lad that I bed wi.
Come awa cannilie nou, tak tent, and byde on the touer,   40
makna yer bairn an orpheling-wean and yer wifie a widdaw.
Battle yer fowk til the fecht at the fig-tree, whaur they micht spiel up
aisiest intil the broch, an rin in whaur the waa has been thirlit.
Thrice dounby they assayt an onfaa wi the wale o their fechters,
roun thae twa they caa Aias and kenspeckle Idomeneeus,
roun the twa sons o king Atreus and Tydeus' feerichan laddie.
Aiblins a chiel wi the second-sicht had gien them a tellan,
aiblins they lippent i thochts o their ain and canny devysans."

Syne muckle Hektor answerit her, wi his bassanat skinklan:
"Wifie, it's me'll tak tent til aa thon. But I'm fairly affrichtit   50
whit'll be said by the menfowk o Troy and the lang-skirtit weemen,
giff I byde howdrand awa like a smeddumless cuif frae the battle.
Na, ma hert says me na. I was gleg aye to be wurdy,
foremaist aye i the fechtan amang the prime o the Troymen,
winnan renoun tae ma faither an meikle renoun to ma nyawn sel.
"Weel I ken this i ma hert, an ma ingyne tells it me trulie:
Tyde sall betide quhan Ilios toun that is haly sall periss,
Priam tae an the fowk o king Priam, guid wi the ash-spear.
Less, for aa that, am I fasht by thon dule o the Trojans ahint me,
neitherans Hekabe's dule, that's ma mither, or dule o king Priam,   60
neither ma brithers' weird, that for aa they are mony and bonnie
doun sall faa i the stour an dee at the hanns o their faemen,
 less for aa thir nor for ye, quhan some bress-sarkit Achaian
luggs ye greitan awa, takan frae ye the day o yer freedom.
"Thonder in Argos syne ye'll tent the loom til anither,
rin to the well in Messeis aiblins or far Hypereia,
sair and aften affrontit, a strang lourd weird 'll be on ye.
Aiblins a body'll say, that sees ye greitan fou sairlie:
'Thon yin's Hektor's wife, him that aye was the wale o the fechters,
Troylann's bauld chevaliers, quhan for Ilios toun they did battle.'   70
Siclike aiblins they'll say, an a new dule then'll be on ye,

want o a man lik me to keep aff ye the season o thralldom.
God, quhan I'm deid, i the murlit mools I'd wuss to be yirdit
or I suld hear yer skreigh o distress and yer waefu mischievan."

Sae spak gesserant Hektor, and raxt out his hann til his bairnie.
Och, but the wean outskraugh, sclentan back on the breist o his nourrice,
fairlie dumbfoonert he was at the sicht o his daddie that loed him,
fleggit sair at the bress and the crest wi its wallopan horsehair,
kelteran doun frae the tap o the bassanat, unco the sicht o't.

Lang then the baith o them leuch, his dad and the leddie his mither.   80
Syne the begesserant Hektor releaseit his bree frae the helmonte,
dounpit it then on the broun derk yird, whaur it bonnilie skinklit.
Kissan the bairn that he loed and dannlin't a wee in his airms,
spak he a prayer richt herty to Zeus and the lave o the godheids:

Zeus and aa ither gods, let this bairnikie be like ma nain sel,
kenspeckle whan he's a man owre aa the menfolk o Troylann,
firrfu lik me in his micht an the maister o Ilios burgh.
Syne may somebody say 'He's better a sicht nor his faither,'
quhan he comes up frae the war. May he come wi wappens aa bluidie,
graith o a foe he's slain, an the hert o his mither be blythened."   90

Siclike spak he, and neist gied back his son til his wifie,
ntil her hann that he loed. At her breist she happit him saftlie,
lauchan and greitan at yince. And her man was ruth at the sicht o't,
straikit her then wi's hann and spak til her couthie and hertlie:

Hinnie, dinna be fasht owre sairlie for me i yer spreit nou.
Nae man'll senn me tae Hell gin it's nae the time that is fateit.
Nae man, trulie I tell ye, sall flee frae his weird that is weirdit,
either the cuif nor the guid man, the weird that is his frae his birth-tyde.
You ye maun gang awa hame, and tak tent till yer ain kind o jobbies,
wirliego, loom an the lave. An see that the lassies are eident   100
entan their wark. The war and the battall the men'll tak tent til,
he abune aa, and the lave that are bairnies o Ilios burgh."

Sae spak gesserant Hektor, and liftit the bassanat blythlie,
horse-hair-crestit and aa; and his dear wife gaed awa hamewith,
turnan aften to luik at her man, aye greitan fou sairlie.

(l. 11) Skamandros is ane o the meikle flumes o the Trojan howe. Astyanax, "Maister o the broch," a by-name gien til the bairn out o honour til his faither.
(l. 59) The Greeks had a notion o gaean backward intil the time coman, the Gaels o gaean uphill.

syne: then *yetts:* gates *beguid:* began *howe-lann:* valley-land *weel-tochert:* dowered *bress-graithit:* bronze helmeted *wonned:* dwelt *tapetless:* heedless *loed:* loved *starnies:* stars *lauchan:* laughing *grat/greitan:* cried/crying *lourd:* heavy *aiblins:* perhaps *yince:* once *yirth:* earth *dree:* endure *weirdit:* fated *dule:* grief *lang syne:* long ago *herriet:* plundered *thraipfu:* prosperous *aigis:* shield o the god *corp:* corpse *tulyie:* squabble, tussle *kye:* cattle *yowes:* ewes *flesches:* fleeces *forbye:* besides *lave:* rest *spiel:* climb *thirlit:* pierced *chiel:* fellow *bassanat:* helmet *skinklan:* glittering *howdrand:* hiding *smeddumless:* cowardly *gleg:* sharp *meikle:* much *ingyne:* mind *tyde:* time *stour:* dust *faemen:* enemies *wuss:* wish *yirdit:* buried *gesserant:* sparkling *sclentan:* leaning *dumbfoundert:* amazed *fleggit:* startled *unco:* unusual,remarkable *begesserant:* glittering *bree:* brow, face *skinklit:* glittered *virrfu:* vigourous *neist:* next *gya:* gave *happit:* wrapped *spreit:* spirit *mirliego:* spindle *eident:* diligent

Frae Catullus, V. "Vivamus, Mea Lesbia, Atque Amemus…"

Lassie, c'wa

Lassie, c'wa, let's live in houghmagandie.
The life o luve's the life for you and me.
Gif unco-guid Kirk-Elders caa us randy
we'll fashna for their snash but ae bawbee.
Suns can gae doun and rise as bonnilie,
but us,— when yince-for-aa our wee bit licht
gaes doun, we're hapt for aye in ae lang nicht.

Gie me a thousand kisses, plus a hunder.
Anither thousand, nou a hunder mair.
C'wa, anither thousand, plus a hunder.   10
Syne when we've scryveit sae monie thousands there
tapsieteerie we'll whummle the sum wi care,
sae's we'll nae ken, and nae ill-gaishoned hizzie
mischieve us jalouslie for beean sae busy.

houghmagandie: a jocular word for sexual intercourse, fornication   *unco-guid:* self-righteous   *snash:* sneering   *bawbee:* a half penny, coin   *hapt:* wrapped   *syne:* then   *scryveit:* wrote   *tapsieteerie:* upside down   *ill-gaishoned:* malicious   *hizzie:* hussy

Frae Catullus, VIII, "Miser Catulle, Desinas Ineptire..."

Catullus man, ye maunna

Catullus man, ye maunna gang sae gyte.
Scryve't doun for tint, nou that ye see it's fled ye.
Umquhile the sun shone on ye, braw and whyte,
ye aye gaed eftir whaur the lassie led ye, —
"I'll loena onie ither lass sae dear".
Thon time ye'd monie a ploy to your delyte
that ye socht out, – the lassie wasna sweir.
Ay, ye had sunsheen yince, richt braw and whyte.

But nou she's sweir. Ye canna help it, sae
be thraward as weel. She flees, but dinna chase her. 10
Makna your life forfairn wi dule and wae,
wi tholesome sweirty ettle to outface her.

Guidbye, ma lass. Catullus nou is sweir.
He'll nae think lang, or speir agin your will.
But sair ye'll greet, nou naebody'll speir
onie nicht for ye, limmer. Eerie and dull
your life's be nou. What lad'll come ye near?
Wha'll think ye bonnie? Wha'll ye cuddle nou?
Whas lass be caad? Wha kiss? Or pree whas mou?

Och, c'wa, Catullus, stievelie nou. Be sweir. 20

gyte = foolish, insane *tint:* lost *umquhile:* formerly *sweir:* unwilling, stubborn *yince:* once *forfairn:* forlorn *dule:* grief *tholesome:* patient *ettle:* try *speir:* ask *limmer:* hussy, mistress *pree:* sample, kiss *stievelie:* obstinately

Frae the Latin o Sulpicia, Elegidion VI

I wish, my jo

I wish, my jo, ye'll never mair
   loe me sae weel and trulie
      as ye hae dune days twa or three
gif ever I've been in sic despair
   at daean oniething unrulie,
      when ramstam youth misguideit me,
as that yestreen I left ye lane.
   I was ettlan to hide the stouan pain,
my luve o ye that brunt owre sair.

jo: darling *loe:* love *ramstam:* headstrong *ettlan:* trying *stouan:* throbbing

Frae Propertius. Elegies II, xi.

Ithers may scryve

Ithers may scryve, or lea ye ligg unkent.
   The man that roosted ye wald saw sand wi seed.
   Thon last black kistan-day, yince ye are deid,
forbye yoursel sall soop aff ilk waement.
   Wi mudyeon for your banes the passer-by sall pass,
   nae even say, "This grieshoch was a skeely lass."

scryve: write *lea:* allow *ligg:* lie *kistan-day:* when the body is prepared to be viewed preceding the funeral *forbye:* besides *soop:* sweep *waement:* lament *mudyeon:* sneering grin *grieshoch:* ash *skeely:* talented

Frae the Latin o Emperor Gallienus

Lasses and Lads

Lasses and lads, crouse and herty,
swyte your sauls out, c'wa wi the party.
Saftlie woo,
like the croodlan doo,
tellan her charms.
Cuddle your belle,
tichter nor grip the ivy's arms,
kissan her mou
closer nor steeks the eyester-shell.
Nou tae your ploys, but dinna fash   10
tae smoor the licht.
It sees ilk ongaun o the nicht,
but that's aaricht,
the morn's morn it doesna clash.

crouse: cheerful   *doo:* pigeon   *steeks:* shuts   *smoor:* smother, cover
morn's morn: next morning   *clash:* gossip

Frae the Greek of Aeschylus, Agamemnon 429-455

Choric Threnody

Aa owre the hale o Grewe whaur they gaed out
a dule the hert canna thole
is in ilka hous. Monie the stang
thirls tae the melt.
Ilk ane kens wham he sent awa,
but insteid o men
graith and greishoch
wins back hame til ilk ane's hous.

The Weir-God, a siller-swapper o corps,
haudan his wechts i the fecht o spears,   10
sends hame brunt frae Ilios
tae their friends a lourd
bit mowe, sair-greitit-owre,
o grieshoch, the warth o the man,
pittan it i the urns, aisy tae be pitten.

Syne they mak mane, roosan this ane
for a canny fechter, and this ane for faaan
brawlie i the brulyie,
aa for the wife o anither.
But thon they'll mounge stowlans. A dule o jalousie   20
stends eftir the vengeabil sons o Atreus.
Anither wheen thonder about the waa
hae lairs i the Trojan yirth,
bonnie men that were. And the fremmit land
has yirdit its owreharlers.

Grewe: Greece *dule:* grief, disaster *thole:* endure *stang:* acute pain
thirls: pierces *melt:* spleen *graith:* armour *grieshoch:* cinders *siller-swapper:* money-changer *corps:* bodies *haudan his wechts:* holding his scales *friends:* relatives *lourd:* heavy *mowe:* dust *greitit:* wept
mane: moan *roosan:* praising *brawlie:* magnificently *brulyie:* close confused conflict *mounge:* mutter *stowlans:* furtively *stends:* stalks
vengeabil: revengeful *wheen:* group *lairs:* graves *fremmit:* aliens
yirdit: buried *owreharlers:* conquerors

198

Aristophanes in Scots: Frae Choruses o The Birdies

I the Wild West there's a region
caad the Gorbels, by the Clyde,
whar they breed a hero legion, –
razor-slashin is their pride.
Fans o Celtic and o Rangers
like their bottles, fou or tuim,
bonnie fechters aa. But dangers
lurk in streets whar lamps are dim.
There the horror-comic heroes
tak a bash wi cosh and cheen;   10
here sic smashers canna steer us, –
Embro's polis is owre keen.

Ye may see in dear Auld Reekie,
through the Hous o Parliament,
lawyers thrang, a sleekit, cliquey,
pin-stripe-breekit regiment.
There come Law Lords, supreme dignit-
aries that decern the pleas,
Deputes, Writers tae the Signet,
Advocates, and SSCs.   20
As the lawyer breeds that thrang here
uis their tung tae swell their wame,
while their clients, richt or wrang here,
pey the fees out juist the same.

tuim: empty   *steer:* disturb   *thrang:* crowd   *wame:* belly

Translations from Italian

Frae the Second Canzone o Dante's "Vita Nuova"

"Mentre Io Pensava La Mia Frale Vita…"

    Ae time that I our flownrie life appraisit
and saw hou brief and bruckil its duratioun,
i ma hert, whaurin he wones, Luve sabbit sairlie,
and wi Luve's sabban then my saul was frazit,
sae that I sychit and spak in conturbatioun:
"Siccar my luve maun dee, maun dee fu shairly".
At thocht o that I was dumbfoundert fairlie,
I steekit my een, that were forfairn and drowie,
and my hale spreit was dowie,
ilk facultie disjeskit and forwandert.   10
Syne as I ponderit,
frae trowth and kennan furth forvayt unwarelie,
phantouns o brayn-wud weemen drave at me,
and skraugh, "Yoursel maun dee. Ay, ye maun dee".

    Then saw I monie a dubie ferly, glaikit
wi slidder phantasies I gaed amang.
I kenna in whatna rowm I seemit to be,
whaur sheylit weemen cam stravaigan, traikit
wi makan waefu mane and greetan lang,
whas een wi grame flaughterit maist fierilie.   20
Howdlins a mirk owrehailt the sun's bricht blee,
the starns atour the firmament sae lither
waementit ilk til ither;
I saw the birds fleean i the lyft doun drap,
the hale yird quok and lap.
Syne cam a deid-wan chiel, spak hairsilie:
"Hae ye na heard the bruit o it frae onie?
Deid is your leddie, that was verra bonny".

flownrie: fragile *bruckil:* brittle *wones:* lives *frazit:* dismayed *sychit:* sighed *siccar:* surely *shairly:* surely *dumbfoundert:* amazed *steekit:* shut *forfain:* unhappy, forlorn *drowie:* indistinct *spreit:* spirit *dowie:* dispirited *disjeskit:* fatigued *syne:* then *forvayt:* wandered *braynwud:* stark mad *dubie:* obscure *ferly:* potent *glaikit:* dazed *slidder:* cunning, cajoling, slippery *rowm:* place *sheylit:* with the face distorted, distraught *stravaigan:* wandering *traikit:* lost, wearied *mane:* moan, lament *greetan:* crying *grame:* passion, rage *flaughterit: fluttered *mirk:* darkness *blee:* complexion *starns:* stars *atour:* around, across *lither:* nebulously opaque *waementit:* mourned *lyft:* sky *yird:* earth *chiel:* fellow *bruit:* rumour

Translations from French

Frae the French o Paul Valéry, "Le Bois Amical"

The Couthy Wuid

Chaste and pure were the things we thocht,
side by side, alang the loanies,
in ithers' hands, richt canty cronies,
amang derklan fleurs, speakan nocht.

Stendan on like troth-plicht fowk,
our lane, out-throu the parks' green nicht,
we bruikit thon fruct o ferly sicht,
the mune, sae kind til ilka gowk.

And syne, we dee'd upo the fug,
far aff, our lane, i the saft skug   10
o this reeshlan wuid, couthy and plat;
and heich amang thon merchless gleid
we fand ilk ither, and we grat,
thou trusty fere o the dumb-deid.

loanies: paths *canty:* cheerful *cronies:* boon-companions *stendan:* striding *troth-plicht:* engaged to be married *our lane:* by ourselves *bruikit:* enjoyed *fruct:* result, fruit, benefit *ferly:* wondrous, marvellous *syne:* then *fug:* moss *our lane:* by ourselves *skug:* sheltered spot *reeshlan:* rustling *plat:* plain, straightforward *merchless:* unbounded, infinite *gleid:* brilliant light *grat:* cried *fere:* companion *dumb-deid:* silence

Frae the French o Paul Valéry, "Le Cimetière Marin"

The Kirkyaird by the Sea

This lown riggin-side, whaur whyte doos gang,
quhidders amang the pines, the graves amang;
thonder perjink midday compounds frae fires
the sea, the sea, that's aye begun anew.
Braw guerdon eftir musardry to view
canny and lang the verra Gods' lown lires.

Wi what pure wark fine fuddrie-leams consume
monie an unseen diamant frae the spume.
Hou lown a peace is kendlit keethanlie.
When the sun liggs abune the abysm o swaws,   10
pure craturs o an everbydan cause,
time skinkles and the dream is savendie.

Savendle thesaur, Pallas' simple shrine,
thou mass o calm, seen siccar no to crine,
proud gloweran watter, ee that hains inside
sae meikle sleep ablow a fiery pall,
O my ain lowness! ... Biggin i the saul,
thousand-tiled gowden summit. Riggin-side!

Time's temple that a single sych can sum,
to this pure point I sclim, I'm uisd to come,   20
encircled wi my sea-stravaigan glance;
and like my final offerin to the Gods
thon seelfu skinklin saws, like grain on clods,
owre the deep hicht a Sovran arrogance.

As a fruct dwynes awa at a bite,
turnan its absence til a delyte
intil a mou whaur its form smoors,
I am braithan here my future fume,
and the luift sings to the saul gane tuim
the turnin to tumult o thir shores.   30

Braw luift, true luift, luik at me as I change.
Eftir sae meikle pride, sae meikle strange

thowlessness, and yet fou o virr,
I gie mysel owre to this gesserant spase.
On the deid fowk's houses my shadaw gaes,
makan me chief wi its dwaiblie steer.

My saul laid bare to the solstice-brands,
I haud ye up, wi your pitiless hands
thou wonderfu justice o siccan licht.
I restore you pure to your first place.   40
Luik at me! ... But reflectin rays
requires a dull half o shadaw-nicht.

For me my lane, me lane, in mysel
by a hert, whaur the springs o poetry well,
atween tuimness and the pure event,
I byde on the echo o my inner pouer,
wersh cistern, sonorous, obscure,
soundan i the saul a chasm never rent.

Do ye ken, fause prisoner o fullyeries,
gulph that swalws thir thin trellises,   50
owre my steekit een, secrets that blin,
what corse trails me til its thowless end,
what brou draws it to this bane-rife grund?
A bit sperk thonder thinks o my absent kin.

Steekit, consecrat, fou o fire but fuel,
a fragment o yird offered to the licht's rule,
I like this place, wi its brands' royal waves,
biggit frae gowd and stane and derk-leaved glades,
whaur fouth o marble sooms owre fouth o shades,
thonder the leal sea sleeps atour my graves.   60

C'wa, my grand bitch! gar misbelievers skail!
When I'm my lane smilean I tell my tale
o ferlie sheep lang I hae herdit here,
the whyte flock o thir my laigh lown lairs.
Keep aff the doos wi their auld-farrant airs,
and thowless dreams, and angels gleg to speir.

Aince here, the future is but indolence.
The golloch-scartit drouth liggs here intense.
Aathing brunt up, forduin, taen intil air,
intil ane essence stark ayont our thocht.... 70
Life becomes merchless, fou wi want o ocht,
wershness is douce, the spreit is clear and rare.

The dernit deid ligg cozy in this yird,
that warms and dries their mystery interred.
Midday abune, Midday without a steer
thinks in himsel, self-congruent, cordial....
Thou complete heid and perfect coronal,
I am the secret change inside you here.

You've nane but me to haud in check your fears.
My penitence, compulsion, douts and fears 80
are flaws to mar your diamant's majestie.
But in their nicht, wechtit wi marble stane,
a drowie fowk doun at the tree-ruits lain
hae sideit wi you in slaw solemnitie.

They hae dwyneit intil a thick nonentitie,
the reid clay drank the whyte identitie,
the gift o life has gane intil the fleurs.
Whaur are the deid anes' turns o phrase we kent,
their individual sauls, their personal sclent?
The larva spins in the tears' auld course. 90

Kittlit lassies' skreighins, blyth and keen,
bricht whyte teeth, blue and greetan een,
the loesome breist whaur the reid lowelicht lay,
the bluid that leams frae the surrendered mou,
the final gifts, the hands that guaird them true,
aa gangs to grund and comes again in play.

And you, great saul, do you hope for some dream
that sanna hae this bricht delusive leam
made here for carnal een by the gowd and the sea?
D'ye think ye'll sing when ye're a reekie wraith? 100
Fegs! Aathing flees! Here's me a porous graith!
And mystical Impatience tae maun dee!

Sable and gilt, thin Immortality,
thou lykewauk-kimmer, laureat monstrouslie,
makan o cauldruif daith a mither's lap,
the bonny lee, the pious stratagem!
Wha kensna them, wha scunnersna at them?
This tuim beld skull, this ever-girnan chap!

Profound faithers, ye untenantit skulls,
dounwechtit wi sae monie shuilfulls, 110
wha are the yird and taigle up our feet,
the true smurler, the worm nane can dodd,
is no for you, sleepan ablow the brod,
he lives on life, my life, and winna lea't!

Luve, aiblins, or self-hate, it may be?
His secret tooth is come sae near to me
that onie name could set him weel the day.
Why fash? He sees, desires, taks thocht, and grips!
He likes my flesh, he sups wi nuptial lips.
skairin his life is aa the life I hae! 120

Zeno, cruel maister of Eleatic thocht,
hae ye thirlit me wi thon arrow aflocht,
that dirls and flees and doesna flee a bit?
The sound bairns me and the arrow slays.
And the sun, Och! ... a tortoise-shadaw's pace
for the saul, Achilles stickit wi fiery fuit!

Na, na! Stand up! Intil the time ahead!
Brak up, my bouk, this pose o thochtfu heed!
Drink, apen breist, the newborn wind's upspring.
A sudden freshness, a breith frae aff the sea, 130
gies me my saul again.... Saut potencie!
C'wa, let us rin to the swaw wi virrfu fling.

Ay, meikle sea, deliriouslie arrayed,
thou panther-hide, thou gairit goddess-plaid
o myriad myriad solar deities,
absolute Hydra, fou wi your blue lire,
bitean your tail o skinklan sperks o fire
amang a dirdum lown as silence is.

The wind wins up! ... I maun ettle to live!
The merchless air apens and steeks my breve.   140
Abune the craigs swaw-pouther daurs be sprayed.
Flee awa nou, ye licht-bumbazeit blads.
Brak, brak, ye swaws. Brak wi blyth water-flads
this lown riggin-side whaur reivan jibsails gaed!

Explicit feliciter a.d. xii. Kal. Sept. MCMXLV.

lown: quiet *riggin-side:* roof *doos:* pigeons *quidders:* palpitates
perjink: exact *guerdon:* recompense *musardry:* meditation *lown*
lires: calm surface *fuddrie-leams:* lightning-flashes *kendlit keethanlie:*
conceived apparently *liggs:* lies *swaws:* waves *skinkles:* sparkles
savendie: intelligence *savendle:* stable *thesaur:* treasure *seen siccar*
no to crine: manifestly certain not to shrivel *gloweran:* frowning
hains: keeps *meikle:* much, a great amount *ablow:* below *lowness:*
silence *biggin:* building *sych:* sigh *sclim:* climb *sea-stravaigan:* sea-
wandering *seelfu:* serene *bruikin:* enjoyment *crines:* shrivels *fruct:*
fruit *dwynes:* dwindles *smoors:* gradually dies *luift:* sky *tuim:*
empty *thowlessness:* indolence *virr:* energy *gesserant spase:* brilliant
expanse *chief:* intimate *dwaiblie:* feeble *steer:* stirring *brands:*
torches *my lane:* by myself *tuimness:* emptiness *wersh:* bitter *dern:*
hidden *fullyeries:* foliage *swalws:* swallows *steekit:* closes, shuts
corse: corpse *bane-rife:* full of bones *yird:* earth *fouth:* abundance
sooms: floats *leal:* faithful *atour:* around *gar:* make *skail:* scatter
ferlie: mysterious *laigh lown lairs:* low quiet graves *auld-farrant:* sage
gleg to speir: quick to ask, inquisitive *golloch-scartit:* insect-scratched
drouth: drought *forduin:* exhausted *stark:* strong *merchless:* infinite
douce: sweet *spreit:* spirit *dernit:* hidden *douts:* doubts *drowie:*
indistinct *wechtit:* heavy *sclent:* inclination *kittlit:* tickled *reetan:*
crying *leams:* shines *sanna:* shall not *reekie:* smoky *graith:* apparatus
lykewauk-kimmer: deathbed-comforter *cauldruif:* chilly *beld:* hairless
ever-girnan: grimacing *chaft:* cheek, jaw *shuilfulls:* shovelfuls *taigle:*
entangle *smurler:* nibbler *dodd:* discomfit *ablow the brod:* below the
table *winna lea't:* will not leave it *aiblins:* perhaps *set:* suit *skairin:*
sharing *thirlit:* pierced *aflocht:* flying *dirls:* vibrates *bairns:* gives
birth to *bouk:* body *virrfu:* energetic, vigorous *gairit:* patched *lire:*
body-surface *dirdum:* tumult *maun ettle:* must try *steeks:* closes
breve: book *swaw-pouther:* wave-powder *licht-bumbazeit:* dazzled
blads: sheets, pages *water-flads:* chunks of water *reivan:* plundering

Translations from German

Frae Hugo Von Hofmannsthal:
"Wo kleine Felsen, kleine Fichten..."

Whaur monie a wee bit spruce and craig

Whaur monie a wee bit spruce and craig,
stands agin the lyft sae free
ye can come and ye can see
us makars, fou wi sangs, stravaig
about wee loanikies, like bairns.
Are na we, mair nor ithers,
the richt cantie tapitless bairns,
we mair bairnielike nor onie
o thir lassies and their brithers?
Are their ploys their real concerns,   10
thir ither anes, that are sae monie?

lyft: sky *makars:* poets *stravaig:* wander *cantie:* cheerful *tapitless:* heedless

Frae Theodor Storm: "Die Stadt"

Grey are the sands

Grey are the sands, and grey the sea,
whaur the toun liggs endlang;
a lourd haar smoors ilk riggan-tree,
and throu the dumbdeid sounds the sea
aye wi an aefauld sang.

In voar nae lintie sings sae blye,
nae wuids whush i the merse;
a hairst-nicht whiles, wi skreighan cry,
stravaigan geese flee owre and by,
the lang links blaw wi gerss.   10

And yet ma hale hert hings on ye,
ye grey toun on the sea;
for me Youth's charm and glamarie
bydes aye about ye, lauchanlie,
ye grey toun on the sea.

liggs: lies *lourd:* heavy *haar:* North Sea fog *smoors:* smothers, covers
riggan-tree: roof *dumbdeid:* silence *aefauld:* monotonous *voar:*
spring *blye:* blithe *hairst-nicht:* autumn-night *whiles:* sometimes
stravaigan: wandering *blaw:* bloom *glamarie:* glamour, magic
lauchanlie: laughingly

Frae the German o Emanuel Geibel

The mowdie

The mowdie fae his couthie neuk
heard a laverock sing,
and said, "Thon wheeplan and fleean
is a daft-like thing."

mowdie: mole *laverock:* lark *wheeplan:* whistling (also sweeping, flying)

Frae the German o Erich Fried

Hame frae Stalingrad

(Til the melodie: "Es dunkelt schon in der Heide")

The gloaman comes owre the muirland
   it's time to haud back hame:
we've boozed up aa the reid wine,
   we lea the whyte alane.

I heard a heuk douncaaan
   the corn wi its reeshlan duint:
I heard a corbie crawan,
   'My honour I hae tint'.

And hae ye tint your honour?
   Sae tint I my guid faith.   10
Our weird has gien the baith o us
   a bluidreid reekie daith.

A croun as reid as roses
   whaur I hae stuid sall faa:
the braid houms o Ruskinland
   are smoort wi an unco snaw.

The snaw is thowan rowthie,
   it rowes wi graimfu spate:
it rairs at my sweethairt's chalmer,
   sae she maun lowse the yett.   20

It thrangs my sweethairt's gairden,
   whaur's neither lass nor loon.
She suldna byde on me mair, —
   soom hame, my wee reid croun.

gloaman: twilight   *haud:* direct oneself   *boozed:* drunk   *heuk:* sickle
douncaaan: cutting down   *reeshlan:* rustling   *duint:* stroke   *corbie:* crow
tint: lost   *weird:* fate   *reekie:* smoky   *houms:* plains   *smoort:* smothered
unco: excessive   *rowthie:* abundantly   *rowes:* rolls   *graimfu:* wrathful
spate: flood, swell   *chalmer:* room   *lowse:* lose   *yett:* gate   *thrangs:* floods
loon: lad   *byde:* wait   *soom:* swim

Frae the German o Erich Fried
eftir the portraict by Pieter Breughel

The Bairns' Slauchter o Bethlehem

Bethlehem is a Fleming toun.
   Word comes the bairnies maun be slain.
Ae squad bydes at the corse, and round
   the houses the lave grip ilk wean.

The snaw scrunches atour their shuin,
   and thows in dubs throu ilka chalmer...
An auntran skreigh or a graimfu din...
   Syne calm as eeswal, ay, or calmer.

A man can thole rowth o dule,
   wi dragoons standan alang the street   10
to speir for grace wald set a fule.
   But the weemenfowk byde and greet.

They canna lea their bairns ligg,
   they speir at the trees, the dogs, the snaw.
The luift and the yird around sae big
   and the reid daithwound sae smaa?

Can ye credit – a blaw that brings nae bluid
   is eneuch, or ae straik o a knife?
And sae sune duin? The Lord beguid
   to tak a day to mak thon life.   20

The bairnie's dozent and maks nae quhither,
   the mortclaith-luift smoors aa the place
wi clorty smytes, the frichtit mither
   blaws them aff the cauld wee face.

bydes: waits *corse:* market-cross *lave:* rest *atour:* over, around *chalmer:* room *auntran:* occasional *graimfu:* wrathful *syne:* then *rowth:* abundance *dule:* grief *speir:* ask *set:* becomes *ligg:* lie *luift:* sky *yird:* earth *duin:* finished *beguid:* began *mortclaith:* funeral-pall *smoors:* smothers *clorty:* dirty *smytes:* flakes

*Frae a German owreset by Lili du Bois-Reymond o an
English Sonnet o the First World War whas autour isna kent*

On the Daith o a Young German Scholar

Ye were my fier, albeid we never met.
   Your faither brocht me ae day as his guest,
and nichtartale, the simmer suin dounset,
   gya me your chalmer to my place o rest.
And syne I felt fresh wauchts o your ingyne,
   like fleurs Persephone sends furth for seil,
and kent that your fiers were auld fiers o mine, —
   Aeschylus, Plato, Sophokles, Virgile.
Sae I was mindit, come anither year,
   to be acquent. But nou ye're gane awa   10
   to thae lown parks whaur asphodelnies blaw.
Ye answerna my voice ye canna hear.
Ligg lichtlie, yirth. Hain aye i your lown peace
the grieshoch o sae braw a sacrifice.

fier: comrade *nichtartale:* at night *gya:* gave *chalmer:* room *syne:* then *wauchts:* draughts *ingyne:* spirit *seil:* blessing *lown:* quiet *blaw:* bloom *ligg:* lie *yirth:* earth *grieshoch:* ashes

Frae the German o Ludwig Uhland

On a Bairn's Daith

For Dauvit Murison

(1) Aberdonian:-

    Saftlie ye cam and gaed. Awa frae men
      ye flittit aff, eftir nae lang abode.
    Faur fae? Faur til? We speir, but anerly ken:
    Out o God's haund intil the haund o God.

(2) Lesbian:-

        Ἠλθές ποτα μολθάκως σύ,
        ξέννα, καὶ ἀπῴχεο αὖτε
          γᾶς πεποταμένα.
        πόθεν; ποθι; τόσσον ἴδμεν —
          θέων ἄπυ κής θέοις

(3) Ionic:-

'Ρίμφα μάλ' ἦλθες ἀπῴχεό τ' αὖ μαλακοῖσι πόδεσσι
    ξείνη ἀπόπτολις ὣς γῆν προλιποῦσα βροτῶν.
'Αλλὰ πόθεν; καὶ ποῖ; Μοῦνον τόδε γ' ἴσμεν ἀληθές —
    ἦσθά τις ἀθανάτων εἶ τε παρ' ἀθανάτοις

Frae Paul Heyse

Eftir the Daith o a Bairn

I thocht I heard ye chap upo the door,
   and rase til apen, as gin yince again
ye stuid there speiran, like ye uisd afore,
   sae couthilie, "*Daddie, can I come ben?*"

Ay, and yestreen stravaigan on the sand
I felt your wee bit hand het i my hand,
And whar the chad was rown i the swaw
I spak out loud, "*Tak tent and dinna faa.*"

chap: knock   *rase:* rose   *yince:* once   *speiran:* asking   *ben:* through   *stravaigan:* strolling   *chad:* shingle   *rowan:* rolling   *swaw:* wave   *tak tent:* take heed   *dinna faa:* do not fall

Frae Christian Morgenstern

A black birdie flees owre the warld,
that sings daith-eerilie
Gin ye hear him, ye hear nocht mair avaa,
gin ye hear, ye s' be wae for evermair,
ye downa see the sun again.

I the howedumbdeid, the dumbdeid throu,
he rests himsel on the finger o Daith.
Daith straiks him saftlie and says til him:
Flee on, birdie! Flee, my birdikie!
And he flees aff wheepan owre the warld.   10

avaa: at all   *howedumbdeid:* dead of night

...

Suddron frae that Samyn Makar

How the Stillness oer the Width of Water hitherwandering comes,
   where the Day's belated rosy Glow outdims, outswims.
How the Stillness oer the Width of Water hitherwandering comes,
   while the sombre-russet moon looms up from dusky Mountain-Domes.
How the Stillness oer the Width of Water hitherwandering comes.
   Wrathful shrieks a Bird, and ceases, deep in Woodland Glooms.
How the Stillness oer the Width of Water hitherwandering comes.

Frae the German o Heine

I loe a fleur

I loe a fleur, but I kenna whilk ane,
   whilk gars me smert.
I rin tae the fleurs, and keek in ilk ane,
   seekan a hert.

I the bricht o the gloaman the fleurs are smellan,
   the nichtigal trills.
I'm eftir a hert as proudlie swellan
   as my ain hert thrills.

The nichtigal trills, and I ken brawlie
   what her bonnie sangs say.   10
The baith o us are sae wae and lawlie,
   lawlie and wae.

loe: love *gars:* makes *keek:* peep *gloaman:* twilight *nichtigal:* nightingale *brawlie:* excellently *wae:* woeful *lawlie:* low in spirits

Frae the German o Goethe

Travesty in Lallans: Mignon's Song, "Kennst du das Land..."

Ken ye the countrie whaur the citrons grow?
Gowd orangers in mirlan fullyerie lowe,
a saft wind blaws frae lyfts blue aa the day,
shiftless the myrtle stands, and heich the bay.
D'ye ken it weel? Thonder's the land for me,
thonder, ma jo, I'd fain stravaig wi ye.

Ken ye the hous? The pillart ruif sae braw,
ilk glistran chalmer and the leaman haa.
There marbyr pictures stand and glentan say
"What's happent ye, bairn, that gars ye luik sae wae?" 10

D'ye ken it weel? It's thonder I wald be,
stravaigan aye, and ye there bieldan me.
Ken ye the mountain and the haarie brig?
The mule glamps blindlins on the mirky rigg,
the auld wurm's fode in oorie spelunks bydes,
doun draps the cleugh and owre't the spate-linn rides.
Ken ye it weel? Thonder our wey maun be,
Och, faither, let us gae stravaigan free.

fullyerie: foliage *lowe:* burn *lyfts:* skies *jo:* darling *stravaig:* wander *chalmer:* room *leaman:* radiant *glentan:* glancing *gars:* makes *oorie:* dank *spelunks:* caves, caverns *cleugh:* chasm

Translations from Lithuanian

Kościuszko's son

Kościuszko's son liggs i the wuid shot deid.
Aa's richt by him, he liggs i the wuid shot deid.
Dod, he was aye a bauld untentie laddie,
wha heeditna his faither or his mither
or onie ither o his noble clansfowk.

Gae, scryve a line to faither Kościuszko,
and gar him scryve til us a braw bit letter,
to let us ken whaur we maun hae him yirdit.
Heich on a hill, under the bield o an aik-tree,
i the whyte sand, aye i the saft whyte sand-drift.   10

Under the aik-tree thonder, i the whyte sand-drift.
The muckle aik-tree, it sall be his faither,
the saft whyte sand-drift, it sall be his mither,
the pines sae buirdly they sall be his brithers,
saft-drappan sauch-trees they sall be his sisters.

Kościuszko: early 19th century Polish nationalist

liggs: lies *untentie:* unattentive *scryve:* write *gar:* make *yirdit:* buried *buirdly:* resolutely *sauch:* willow, poplar

The Gods' buss, epple-ringie

The Gods' buss, epple-ringie, blaws
amang the rue i the gairden-waas.
A cowzie nor' wind cam wi a whuss
and rave a ryce frae the Gods' buss.
There breenged at a gallop a young laddie
and lowsit i the gairden his broun cuddie.
The shelt stravaigit i the gairden fair,
and the laddie gaed aff to the lassie rare.
The naig dountrampit the rowthie rue,
and the laddie preed the lassie's mou.   10
Fraemang the rue caa aff the cuddie,
frae the bonnie lass caa aff thon laddie.

epple-ringie: southernwood, lad's love *cowzie:* boisterous *rave:* tore
ryce: twig *breenged:* rushed, plunged *lowsit:* set loose *cuddie:* gypsy
word for a donkey, thence generally any small or inferior animal of the
equine sort *shelt:* small horse *stravaigit:* wandered *rowthie:* plentiful
preed: sampled *caa:* drive

Britherly Fareweel

Nou three crousie cockerels craw,
the brither graiths his horse sae braw.
   Wauk up, sister, frae your bouer,
   wauk, ye slamber lily fleur.
It's I tae the weir maun ride awa.
Mither, licht the candle sheen,
I maun wash my face and een,
   and syne tak britherly fareweel
   o my wee tittie, fond and leal.
Aiblins we'll never mair convene.   10
Whas kist nou are ye buskan there?
Whas linen are ye fauldan fair?
   I canna tak it wi me, lass,
   my brithers waldna lea me pass
wi sic gear tae the battle sair.
The King'll gie us cleidans shairly,
glaives for our whyte haunds, tempered rarely.
   Syne we'll busk oursels sae braw
   wi meikle graith o weir and aa,
aa faither's sons they'll think us fairly.   20
The warld micht burst upon us three
and kings plowter in bluid tae the knee,
   we'll byde the steer sae stieve and bauld,
   ne'er sall our reid bluid rin cauld,
and aiblins we'll win the victorie.

crousie: merry *graiths:* harnesses *bouer:* bedroom *slamber:* delicate *weir:* war *syne:* then *tittie:* sister *leal:* faithful *aiblins:* perhaps *convene:* meet *kist:* coffin *busk:* trim *fauldan:* folding *lea:* allow *cleidans:* clothing *shairly:* surely *glaives:* swords *meikle:* a great amount, much *graith:* equipment, trappings *plowter:* flounder, squelch *steer:* disturbance *stieve:* firm *bauld:* bold

Translations from Chinese

"Shi King": The Second o the Odes o T'Ang

Rowans are rowthie

Rowans are rowthie heich on the braes,
elms i the hauch grow swack.
The laird has an aumry o braw cleidan,
but never a coat til his back.
The laird has Clydesdales and a muckle cosch,
but he rides never ava.
In daith he maun part wi the hale jing-bang,
ane ither sall joys them aa.

Bierly birks abune on the brae,
yews dounby i the den.   10
The laird has a spence and a pillart haa,
neither bruim nor wattle they ken.
The laird has a fiddle and a braw bag-pipe,
but pipesna nor fiddles sae fine.
In daith he maun part wi the hale jing-bang,
ane ither sall bruik them syne.

Spirlie the ash sclims on the brae,
sauch-trees sough at the well.
The laird has a fouth o meat and drink,—
why suldna he pleasure himself,   20
ilk day dirlan the clarsach-strings,
merry as lang's he's spared?
For he'll dee his daith and quit his hame,
whaur ane ither sall come to be laird.

---

rowthie: plentiful, abundant *swack:* strong *aumry:* cupboard, wardrobe
cleidan: clothes *cosch:* coach *joys:* enjoy *bierly:* robust, strapping
spence: drawing-room *bruim:* broom, thatch *bruik:* enjoy *syne:* then
spirlie: spindly *sclims:* climbs *sauch:* willow, poplar *sough:* whisper,
murmur *fouth:* abundance *dirlan:* vibrating, plucking

"Shi King": The Second o the Odes o Wei

The Hermit Bonze

Biggan his bothy by the muirland burn,
   thonder the lord o state finds freedom nou,
waukruif or sleepan wones in musardry,
   braksna his life-long aith, but hains it true.

Biggan his bothy on the mountain-bord,
   the great man there wi ballant and auld sang
pleasures himsel his lane baith nicht and day,
   braksna the aith he'll hain his life-time lang.

Biggan his bothy thonder on the braes,
   centred on that he bydes, far aff frae men;   10
baith day and nicht keeps his ain companie,
   braksna the aith nae ither man sall ken.

biggan: building *bothy:* hut *waukruif:* awake *wones:* lives *musardry:* meditation *hains:* keeps *bord:* edge *his lane:* alone

"Shi King": The Ninth o the Odes o Wei

The Rich Spinster's Sang

   Puir friendless tod,
owre thonder at the cruives o K'i.
   Ech sirs, the pitie o't,
a breekless man's nae sicht tae see.

   Puir friendless tod,
breistan the spate at the fords o K'i.
   ech sirs, the pitie o't,
nae belt about his middle had he.

   Puir friendless tod,
owre thonder on K'i's banks sae bonny.   10
   Ech sirs, the pitie o't,
plaid, sark or coat, he hadna onie.

tod: fox *cruives:* fish-dams *spate:* flood, swell *sark:* shirt

The Auchtand o the Odes o P'ei
   (by a leddie for her man at the war)

The phaisant cock has flown awa

The phaisant cock has flown awa,
   och, but his wings gaed slawlie.
Richt sair, I ken, man bonnie man,
   thon twynan made ye lawlie.

The phaisant cock has flown awa,
   alowe and abune he skraikit.
My lord was leal aye, and ma hert
   wi rowth o dule is traikit.

Goaman lang at the sun and the mune,
   ma thochts run free and swack;   10
they tell me it's a weary wey.
   Ken ye how he'll come back?

Ye ken, that were his trusty feres,
   his mensefu braverie,
nae ill-gaishon'd gredur about him?
   What did he unhonestlie?

twynan: separation *lawlie:* low in spirits *leal:* loyal *rowth:* abundance
dule: misery, grief *goaman:* heeding *swack:* abundant *feres:* companions *mensefu:* well-mannered *ill-gaishon'd:* malicious

Translations from Russian

Frae the Russian o Pushkin

I loed ye yince

I loed ye yince, and aiblins i ma hert
thon luve's nae aathegither dwineit awa.
But dinna let it fash ye onie mair,
I waldna seek to gar ye greet ava.
I loed ye tungless, loed ye hopelesslie,
whiles unco jalous, whiles owre blate to woo ye.
I loed ye yince, sae tenderlie, sae trulie,
as gie't ye God some ither chiel may loe ye.

loed: loved *yince:* once *aiblins:* perhaps *dwineit:* wasted away, dwindled *gar:* make *greet:* cry *whiles:* sometimes *unco:* unusual, excessive *blate:* shy, timid *chiel:* fellow

Ich liebte dich. Mag sein dass jene Liebe
brennt noch und funkelt mir in diesem Herz.
Doch huet' du dich vor jedem traur'gen Triebe,
ich moechte wohl dir machen keinen Schmerz.
Ich liebte dich ganz hoffnungslos, verschwiegen,
durch Eifersucht gequaelt, und sonst durch Scheu.
Dir treu und zart all' mein' Gedanken stiegen.
Gott gib dir einen ander'n Mann so treu.

The Black Shawl

Wudlike I luik on the black satin shawl
and sorrow is ryvan my cauld-stricken saul.

When I was a callant, a daft thochtless ass,
I loed wi a passion a young Grecian lass.

She kissed and caressed me, sae gentie and gay,
but sune I was weirdit to see the derk day.

Ae day my guid cronies were speirt til a splore,
a scunnersome Jew cam and chapt at the door,

and rouned i my lug, "*While ye birl at the wine*
een nou ye're betrayed by the fause Grecian queyn." 10

I gya til him gowd, and banned him fu sair,
and cried my leal servant to busk and prepare.

Awa then we gaed, I pit spurs to the shelt,
and smoorit the saft-hertit pitie I felt.

As sune as I saw the door-stane o the Greek
derk were my een, I grew dizzy and sick.

My lane in ben to the chalmer I pass,
an Armenian is clappan the fause-hertit lass.

I sawna the jo, the steel fell wi a whiss,
the loon wantit leisure to brak aff his kiss. 20

A gey while I strampit the corp o the man,
and luikt at the lass, ohn speakin and wan.

I mind yet on her prayers, bluid ran on the stane, —
the Greek lass was gane, and my luve o her gane.

I tuik the black shawl frae the deid lassie's heid
and silently dichtit the dagger sae reid.

Syne my man, when the gloaman cam haarie and raw,
up and threw the twa corps i the swaws o Danaw.

Sin that time I kissna een that are bricht,
sin that time I kenna the lusts o the nicht. 30

Wudlike I luik on the black satin shawl,
and sorrow is ryvan my cauld-stricken saul.

wudlike: like a madman *ryvan:* tearing *callant:* youth *loed:* loved *gentie:* delicate, elegant, sprightly *weirdit:* fated *cronies:* boon-companions *speirt:* invited *splore:* merry party *scunnersome:* loathsome *chapt:* knocked *rouned:* whispered *lug:* ear *birl:* ply drinks *queyn:* girl *gya:* gave *banned:* cursed *sair:* sore *leal:* loyal *busk:* make ready *shelt:* pony *smoorit:* smothered *door-stane:* threshold *my lane:* alone *chalmer:* room *clappan:* embracing *jo:* sweetheart *loon:* fellow, lad *wantit:* lacked *gey while:* considerable time *strampit:* marked, embossed *corp:* corpse *ohn:* without *dichtit:* wiped *syne:* then *gloaman:* twilight *haarie:* foggy *swaws:* waves *Danaw:* Danube *lusts:* pleasures

...

Dearer the fleurs o hairst's dwynin
  nor voar's first flourischan schene.
    They wauken dowie musardrie
      in ilk ane's spreit mair vivuallie.
Een sae, whiles, the hour o twynin
  is viver nor a new convene.

hairst: autumn *dwynin:* dwindling *voar:* spring *schene:* brilliance *dowie:* melancholy *musardrie:* meditation *spreit:* spirit *vivuallie:* vividly *twynin:* separation *viver:* more vivid *convene:* meeting

...

Amang the fullyerie's shadow-ferlies
  and clover's daithless fouth
I fand a lowean fire frae heaven,
  brunt throu wi luve's drouth.

fullyerie: foliage *ferlies:* marvels *fouth:* abundance *lowean:* burning *drouth:* dryness, thirst

To A. P. Kyern

I remember the marvellous meeting,
   before me I saw you appear,
a glimpse, a vision fleeting,
   the Spirit of Beauty clear.

Hopeless, sad, and surrounded
   by turbulence, grief, and care,
in my ears your soft voice sounded,
   I pictured your features fair.

Years passed, and my dreams confounding,
   Rebellion stormed through the air;   10
I forgot your voice soft-sounding,
   your features heavenly-fair.

In dark exile, desolation,
   my days passed slow and sad;
no Deity, inspiration,
   life, pity, nor love I had.

My heart is awake and beating,
   there again I see you appear,
a glimpse, a vision fleeting,
   the Spirit of Beauty clear.   20

My soul swells with elation,
   returning to earth above,
to Deity, inspiration,
   pity, and life, and love.

Frae the Russian o Kondrati Fyedorovitch Rileyev

Octobrist Manifesto

Freedom! Your proud inspiration, —
   the fowk feel na what ye are.
Wheesht to revengfu consecration,
   nane maks a steer agin the Tsar.

Hauden doun by deils' repression
   aneath a lifelang wecht o steel,
their douce herts feel na their oppression,
   their hairns canna think it real.

Slavish Russia I hae viewit
   thrangan the kirks frae near and far,   10
jinglan censers, wi their craigs bouit,
   the Russians worshippan their Tsar.

---

steer: stir, disturbance   *wecht:* weight   *douce:* gentle, sober   *hairns:* brains   *thrangan:* crowding, flooding   *craigs:* necks

Frae the Russian o Nyekrasov

A Mother's Tears

Viewing the terrors of the strife,
   with each new victim of the battle,
I mourn not friend, I mourn not wife,
   I mourn not heroes killed like cattle.
Widowed wives one may console,
   the best of friends give over sighing,
but somewhere there remains a soul
   that still remembers till her dying.
Among the vulgar and absurd
   eye-serving tricks of our deceiving,   10
in all the world is seen and heard
   one kind of true and holy grieving, —
unhappy mothers' hopeless crying.
They can't forget their children's dying
   among the battle's bloody maze.
   The weeping willow cannot raise
her downcast twigs for all her trying.

Translation from the Welsh

Frae the Welsh hymn by D. Gwenallt Jones

Wales

Saunts o lang syne ligg in stour nou,
   martyrs sleep here neist your hairt:
ye that gae them life and motion
   faulds them here for rest apart.

Angels here at kirk and mercat
   left their fuitprents plain tae view:
here the Halie Spreit cam nestan
   mangs your wuids a cushiedoo.

Makars i the stormwinds' sychin
   heard the Victim's agony: 10
throu the oorie forest shadaws
   saw thon corse upraised on hie.

New uprisen He made your springtime,
   sauvit made your simmer green:
owre your cauldruif bens o winter
   perfit Grace has woned serene.

Providence poured doun its dauchfaa
   owre your cornfields' springan breer:
aa your graith shone wi His glory,
   leaman frae your horses' gear.   20

Aaweys airtit, eident gangrels,
   sailed your ships outowre the sea,
wechtit tae their benmaist haulds wi
   troggin brocht frae Calvary.

God had gien you arles for service,
   made you witness for His plea:
owre your yetts His covenants scryvit
   stand til aa eternitie.

Ye hae loed your saunts undeemis,
   nou they thrang in luve tae sing: 30
you hae gethert them thegither
   here ablow their mither's wing.

saunt: saint *lang syne:* long ago *ligg:* lie *stour:* dust *neist:* next *gae:* gave *faulds:* folds *cushiedoo:* wood pigeon *makars:* poets *sychin:* sighing *oorie:* dank *corse:* corpse *sauvit:* saved *cauldruif:* chill *woned:* dwelt *dauchfaa:* dewfall *breer:* growth (from seed) *graith:* harness *leaman:* radiant *aaweys:* in all directions *airtit:* headed *eident:* diligent *gangrels:* wanderers *wechtit:* heavy *troggin:* wares *arles:* goodluck pence *yetts:* gates *scryvit:* inscribed *loed:* loved *undeemis:* countless *thrang:* crowd *gethert:* gathered *ablow:* below

Translation from the Hebrew

Frae the Hebrew

The 23rd Psalm o King Dauvit

The Lord's my herd, I sall nocht want.
   Whaur green the gresses grow
sall be my fauld. He caas me aye
   whaur fresh sweet burnies rowe.

He gars my saul be blyth aince mair
   that wandert was frae hame,
and leads me on the straucht smaa gait
   for sake o His ain name.

Tho I suld gang the glen o mirk
   I'ld grue for nae mischance,   10
Thou bydes wi me, Thy kent and cruik
   maks aye my sustenance.

Thou spreids ane brod and gies me meat
   whaur aa my faes may view,
Thou sains my heid wi ulyie owre
   and pours my cogie fou.

Nou seil and kindliness sall gae
   throu aa my days wi me,
and I sall wone in God's ain hous
   at hame eternallie.   20

---

fauld: fold   *caas:* drives   *rowe:* roll   *gars:* makes   *straucht smaa gait:* straight narrow track   *mirk:* darkness   *grue:* feel a chill of horror   *bydes:* dost remain   *kent:* shepherd's long pole for leaping hedges, etc   *cruik:* crook   *brod:* board, table   *meat:* food   *faes:* enemies   *sains:* dost bless   *ulyie:* oil   *cogie:* bowl   *seil:* blessing   *wone:* dwell

The Coolin: An Assonantal Projection into English, from the original Gaelic of Sorley MacLean's 'An Cuilithionn'

Dedication

Christopher Grieve, "MacDiarmid",
if I had even the leavings
scraped from the scum of a particle
of your keen mind, deep and ample,
I would lift the awesome Coolin
skyward in radiant tumult,
I would set the Island yelling
with a fateful shout in the heavens.
And you, glorious Macdonald,
had I a third of your potency   10
I would steer our fine Skye vessel
head on to Europe's war-welter.

First Movement

Scurr Alasdair the scurr that's loftiest,
but Scurr nan Gillean the best scurr of all of them,
the dark-blue scurr, wide-jawed and massive,
the scurr of branches, narrow, antlered,
the awesome scurr, great and dangerous,
the scurr of Skye that is my favourite:
best of places the world over
for me to be on your high shoulders,
grappling your rocky stark-grey gullet,
my fight with your hard chest, craggily surging.   10

Dedication:
(l. 5) The Cuillin range in Skye: symbol of Communist aspiration.
(l. 9) Alasdair Mac Mhaighstir Alasdair, 18th century Gaelic poet and Scots patriot.

Clambering there from the corrie upward,
foot on shelf, chest to boulder,
finger in fissure, mouth to overhang,
on shaking foot-holds head not dizzy,
arm tough and bold, never turning
till it reach the skyline of your fifth summit,
where there will break on the head of my struggle
the great grey sea of gabbro surges,
the knife-edge of thin high ridges,
the dark steel belt of furious billows, 20
an ocean's welter packed among cliff-sides,
its eternal maws the chasm-gizzards,
its spouting perpetual in the rocky turrets,
scurrs thrown up its endless surging.
I see the fine Isle, jewelled with charms,
that was seen with yearning by Big Mahri:
in the scattering of mist from the head of Garsven,
crawling over waste scree-shoulders,
the fate of my people rises before me,
the lovely Island's dreary story. 30

The loch of lochs is in Corrie Laggan
except for the freshets of Corrie a-Vattie;
the best of freshets in the whole world
springs in the white green Fyoon Corrie:
the freshets' plenty and fresh youths' scarcity
daily and nightly keep me wakeful,
my anguish the loss of our country's people,
banishment, plunder, the crofters' clearing.
I see the Great Isle's winding shore-lands
and a hoodie-crow squatting on every fortress, 40
black hoodie-crows, soft, crass, and squinting,
- all eagles in their own opinion:
a flabby hoodie-crow is crouching
on the slippery roosts of a certain tower,
a lying hoodie down in Portree there
smarmily flatters that sleekit female.

(l. 26) Mary MacPherson, poetess of the Land League.
(l. 43) Flora Macleod of Dunvegan.
(l. 45) Headmaster of Portree school.

This wall was built by the Devil in person
60 to put in hiding the ~~fortress~~ Castle-Headland,
the Laird of Dunvegan fleecing his tenants,
Macleod plundering with reverend protection,
clearing crofters and planting instead of them
brute beasts. And thanks to the same Devil
that I'm not in sight of Loch Slapin
where Macdonald caused long-drawn anguish;   Lord Macdonald of
slavery came in at his lordship's commandment,   Sleat
the crofters were cleared and sheep planted.
But O for Dunvinish, girdled with precipices,
70 the foul shame of the Isles was checked there,   references to
where a kick-up was made by the folk of Glendale   crofter risings
enough   about 1880
~~fit~~ to shatter Castle Dunvegan.
And O my country, the Braes of Clan Nicol,
where was renewed the withered vigour,
a bold movement of attack was made there   the Battle of the Braes,
that brought Scotland to the turn of waking.   crofters against police.

Here's a croft to please my temper,—
a part of Minginish in Heaven;
a bit of Trotternish in glory
80 would make my wished-for portion;
a piece of Waternish in the Kingdom
would excel the Green Isle in virtue.   Green Isle: Celtic Paradise
Bracadale of the rain-green ~~pastures~~ grazings

This wall was built by the Devil in person
to put in hiding the Castle-headland,
the Laird of Dunvegan fleecing his tenants,
Macleod plundering with reverend protection,　　　　50
clearing crofters and planting instead of them
brute beasts. And thanks to the same Devil
that I'm not in sight of Loch Slapin
where Macdonald caused long-drawn anguish;
slavery came in at his Lordship's commandment,
the crofters were cleared and sheep planted.
But O for Dyoorinish, girdled with precipices,
the foul shame of the Isles was checked there,
where a kick-up was made by the folk of Glendale
enough to shatter Castle Dunvegan.　　　　60
And O for my country, the Braes of Clan Nicol,
where was renewed the withered vigour,
a bold movement of attack was made there
that brought Scotland to a turn of waking.

Here's a croft to please my temper, -
a part of Minginish in Heaven;
a bit of Trotternish in Glory
would make my wished for portion;
a piece of Vaternish in the Kingdom
would excel the Green Isle in virtue.　　　　70
Bracadale of the rain-green grazings
would put beauty on Hell's pavements.
I would hear from the bottom of the pit of torment
the bridled Vattirshtain Stallion snorting.
Brown-green Slate, with its lovely women,
wide great Strath, with its noble pinnacles,
to them I would give my love together,
and Blahven's bald skull over the estuary.
But give me myself Brittle Shoulder,
though it should cost as much, or more so,　　　　80

(l. 54) Lord Macdonald of Sleat.
(l. 59) Referring to crofter risings about 1880.
(l. 63) The Battle of the Braes, crofters against police.
(l. 70) Green Isle: Celtic Paradise.
(l. 74) A rock in North Skye: symbol of heroic Scotland.

as the Scorribreck sheep and three-fold over
the sum that was once paid out yonder
on account of the debts of his noble Lordship.
As soon as the place was my property
I would stand there above Shesgach Corrie
and take a view of the rocky Coolin,
the whole length from the Naze of the Skooman
to the gully that splits Scurr an-Ettin.
Then I would call Michael and tell him,
and Gabriel too, at their pleasure, 90
to help themselves to what they wanted,
east and west, southward and northward;
I would give to them and to every pair
of angels and high arch-angels
their hearts fill, fully and freely,
of sheep and cattle and moorland sheep-fanks
that they might clear out of my neighbourhood
and leave Skyemen in their own place.

Then everything would be in order
if only I were Seton Gordon; 100
I would make descriptions deftly
just to the taste of bourgeois gentlemen.

And all would be smooth and graceful
if only I were Kennedy-Fraser,
I would spin adulterated music
to soothe and wheedle their ears with its crooning.
And you, no doubt, if I happened to mention you
I'd be making silk of your precipices
and Fairy-Music of the Spectral Terror,
I would drink only the Well of the Gentry. 110

But who on earth would be pleased about it
supposing I were Neil Macleod?
For what he saw was gloomy corries
along with his travailed country's sorrow.

(l. 82) A Macdonald estate sold for debt.
(l. 100) Author of descriptive zoological and sporting books.
(l. 104) Arranger of expensive volumes of *Songs of the Hebrides*.
(l. 112) Skye poet, late 19th century.

Some cursed the glens they had to be leaving
that bracken alone might thrive freely;
and, if they cursed, their prophecy is heavy
upon the towers that are highest at present.

I see the Castle of Dunvegan
all one leaping-flame of bracken,   120
I see the great Armadale mansion
luxuriant, foundation and battlement.

I see old townships of Brae Eynort
like rivers of bracken with the spate rising,
and I see the Gaels' pale Twilight
reaching heaven with its bracken-lightning.

But I saw Kennedy-Fraser polluting
with that plant's blossom of true music,
I see a talkative little old woman
and about her mouth its green froth drooling.   130
Since all these have been seen truly
I'm damned if I'll seek a superfluity.

But what, - if this be a civil inquiry, -
is the pitch of filth in the worthy Island?
I say: a creature that's no Skyeman,
that toadies the refuse of ancient chieftains,
a black hoodie-crow, vain and sleekit,
prone to jealousy, a paltry creature,
pusillanimous, scheming, sneaking,
slippery, boastful, hollow, greasy,   140
turning, twisting, fawning, feeble,
plausible, snobbish, sweet, deceitful.

He said I would never rise to a bourgeois
because my tongue was so brutal,

(l. 121) Lord Macdonald's castle.
(l. 125) Reference to the literary 'Celtic Twilight', 1890-1910.
(l. 129) Mrs Macleod of Dunvegan.
(l. 135) Headmaster at Portree.

and I know I shall never attain the smoothness
of his tongue's demure purity.

Never mind, I'll say no more,
though he traversed Inverness all over
licking advancement, the way a stoat
sucks shell-less eggs' slavery matter.   150
He sucked many from every party.

A day was mine on Scurr a' Ghretty,
I stood on the high notched knife-edge steadily
looking down on the Corrie of Loneliness,
and all around me the mist pouring:
and once, where the rain-drift was broken,
a glimpse of gold gleamed for a moment
on the wings of an eagle passing below me
along the precipice-flanks slopingly.
But for me beyond all birds' glory   160
is the Bird of Skye with its golden brightness.
I turned round, and there behind me
was Minginish in range of my eyesight
and yonder green Bracadale lying,
Dyoorinish, and Trotternish sidelong:
the fine Isle's glory rose to my mind then,
arose, but another thought beside it –
What sense has my passion to any Skyeman
bourgeois-ward busily climbing?

In a large ball-room down in London   170
mustered the bourgeois of Clan Macleod,
a little yattering English female
arranging a spree for the festive crowd.

From Heleval More to Scurr Hoolum
cried out each hill and meadow-strip

(l. 148) County Education Authority centres at Inverness town.
(l. 161) Skye means the Winged Isle.
(l. 171) Clan Macleod Society featured in 'Picture Post'.
(l. 172) Mrs Macleod of Dunvegan..

for joy at the way things have happened
since the far-off days of the Big Ship.

Many a bluff and spring was mourning
from Ardmore to Brooach na-Free,
many a homesick spirit travelled   180
from far lands and the great sea.

On gusty winds from the West sweeping
was heard a faint eerie voice:
"Ben Hota-Goramul and its handsome menfolk,
Ben Dooagrich, dearest of joys."

Bare cold bones were resurrected
from the Vatersay Strait's welter of sea,
their brittle hardness made a harmony
of rattled laughter with the bourgeois glee.

There came the spirit of Neil the poet,   190
mourning the glen where he was a boy;
and there came Big Mahri Macpherson
to make mention of Macleod's ploy.

[verse missing]

There came that jewel, John Macpherson,
from St Congan's kirkyard down in the Glen;
his pleasure was not increased much
hearing the tattle there was then.

One evening I stood on Scurr na-Banacheich
and from the gloaming rose up phantoms:
on each side of the Coolin pinnacles hovered   200
the wan ghost of a folk-robber.

(l. 177) In 1739 the Skye chiefs began to transport their people to the West Indies.
(l. 185) End of a list of rimed place names made up by a transported girl.
(l. 187) In 1820 the emigrant ship, 'Annie Jane', sank in Vatersay Kyle.
(l. 190) Neil Macleod - reference to a song of his.
(l. 194) Crofter leader, c. 1880.
(l. 195) In Glendale.
(l. 201) Evicting landlords.

Straddle-legged on Scurr a-Ghretty
a riff-raff of the Lairds of Dunvegan,
and high up on the Tusk of the Baptist
an ugly gang, the Macdonald Barons.
South-west, on the head of Garsven
appeared to the view Dr Martin,
Macalister of the Aird's phantom
stalked about the top of Blahven;
Big Ewen Macaskill on Scurr an-Skooman   210
gazed down on Roo an-Doonan,
and Cameron standing near
watched Minginish, that they had fleeced.
Eastward, on Scurr nan-Gillean's skyline
arose Major Fraser's likeness;
and down on their hunkers high on the Pinnacle
sat Ballingal and Mr Gibbon;
on the flank of the Brooach all alone
were Red Alasdair and Tormore;
Mackay and Rainy on Dun Cana,   220
by no means gentler phantoms.

And below in every corrie under them
the fawning liars who kept them company,
who earned the cream of the big profits,
every factor, gent, and lawyer
who came and guzzled and licked around them,
harrying, thieving, plundering scoundrels.
From every corrie and scurr of the Coolin
the one hymn swelled in unison:
"In the track of wealth and honours forever   230
march devoutly the gifted and clever.
Up they come and receive satiety,
that's Noblesse Oblige and the Law of Society."
Belched about me their harsh mocking –
"Lazy crofters, their system's shocking.
Crush 'em, clear 'em, sweep 'em all out,
smash 'em, hunt 'em, chase 'em about."
The spectral troop then set to dancing,
a fine frolic and most romantic;
the mourning cries of the exiled tenants   240

mixed with the drunken din of the gentry.
Over the width of sea and forest
the grey Pope of Rome responded,
likewise General Franco of Spain
and warily wily Chamberlain;
resounded the triumph-shout of Odin;
Vienna appeared, and Barcelona,
Shanghai, Hamburg, Harbin, Calcutta
came to my vision, Borreraig, London,
Prague appeared, Naples and Munich,   250
every poor room the sun looks on
where is heard the distressed cry of the needy,
like that cry of agony Archibald Geikie
heard in Strath and reported fearlessly.
And even if other speakers
cleave the mist, Marx and Lenin,
Thaelmann, Maclean, Dimitrov, Macpherson,
Mao Tse Tung and the men about him,
that devilish symphony would drown both
the voice of the wise and the yell of anguish.   260
Even if I had power and manhood
like Stalin's, chest to chest with agony,
I would be crushed by that din's shrillness
while the great Coolin swirled dizzily.

On Scurr Alasdair amid the glitter,
the full moon's silvery brilliance,
that cry clave to me as I listened,
pierced and ruined the pith of my spirit.
And though our Ben Lee stood towering
above the peaks and braes around it,   270
and though I saw the rocks of Valtos
soaring higher than any swan-troop,
though the Three-Burns' Ford should flow
like the Volga, full and slow,
the Coolin's harsh screech distressfully

(l. 246) Nazi Neo-Paganism.
(l. 254) The geologist, whose protest is reprinted in *100 Years in Strath*.
(l. 273) Place of struggle in the crofter rising.

would cleave to my listening ears and vex me.
And though I heard in a hall one evening,
at Portree that I know and love dearly,
Donald MacCallum, the old hero,
that agony cry will linger forever.   280
Till the Red Army all together
crosses Europe at a war-march-step
that dirge of misery will penetrate
through my ears and through my entrails.

Thousands of poor men decay,
mouldering corpses down in Spain;
in China hundreds of thousands of carcasses,
far off the effect of their sacrifice;
many a Thaelmann in Germany yonder,
one or two John Macleans in Scotland,   290
Macpherson beneath the turf of St Congan's,
the Great Isle like a skeleton tottering,
myself at the sport of climbing rocks here,
and Scotland in sickly sleep rotting.

Second Movement

Rocky Coolin, awesome monster,
you are with me in spite of horror.
The first day I scaled your swart fortress
I thought the Last Doom would fall on me;
the first day I kissed your profile
it looked like the Red Spate of Noah;
the first day I took your mouth and kissed it
Hell yawned with both jaws viciously;
the first day I lay on your bosom
I seemed to see loaded fully   10
the heavy skies, ready to go off
and ruin the earth with one explosion.
   Climbing the Brooach na-Free's blade-back
I saw the country's wildness naked,
black-red clouds mantling heavily,

(l. 279) The Rev. Donald MacCallum: put in gaol for inciting the crofters.

the winds' mouths blustering tempest;
on the girdling summits of the awesome mountains,
a dun opening in the heaven lowered
under the low dense red-black pall
of surly cloud-banks, grizzled and swart,   20
a congregation of the horrors of the elements,
a Highland Games of the gathered tempests.
Wintry snorting of squalls skirling
around sullen savage pinnacles;
yelling gusts quivering and quaking
round summit battlements, grey and naked;
the flanks and thighs of the bare Coolin
stripped for the giant wrestling-duel,
fleshless but for the scree covering
hurled headlong in mounds of rubble,   30
down from your hip and your knees scattered
to the bottommost depth of gloomy chasms.
With Coolin's giant son for contrast
Goll and Fyoon and all the monsters
inspired by human imagination
would be like a louse on a cock-chafer,
compared with Coo-hoolin in his war-clothing.
But what resemblamce has mortal shoulder,
knee or calf, thigh or torso,
to precipice-ramparts, grim and rocky,   40
black with ice and chilly oozings,
to the heaving chest of high moorlands,
their arrogant crags surging upward
like the mother-breasts of the wide world
erect with the universe's lustfulness?
I saw the Red Mountain's Horn
rise in a fury of challenging scorn
through the tumult with which the skies were torn,
and I saw tossing the stars in spindrift
the trinity of Skooman arisen.   50

  On the twin-crested Black Mountain
a tune came to my ear sounding,
Big Patrick and his music keening

(l. 46) Symbol of Communism.
(l. 53) Patrick More MacCrimmon, the pibroch composer.

all the children of the human species.
And on the Garsven one evening
there came to me another music,
'Muldown' and its theme of love-fullness,
breaking the heart of melodic beauty.
   In the sun's white down-lying
the westward sweep gave to my eyesight   60
the seas beyond Barra shining
encircling our ancestral islands,
and the Great Isle jewelled with charms,
the way homesick eyes imagined it,
sighting America but yearning after
Groola, Broonal, the twin hills of Scarral,
that surged yet in the blood's beating;
Dyoorinish and its high sea-capes,
Minginish with its ample bosom,
soft Bracadale's pap-hollows in beauty,   70
washed by the hidden kiss of the ocean,
the great Aird of Strath Swordale,
the long smooth thigh of the cold hill-range
where heather and grass lie jewelled richly
like my darling's hair in its golden glistening.
   From the sweet-gale of the Castle-Headland
in keen fragrant wafts ascending
the love and grief of the land's people,
scattered by their exploiters' greediness.
On the green braes and pastured field-slopes   80
the mist of History twining and creeping,
heart, blood and flesh of my people
a nightmare on the fields lying heavily;
Minginish folding together
Vaternish and the Slate Headland,
Trotternish, Raasay and Rona,
Dyoorinish, the Strath and Soay,
side by side in the soft drizzle.
And heavy on the deep sleep of the wilderness,
the hardship and poverty of countless thousands   90
of the crofters, the lowly folk of the region,

(l. 54) Reference to the pibroch, 'Dirge for the Children'.
(l. 57) A famous pibroch.

my kindred, my own people.
And though their fate never made
the bitter world-cry of Spain,
though their lot might never precipitate
a mantle of blood on the face of the firmament,
as Marlowe saw Christ's blood streaming
and Leonhard saw the blood of Liebknecht;
and though no news was brought
on their night of ruin and loss   100
to equal the world-anguish of mourning
when the Asturians went down in glory,
their doom was the doom of the serfs and the lowly,
continual hardship, famine, injustice,
since the duping of the masses in all countries
by the rulers, the State and the legal system,
cheating priests, prostitutes, ministers,
selling their souls for the wages of mischief
the world's bitches are busily earning
since ever the boss-class heaped up treasure.   110
I'd see them all in a drowning-poke,
the ruling class, the lawyers and popes,
thrown out over the Stallion directly,
through the swelling seas' mid-depths descending
down to the Hell reserved for the gentry.
   And, God, if I were at Dunvegan
with a big gun on a cliff-edge there
I'd pound the castle of those wretches
till it lay here and there like a pulpy eggshell.
And if I were down in the Slate district   120
putting to use the same artillery,
I'd hurl its towers' embattled foulness
where they would never succeed in towering!

Another day this on the moorland-summits,
the Asturian folk again insurgent.
Would to God I could see the strength of their challenge

(l. 102) Revolt of 1934 by the Asturian people in Northern Spain against the right-wing Robles regime.
(l. 122) Armadale Castle.
(l. 125) Against Franco.

descending here on the Coolin's masses!
You best of men on the earth's surface,
though your fate was chill with death's dunness,
you brought shame to other men's faces   130
who felt the majesty of your bravery
and suffered to see the burden left on you
through other men's cowardice and lying treachery.
Would that the black Scurr nan-Gillean
and every other scurr and pinnacle
would rise as monuments to your hardship
and your great portentous valour.

Another day this on the moorland-summits,
and the folk of Skye not yet insurgent;
another day this on the mossy field-slopes   140
and the Great Isle losing its people;
another day this dappling the heavens,
but it will not satisfy their yearning;
another day this breaking the skyline
that will not see them joyful and smiling;
another day this comes to my eyesight
that gives no respite to my desirings,
desires that follow each year's cycle
as it creeps onward down to its twilight.
Here am I without my people   150
since the men of Braes failed and yielded,
since never a MacCrimmon nor John Macpherson
this year or last year came to help us;
and still if I attain tomorrow,
I shall have shame for my allotment.

Another day this on the peaks ascending,
great Scotland 'under a beasts' sentence',
her thousands of poor folk exploited,
a butt for cheating rogues' enjoyment,
cajoled, enticed, drugged and doctored,   160
purged and cleansed with unctuous concoctions,

(l. 151) Scene of crofter rising.
(l. 157) Phrase of Alexander Macdonald.

the stock-in-trade of godly divines
who made a bourgeois of Jesus Christ;
and the Press of the capitalists of Clydeside
buying for money soul and talent,
where poetry is rated at the low value
approved by Lithgow and such gentry,
where the name MacDiarmid is never heard of
because he would not pay them dividends,
where dandies and dunces are stuffed to splitting   170
with the food of sickly slum-children.

Another day this on the moorland-mountains
and white Scotland a porridge of foulness,
royal England, republican France,
twin dungheaps of bourgeois Finance,
great Germany in a mythical frenzy,
and Spain a burial-ground for heroism,
the Pope of Rome, oily and slippery,
defending the bourgeois class slickly:
the Polish peasants' clique of rulers   180
the laughing-stock of all Europe.

Another day this on the moorland-summits
and the bourgeoisie jostling each other
at the merry ploy of slitting gullets
on the people's bodies in every country;
another day this on the moorland-summits,
and God beating a retreat dully
in spite of all the Creed's bishops
and sharp Presbyterian ministers;
another day this on the grassy uplands,   190
Bourgeoisdom's red bog engulphing
tens of thousands at once with its gobbling,
the one quagmire of Europe's continent.

(l. 167) Sir James Lithgow, Glasgow shipping magnate.
(l. 176) ref. A. Rosenberg's "The myth of the Twentieth Century".
(l. 191) cf. Christendom.

I see the race of men floundering
chained together in Mararowlin,
Chamberlain, Mussolini, Hitler,
and godly Franco vying with them,
giving directions to each legion
towards their drowning among the peat-hags.
   But och! you Mararowlin quagmire,   200
you were never brought up to phantoms,
although you heard the mountain clangour
the day they waged the Desperate Battle,
though you heard also the sore keening
that day Minginish lost its people.
For our Island what is the use
of another Festubert and Loos?
At Portree there are names by no means sparse
on the monument under the lion's arse.
For permanent possession you got damn-all   210
though you captured Beaumont Hamel.
And if you survive this you will see
other rotters with the O.B.E.
and dowagers guzzling themselves full in
luxurious Sligachan, viewing the Coolin.

Third Movement

   You great morass of Mararowlin,
Fortune has endowed you proudly,
you will swallow Europe's nations,
America's as well, and Asia's;
your talents will increase and travel,
you great red scummy quagmire;
you are streaming now and rising,
drowning in your flood of lying
all that's bountiful, honest, upright,
you palsied slough of every country!   10

(l. 195) A marsh north of the Cuillin: symbol of Bourgeois Capitalism.
(l. 198) The "Non-Intervention" brigades.
(l. 203) Macleods v. Macdonalds, 1601.
(l. 209) Portree war memorial.
(l. 215) A fashionable hotel.

You have grown large, soft, rich and greasy,
gulping the lands of miserable people,
your blubbery mantle, red and scummy,
choking thousands of wretches under.
Many a peak and numerous mountains
you have put under with your foulness;
you have drowned God up in the heavens,
you will drown the Coolin and Braes together;
you dragged Minginish below
and drowned Bracadale long ago.   20
You great swamp, bloody and murderous,
who at all will stop your flooding?
Who ever will muck out the reed
unless the Red Army march for our need?
Who will fling out the shite
unless Stalin descend from the height?

   Many a rose and lily in loveliness
vegetates on the bog's surface,
lovely in flesh and lovely in blood
although they sprouted out of the dung;   30
but the foulness will penetrate the soul
belying the blood's healthy glow.
Many a tree, spreading and sappy,
grows in that alien quagmire;
many a bird, winged and lovely,
perches there before it goes under;
but when it is time for the running to seed
the flowers are swallowed, the birds and the trees.

Mararowlin, I salute you,
you swallowed the great French Revolution;   40
you swallowed Germany, you swallowed Italy,
long ago you swallowed Scotland and Britain;
you swallowed America and India,
Africa and the great plain of China,
and, Great God! it agonised me
that you swallowed Spain's heroic rising.

   (l. 23) reed: cattle shed.

It's certain you are a bog of note
for casting lies in their prophets' throat;
many men have paid you devotion
between the two sides of the ocean; 50
papers in France and Rome, with the Press
of Germany and England no less,
praise your flux long and loud,
a far from solitary crowd;
slick pens of many hirelings sate us
constantly boosting your worth and status;
strumpets of trim alluring figure
stimulate and renew your vigour;
the gentle doves of the B.B.C.
are not behind in your flattery, 60
and the precious bishops all proclaim
your virtues, piety, and fame.

Here's to your health, Mararowlin,
you are endowed greatly and proudly.
And proud you should be, with your due part
of the service of brain without heart;
great men of genius have given you their service
many a day, in spite of regrettings;
Big Patrick and Mozart were at your behest,
you got Shakespeare, Yeats and the rest; 70
it was your misfortune, not deficiency,
that you did not get Shelley and Livingstone.

Come, you children of bourgeois despotism,
dance at Mararowlin together.
Come and sport on its braes merrily,
you'll soon be off the top forever.
Take a trip down to St Congan's
and dance on the hero's grave yonder;
make a journey away to Glasgow,
it's there Maclean's grave grows grassy. 80
Dance heartily, dance merrily,
before you are drowned yourselves in the deluge.

(l. 72) William Livingstone: Islay poet, 1808-1870.
(l. 78) John MacPherson.

Huge is the bog, the plain is huge,
but the Red Peak is forbidden you.

Many a palsied false corruption
skims Mararowlin's surface,
many a consumptive philosophy
is heaped up high on the midden.
Brutal bog, here's a health to you!
You are the bourgeoisie's belching.   90
Fie Fie! God! that's my verdict,
you are the world's great belching.

The shameful story, have you heard it?
Our Stallion has been gelded.
He was overtaken in Mararowlin,
bound with chains round and round him,
many a bourgeois, many a factor
holding him fast down in the quagmire;
his stones and his brain were roughly severed,
the animal was atrociously dealt with;   100
they turned his snorting into a bleating,
he was left on the dungheap among the beetles.
Now that our famous horse has been taken
this bog will drown the whole of creation.
   It's rising now, dancing higher,
sought with great and growing desire,
running over with red scum,
adding still to its virtues' sum;
it has equalled the Goat's Peak in height
since it gained a fresh accretion of shite.   110
And if it swamps the Coolin too
we'll have nothing left to do
but submit to His Bog Majesty
Mararowlin, and bow the knee.

   Has the news reached Glendale parish
what happened to the nimble noble Stallion?

(l. 84) Scurr Dearg as symbol of Communism.
(l. 94) Waterstein Cliff as symbol of heroic Scotland.
(l. 109) Scurr nan Gobhar in the Cuillin range.

Has the news reached the Braes people
of the mettlesome strong animal's treatment?
In Russia and in India the folk are on fire at it,
in France, on the great plain of China, 120
but Scotland has not yet got hold of it,
for she is deaf and blind-folded;
and in England, if the news is heard of,
the dunces will never grasp the sense of it.

Slily the rogues have gelded the beast,
   gelded the poor beast completely,
smiling they tore his stones away
   and managed the crime so neatly.

The men of Skye are all wounded
after the torture of that poor brute; 130
the men of Scotland feel sick and rotten
although the story has never got to them;

the folk of England are a butt for laughter,
they do not understand the matter;
the folk of Europe are all fools
in spite of understanding that news.

The men of Skye are all saddened
though they do not understand the matter.
Do you think that in Glasgow there's any person
who understands and expounds the sense of it? 140

The manly work, have you heard of it,
done for us by the bourgeois gentry?
Far went the fame of their exertions,
they robbed the beast of his vital essence.

I climbed at early dawn on Sunday
to misty battlemented summits;

(ll. 125-128) Parody of the popular Gaelic song, 'Pilot my dog, they blinded his eye'
   — free paraphrase to the same tune.
(ll. 141-152) The first three stanzas here parody the first three stanzas of Iain Lom's
   poem on the Battle of Inverlochy.

I saw the Bourgeoisie mustered,
Macleods and Macdonalds *not* triumphant.

On Horse Corrie Knee mounting airily
I saw you were busy animatedly;150
my country lay devastated,
and that ill-deed was no reparation.

Have you heard the foul scandal,
what they did to the Glendale Stallion?
That's little enough of their greedy malice,
landlords' work, crooked as ever.

Here's to your health, Mararowlin!
you pour over the pavements aboundingly.
If they are caught on the banks of your current
the Bourgeoisie will claim the world.160

I am tortured with grief for the horse of victory
who reared his high head over the billows,
challenged with neighing the mountainous tumult
of the Western Ocean swelling hugely.

Once I heard with exultation
that his head's bristles were dancing and raging
when a banner was raised in the Isle, dappled
with manifold wrongs, scarlet with anger.

God! If I had been in his saddle
when there arose that year's clangour,170
I would have overtaken MacDiarmid
though he storms across the sky fiercely,
I would have overtaken Macdonald
despite the lightning-fire of his glory.

But I have never beheld such greatness,
I must stay in the best place at hand,
a Skyeman, beside Big Mahri.

(l. 167) Crofter rising of 1882.

But I shall not tell her strong temper
that no turn has come on that tide's ebbing.
I shall avoid the charge of boastfulness, 180
for I tell the subsiding of our Isle's glory.

From the high tops of the antlered Coolin
I have seen many a vision of beauty,
some stalking on the steep mountains,
some descending down to their drowning.
Even in that bog's ugliness
I have seen the shadow of loveliness;
I saw youth, music and laughter,
I saw wisdom, honour, valour.
I saw hearts that were generous and kind, 190
heroism, exaltation of mind;
I saw every flower that blossoms,
even the side lanced and tortured;
but never has there been seen a tryst
of Lenin's intellect and the red side of Christ.
That pair are not to be seen together
despite the swamp's vast levels.
To see them both at once you must seek
the bare summit of the highest peak.

My spirit grew chill and pallid 200
with anguish over a sudden fancy
that I saw your face in the vapid quagmire.
My love, my delight, my white darling,
its black bank could not attract you.
My heart flushed flame-rapidly
to see you climb the peak of happiness.
Many a beauty, pure and lovely
has been drowned by that swamp's scumminess,
but it did not drown my white darling,
a sign that its triumph-day is passing. 210

Day will fade on Mararowlin
for all its great proud endowments;
evening will darken over its borders,
its scum will dwindle and sink soggily;

after full flood ebb is due,
the expanse will take another hue;
respite will come from drowning and anguish,
and day will rise on the Coolin's masses.

Fourth Movement

Far distant from the height of the mountains
down to the depths of Mararowlin.
But still the higher the climb rises
deeper and further the climber's eyesight
pierces the stagnant scum of the swamp
into the guts of the drowning-bog.
But why on earth was I entertaining
a hope that the moss would change its nature,
that its might and talent would soon desert it,
that its scum would shrink and sink at ebbing? 10
Is not great proud Scotland
already down under the bog there?
Down in the bog Spain and Italy,
France down, Germany and Britain?
Has it not drowned everything,
good upon evil, under its deluge?
Has it not overcome the world
on all sides with swamping current?
Has it not made the world a Dachau,
polluted white love and valour? 20
There have been seen on the streets of Glasgow,
on the streets of Edinburgh town manifest,
on the crowded streets of London city,
the ultimate issues of the bog's filthiness.
Poverty, hunger, prostitution,
fever, consumption, sick stupor;
they all flourished round its shores,
the bog ran to seed with sores.

One of my feet in Mararowlin,
  my other foot mounts the Coolin; 30
my hands tied beneath the manure-heap
  and my eyes pursuing the swift revolution.

Hardly ever shall I climb
   to the high hunting on the upland levels;
hardly ever shall I be found
   on the mountain-tops where the stars are dwelling.

This spirit of mine is weak and abject,
   distracted, overwhelmed by oppression;
my faint heart has no hope of seeing
   the world's sages leagued together.   40

I shall not wrestle, I shall never struggle
   in single combat with that swamp;
I shall not escape its horrible quagmire
   by the restless activity of sage thought.

Too much of the bog is in my spirit,
too much swamp in my heart's impulse;
too much red scum in my talents,
the grey hue overlaid my valour.

I shall not reach the summit of Beedyen,
   I do not even mention Blahven;   50
I shall not be seen on Scurr nan-Gillean
   on the pinnacle height towards Garsven.

The swamp's night covers my eyes,
   pervades entirely my whole perception;
I have no hope of new bloom
   nor the sun's new whiteness forever.

   Far, far away
      is the day that has never arrived;
   on the Coolin the night is long
      as it tosses agonized;   60
   long the night on the mountains
      that howl with a hard cry;
   long the greying of evening
      on the peak of my love's desire.

(l. 40) Dictatorship of Intelligentsia.
(l. 44) Dialectical materialism, i.e. Marxist philosophy.

Fifth Movement

I heard that there was seen a breaking,
   an alarum waking the wide horizon,
that there was seen a red fresh rose
   over a globe oppressed with violence;
I heard about the River Clyde
   incarnadined with floods of scarlet;
John Maclean too I heard of.
   An everlasting knot was fastened
on every man's heart and brain
   by his inspiration above agony.   10

A great portent has been seen and a prodigy,
the Stallion up on the Coolin snorting,
rising of rocks, bubbling hotly,
the spirit set them heaving and tossing.
The pick of the steeds of rock-pedigree
skipped like a buck on Scurr a-Ghretty:
the great untamed horse was leaping
beyond the furthest bounds of the region;
he put a hoof on Scurr nan-Gillean
while prancing up on the top of Beedyen;   20
he jumped across with power and arrogance
from Scurr na-Hooava to Blahven;
from there he took one swift full leap
right to Garsven's horny peak;
he cut a caper from Scurr an-Ettin,
quitting the desolate wild precipice,
and bounded over into the swamp,
trampling it down like a rutting-bog.
Fresh Stallion, here's a health to you,
you'll smack the bourgeoisie, the wretches.   30
Over the bog you'll bound swiftly,
you're no longer thrown on the midden,
you're not a poor gelded garron.
Great Mararowlin has lost her charm.

(l. 6) Red Clydeside, 1917-1922.

Grey horse, grey horse,
steep head high tossed,
your chest arrogant,
   daring your course:
joyous your racing,
joyous your neighing,   40
joyous your rapture,
   your rapid hoof-force.

Horse undefiled,
with your great grey side,
with your deedsome heart
   speeding your flight:
my love your racing,
my love your neighing,
your frightful affray
   my playful delight.   50

Great ocean-stallion,
my love your grandeur,
with your high spirit,
   your stiff old head:
grey horse and fine,
with your brindled side,
huge steed and wild,
   pridefully bred.

Great horse, your bridle
is flawless iron,   60
your head of steel,
   its sheen my praise:
mighty your prancing
with the limbs of an athlete,
you are our darling,
   our marvel always.

Skye-steed not gelded,
my joy your presence,

(ll. 35-146) These stanzas attempt to represent a pibroch movement.

my choice of jealousy,
   my yearned for prize: 70
steed of the oceans,
exciting devotion,
my heart in commotion
   at your rolling eyes.

Great horse, my darling,
with your mane mantling,
you heard fierce Patrick
   calming down:
great horse of the seas,
riding of heroes,   80
you heard the theme
   of piercing Muldown.

Rugged Stallion,
you heard the thrilling,
the drones' brisk passion
   shrilling wide:
from Patrick More
and Patrick Og,
love and sorrow
   and enormous pride.   90

Horizon-stallion,
my heart of laughter,
you heard that manly
   magnanimous pride:
you heard Macpherson
from your castled steepness,
you heard the hero,
   free-chosen guide.

Grey steed and terrible,
you heard the yelling   100

(l. 78) Reference to a pibroch, 'Blind Patrick's Flame of Wrath'.
(ll. 87-88) The MacCrimmons.
(l. 95) John MacPherson of Glendale.

when came the rending
  of the rebel year:
you heard MacCallum,
noble and valorous,
and Macpherson advancing
  in ardent career.

Stallion of the mountains,
you will be found there
in the time of council,
  when discord has ceased: 110
now on the Coolin
you wait the assurance
and the bright rose-bosom
  full-blown in the east.

Europe's multitude
erected upright
to the breast of Justice
  with its hurts and sores:
the world's menfolk
putting a welcome 120
on the orient spreading
  of the fiery force.

Darling of the skyline,
love of the high peaks,
my beacon prized one,
  your brightness my life:
girdling precipice
of intellect and heroism,
hills of my treasure,
  eternal your strife. 130

O love of Scotland,
soon will lift off us
the bandage that rots us
  with strong vapid trash:

(l. 102) 1882.
(l. 114) The "inevitable" dawn of Communism.

Europe's fond seeking,
sure aid draws nearer,
red flame's live leaping
   that will sweep away ash.

The Coolin's a vision
like an eagle in swiftness,
with a red dragon's vividness,
   a lion's mild pride:
Scotland's glory,
with her flanks' white zoning,
a fire going over
   strath-floor and hill-side.

Far, far away,
   far the way ascending;
the Coolin's way is lengthy
   and the tremor of your exertion:
long the way of the peaks,
   they need many an exploit;
climbing of the bens is hard,
   no lack there of exercise.

Great the battle and bloodshed
   that must be to ransom Europe;
hard the agonised struggle
   till justice is realised truly:
long, long, the perplexity,
   wretched, sick confusion;
long the night of yearning
   till the red sun's gold fullness.

Long, but come it will,
   the gilded sun will pour on us;
the Coolin will rise proudly,
   bountiful, white-glorious:
bitter the night that shadowed
   your glad lustre over;
but dawn will break at last
   on battlements of glory.

Hard the extremity of China,
   of India and my Scotland;
bitter the loss of Spain,
   plain of the great corpses:
hard is Italy's extremity,
   Germany's, France's also;
and England's vile stupidness
   that keeps poor folk wanting.

Connolly is in Ireland
   rising above trouble;   180
John Maclean in Scotland
   a column on the uplands:
Liebknecht dead in Germany,
   with never-dying lustre;
Lenin in Russia the result
   of great judgements consummate.

"If there are bounds to any man
save those himself has set
to far horizons they're postponed
and none have reached them yet.   190

"And if most men are close curtailed
and keep a petty groove
'tis their own sloth that is to blame,
their powers they will not prove.

"Preferring ease to energy,
soft lives to steel-like wills,
and mole-heaps of morality
to the eternal hills."

Sixth Movement

I got hardship without relief
from the day I was put on the Ship of the People;

(l. 2) 'Annie Jane', 1820.

I was in Gesto gathering shellfish
when I was seized, alone and helpless.
Slavery with flogging, I had to endure,
black labour and a sun at noon
that shrivelled my flesh on my bones with its fury,
making havoc of the young bloom
with which my cheeks and brow were covered
before ruin came on my world.   10
   I heard of many a terrible trial
before that time on our Island,
but who got as much, or half of it ever?
God's curse on the Laird of Dunvegan,
may it fall on Macdonald of Slate duly,
and another curse on Norman of Oonish,
the skipper of the ship of those brutes.
God of favours and Christ of grace,
all I asked was not great,
but I got not even the small kindness   20
of a chance to see on the far horizon
Ben Dooagrich, where we had the sheiling
in my youth, nor the graveyard of my people.
Many a thing comes on the poor,
but no-one has suffered my ruin,
though I was happy when I was young,
in spite of poverty, in Macleod's country.
Now, when I rise at dawn's coming,
I see grey fields, level and dull,
where there is violence, misery, drudgery,   30
and the soil itself on the point of bursting
with the murderous heat of the sore sun.
Toil, degradation, faintness, hunger,
these are mine by fate's allotment.
I'll never reach a distant prospect
of my mother's house at Loch Harport,
where there was heartiness and laughter
at cloth waulkings among the family.
I'll never see the Coolin's antlers
rise above Minginish my darling.   40

Sad fullness of grief
is my mood this eve,
and the poor folk's deal in my thought.

Chieftains' fates
give me no pain,
but my dear ones' state and their lot.

The music and tongue
I was used to when young
gone for good like a dull eye-spot.

My eager devotion 50
of reasoned emotion
beyond seas' commotion from my thought;

with Bracadale's
steep grassy braes
and green pastures my brain is fraught;

by Minginish
with its vivid hills
and leaf-springing my will has been caught.

Skye's dear island
with its shapely high peaks 60
and its striped moors lying
  is the joy of my heart.

With that Isle and its Coolin
stately and gloomy,
its fjords circuitous,
  my raptures start.

That Island princely,
with steep cold hillsides,
with restless rivers,
  and mild meadow-part. 70

(l. 41) To the tune of 'Caol Muile'.

The Isle of Welcome,
where hearts are plenteous,
where kindly tempers
    make bounty an art.

Exile is surely a wretched business
when hardship and poverty go with it.
I learned that for myself the day
I sailed off on the "Annie Jane".
We hoisted sail in the Bay of Barra,
a wild day and a night of havoc,   80
and the sails flew out in tattered strips
behind Vatersay with the storm-drift
and the savage sea's spray whirling.
The "Annie Jane" broke into planks
with me and her cargo of my family.
Distant America I never saw,
for the big sea swallowed me with her maw.
Drowning was surely a wretched business,
with no need or benefit in it.

I am the great Clio of Skye,   90
famous above hundreds am I.
Throughout the world I am well-informed,
acquainted with men's fate and fortune.
I was one day in Strath Swordale
and an agony-cry came to my ears,
I heard the lament of the poor people
the Baron of Slate was busy clearing
from Borreraig and green Sooishnish
to the other side of the ocean's tumult.

I am the great Clio of Lewis: 100
I walked as far as there was occasion
on that quick ready way
from Bernera to Stornoway.
I am the Clio of proper arrogance,

(l. 90) Clio: the Muse of History.
(l. 97) Lord Macdonald.

for I saw the Hunt of Park;
I am the subtle, shrewd Clio,
I know whence comes the Revival.

I am the Clio of Harris,
I nibbled among those eastern crags.

I am the sorrowful Clio of Mull, 110
I have seen bracken in floods.

I am the Clio of the Hebrides,
I have seen travail and bereavement;
I heard the great pipe of MacCrimmon,
also the hornless sheep nibbling.

I am the Clio of Scotland,
I knew blindfoldedness and rottenness;
I have seen coalminers in contract-serfdom,
and the red rose of Clyde ebbing
from its mighty great flood of anger 120
when John Maclean raised a standard.

I am the Clio of Ireland;
God, I was tortured entirely
by the Famine of Potato Year,
by oppression, fraud, anguish, and need;
but in spite of misery and violence
I am the great proud Clio,
for I have seen Pearse and Emmet,
Connolly, Wolf Tone, Fitzgerald.

I am the great Clio of England, 130
my lot of no sinecure;
I saw Tyler and John Ball,
Robert Kett and other stalwarts;
I heard Shelley in glorious song
and Byron among his fellow Lords.
I have seen the snobbery of the English,
and Art, and Paul Robeson singing.

(l. 124) 1846/7 of the "Christian" era.

I am the great Clio of Spain,
it is I who know tribulation;
I was in Barcelona and Madrid, 140
I saw heroism and tyranny,
I saw travail and misery
in spite of the struggle of the proud heart.

I am the Clio of France,
I saw the Revolution lost,
I saw the glory of the Commune,
its suffering, heroism, and sorrow.

I am the Clio of Germany;
I saw the troubled mist spreading
on the condition and heart of the human race, 150
Beethoven, Liebknecht, and slavery.

I am the Clio of Italy,
I saw a fearful vision,
crosses along the Appian Way
with Spartacus and the militant slaves;
there I saw as much as was proper,
also the death of Matteotti.

I am the Clio of Greece,
I saw slavery maimed and diseased,
and Metaxas the false liar 160
in spite of wisdom, art, and science.

I am the Clio of India,
I saw untold shame, without limit,
exploitation and propaganda,
the extremity of Nehru and Gandhi.
I saw poverty beyond thinking,
mankind's travail and misery.

I am the Clio of China,
I got my own share of violence.

I am the Clio of the world; 170
I travelled hills, glens, and uplands,
towns, and moorlands lying empty,
but I have not seen much respite.
I have read Plato, Rousseau, Voltaire,
Leonardo, Condorcet, and Cobbett,
Schopenhauer, Hume, Fichte,
Blok, Lenin, Marx, Nietzsche.

The great Clio of the world's masses,
on the Ship of the People I worked my passage,
I was there at the Braes doing battle, 180
and in Leningrad at the Winter Palace
when there came all the Bolshevik warriors
in a spate-stream pouring onward.

    A thrush am I on Paible's floor,
    but I have not got much repose.

    Look out, is it the day,
      and I awaiting the horizon?
    And I biding on the Coolin
      till its tremor's full sufficing?
    Look out, is it the morning 190
      softly dappling the firmament?
    See if that is the red rose
      making golden the hillsides.

I am the Clio of the world;
eternal, continual my journey.
I was present inside the castle
when there came the monkish rabble
to put questions to Galileo;
I heard his ready saying,
"But it does move all the same." 200
I was in Leipzig with heedful devotion

(l. 184) Allusion to a poem of John MacCodrum.
(l. 200) *Eppur se muove* — a myth!

when Dimitrov stood before the Court,
and I heard them more than ever
till that hour I had heard of.
I saw in one living flame
all Man's exultant spirit there,
the hero-soul, lively and stubborn,
the exact disciplined brain of the summits,
triumphant irrepressible intellect,
the sage's heart radiant and vigorous. 210
"History's wheel taking its course,
the universe won't prevail over it."

The wheel describes its circle,
   and misery will turn to triumph.
Ha, I shall one day see
   the ebbless sea's violence,
I shall see the rising of the waves
   and the breaker's huge high frowning.
That day will be for evermore,
   and a roar of joy on the mountains. 220

Clio never left the Dun
   despite her long swoon-misery,
though her joy went with speed
   on mountain-steeps beyond thinking;
she spoke to me and said,
   "The thing you yearn and hope for,
joy's head will surely be seen,
   the desire of the hero-poets."

I saw the bobbing of wretched faces
with the sea's motion, hurt and dismayed. 230
At the Mound there in Edinburgh city
I have perceived the hand lifted
above the sea's welter and drift
to make a clutch at the flitting wisp,
the straw of hope passing with a rush
and the empty heart ready to burst.

(l. 202) Reichstag Fire Trial, 1933. Leading Communist, Dimitrov, conducted his
   own defence.

I have seen on the streets of Glasgow,
   and manifest in Edinburgh city,
I have seen on the streets of London
   the ultimate course of the track of the spirit.   240
Rising up from poverty and hunger,
   from suffering and wounds and violence,
the spirit's great red standard
   not to be cast down after rising.

In Leipzig there Dimitrov brandished
that high-willed venturesome banner
that will waken every diseased spirit
and inspire the downcast with vigour.

The Red Flag's golden hammer
   and sharp sickle intertwined,   250
the mantling blood of Fate's spirit
   raising bitterly the flood-tide.

   Blood and sweat of working people,
the scarlet that will give freedom,
brain's blood of the sage and the poor
that will overcome wealth's crookedness.

   I looked over towards the Coolin,
it trembled under a new movement.
Excelling Dimitrov, your features
were cut on the face of the ancient peaks.   260
The blast of your heart's high-willed vigour
put a heaving on Scurr nan-Gillean,
the surging of all humanity's hopes
shook that mountain's stone-slopes.

If a limit has been set to Man
   except that he has set himself,
and if living man has gone there
   it has known your step.

Seventh Movement

Many a turn the world has taken
since the vision Aeschylus had of the shape
of Hero-Man-God hanged, outraged,
on Caucasus' sharp dangerous mountains.
The god fashioned in man's image,
cruel Jupiter, with squint-eyed tyranny,
sending the ravenous vultures, disciplined
to rend and eat Prometheus' liver;
the human race on the craggy peaks
devouring their own soul to the screeches   10
of savage brutes and winged guzzlers
that got the benefit from that gluttony.
   Jupiter the brutal coward has fallen,
barbarous Jewish Jahweh also,
but a time has never come when the bosses
have failed to find some sort of god
to hang on pious mountain-tops
surpassing men's sacrificed bodies.
Jesus Christ was hanged on a cross,
and Spartacus with his myriad militants;   20
there were many god-vultures in Britain
to tear the flesh of Connolly and Casement;
many a Christ in France and Spain
has been crucified in later ages.

   Shelley said the Caucasian peak
startled at the torment of that hero,
and I myself saw a startling,
the Coolin's breast leaping with rapture
to see Dimitrov alone
making the mortal human soul   30
leap from its husk with sudden bursting
to stop the breath of the whole world.
There died then in that stoppage
aged decrepit bourgeois goddities;
they tumbled down from the desolate pinnacles,
shrieking and howling, down to the abysses.

I saw Dimitrov with his ensign
overcoming horror and terror.
   But the vulture and the buzzard are still busy
swooping about the savage hillsides.					40

   Up the mountain my love went with me
so that she might hear the singing,
the singing of the peaks dangerous to tread;
she heard and half-understood the melody,
and straightway the form of the vulture
came on her white sad loveliness,
and she picked a hole in my side suddenly.

   There are many birds about the hill,
some silent and some singing.

I went out on the mountain-steeps					50
and took with me my own people.
They heard the crying melody's theme
and fell to rending one and all
the great strong famous form
that was there on that precipice hanging.

The bird's beak will rend the blasphemy
that is in the heart of holy knowledge.

On the height of the hills I went walking,
and in my head two loves brawling,
white vultures and foul vultures					60
making havoc of my heart utterly.

I am not the Clio of the world,
death-chill I found the summit.

I am the Clio of the world,
I saw enough toil and suffering;
Before now I have had hardship
with Lenin and his Krupskaya.

The monster has been lifted out of the sea
and put high on the Coolin's peak.
It was curled up when routed out
from the ocean-depths where light is drowned,
but now it has straightened up its form,
leaping to windward in the face of storm.
I saw the serpent leaping proudly
to strike with her fangs the heaven's brow.

I saw Christ going around
on the bare cold top of the mountain.

I saw the others climbing upward
on the sharp crags of the emulous summits.

I saw Dimitrov high on the Coolin,
and the mountain shaking with laughter-music.

A day was mine on rocky Coolin,
I heard the great pipe booming,
the roar of all mankind answering,
brain and heart resolved in harmony.

I heard on the mountains the loud crying,
the freedom-shout of the people rising.

All around me on every pinnacle
were the living dead who won victory,
Toussaint, Marx, More, Lenin,
Liebknecht, Connolly, Maclean together,
and many a spirit proud and ardent
put out in Spain's disaster.

A thousand years were like a wisp
of drifting mist lost in the firmament.
The great Clio was rising eternally,
a million paltry to her perception;
it was she who saw the Coolin boldly
rising on the far side of woe.

Landauer, Liebknecht, Eisner, Toller,　　　　　　　　100
marching on the hills, marching in order;
the Commune of France risen anew
ever marching over the moors:
Connolly and the eternal Easter of Ireland
taking the way of the moorland heights:
Thomas Muir and John Maclean
in death not sleeping, not prostrated:
MacCallum, Donald Macleod, Macpherson,
marching over the hills forever:
in the law court forever Dimitrov　　　　　　　　　110
defying a desperate predicament:
Maclean's funeral in Glasgow winding
over the streets of precipitous heights:
the soldiers of the people pouring out
over the peaks and glens of the mountain:
thousands without name or history,
flawless heroes without flinching,
who looked in the face of death and agony,
the high hills' steadfast ramparts.

The chains of Tatu Ho in steel　　　　　　　　　　120
swinging between perilous peaks.

The measure of the mountains measuring together
Einstein's brain and the live-red spirit,
understanding of the universe and measure of the world
meeting on the bareness of the mountain summit.

The Coolin will be cleansed with fire's vigour
to the steel of the hard rocks of the spirit:
the synthesis that is uplifted
beyond agony, travail and victory,
the rottenness of a whore smitten with syphilis,　　130
and Dimitrov adding to the spirited
mountains of the high human intellect,
and a petty bourgeois, plump and piffling.
The edge of man's spirit will be ground
on the sharp summits of stony mountains.
The heart that cannot ever be rent

(l. 100) All German Socialist/Communist martyrs.

and the brain that cannot be choked ever
are marching together, eternally marching
over the black peaks of anguish.

The stars' distant dim orbit 140
for ever measured on the mountain-tops,
the great intellect in the contest of a poem,
the hard wrestling of a struggling soul,
the heroism of the spirit speeding the course
of the wheel's rapid violent woe:
Einstein high, but more surpassing
Dimitrov, wrestling with agony:
the spirit of Man putting his seal
on the harsh eternity of the peaks.

Rising on the far side of woe 150
more than one Coolin shows:
there is seen the blue Coolin of the Island,
and two other Coolins beside it:
the Coolin of Scotland, ancient Alba,
and the Coolin of our common humanity:
a Coolin trinity pouring its flood,
its surge of peaks, over the world:
a Coolin trinity rising up
beyond the eternal woe of the summits.
   The black rose of the piercing Coolin 160
red with Man's heart-blood's suffusion:
the dim rose of the grey brain
red with the vehement blood's stain:
the white rose of the sage intellect
red with blood free and invincible:
the red rose of hero courage
aflame over mountain summits.

   Black ooze on the rock-precipice,
black labour and bloody sweat;
black ooze up on the firmament, 170
the woe of millions making it dull;
the everlasting woe that has come,

and the woe that has not yet come,
and the woe that is on us at present,
the sore woe, long and deadly;
Christ on the cross hanging nailed,
and Spartacus beside him there;
each thousand years of slow contending,
the salt rose's bitter petals;
the black labour a nightmare,   180
fever, consumption, degradation,
the petals of that terrible rose
a nightmare on the sky's dome.

In spite of all the Coolin shows
rising on the far side of woe;
the exultant Coolin of joyful freemen,
the live-spirited Coolin of heroes,
the high Coolin of the great intellect,
the Coolin of the rough heart of misery.
The variations of the Bairns' Dirge   190
are seen marching on a bright pinnacle,
the ground-themes of Muldown
marching high on the bare mountain.
Lucretius, Beethoven, Jesus,
going in procession, Lenin, Liebknecht,
Maclean and Connolly, their flesh kindling
a heather-fire of joyful brilliance;
the great serpent stiff and erect,
striving upwards to the height of heaven:
the gold-lit eagle of the the bens,   200
the wild stallion of the glens.

    Coolin of Skye,
    mountains of ire,
    savage and wild,
       your outcry thrilling.

    Coolin of stone,
    peaks unthrowable,
    mountains of sportiveness,
       your roar goes shrilling.

Coolin of the skyline, 210
sharp belt of high peaks,
Coolin of mightiness,
   fine end of dull yearning.

Summit-circuit
of the human spirit,
danger-precipitous,
   your hope's pith burning.

Coolin of desiring,
rain-crest of the high tops,
unblemished, undeclining, 220
   without eyes' squint turning.

Exalted Coolin,
your bosses luminous,
fine cliff, the true theme
   of wooers' discerning.

Ancient summit
of agonized struggle,
Coolin resurgent,
   your pride-urge ramping.

Wooed pinnacles 230
of unresting intellects,
strong torso stripped white
   beyond misery's cramping.

Naked brain,
above injury's pain,
above poverty's strain,
   above fate's culmination.

Soul steel-hard,
above pulsing of laughter,
above shock of agony, 240
   above factious laceration.

Heart of iron,
eternal mind,
above jealous ire,
   your fine brain's domination.

Coolin swart-stark,
wintry storm-darkness,
smoke blackness surpassing
   suns' stark lamination.

Darkness' radiance,   250
light of sages,
peak unabaseable,
   stream-spate of creation.

Coolin rock-range,
heart of sorrow
benign consciousness
   above wrong's cumulation.

The Ship of the People
taking the stream-spate
on old torn scree-slopes'   260
   cleared desolation.

The vessel of a multitude
windward working
over reefs in the currents'
   blue undulation.

Great Ship of Renewal,
and her rudder's fury
raising the spume
   above gloom-crags' elevation.

The World's Ship   270
not veering or flinching,
not steering squintly
   before a wind of elation.

The Coolin untranquil,
a consummation of talents,
a secure hardness,
  a surpassing-white ovation.

The Coolin of ages,
a soul growing greater,
a full-teeming brain,   280
  a white pain of animation.

Coolin-Stallion
rock-steed of the marches,
rampant charger,
  fast without motion.

Coolin of welcome,
in my thoughts forever,
famed mankind's yearning,
  wide-spread devotion.

Stallion of the hills,   290
great horse without bit,
red stag and slim,
  stintless ocean.

Coolin trinity,
Stallion of vigour,
eternal horse-pinnacle,
  big in each notion.

Coolin of History,
spirited, vigilant,
rock unwithered   300
  amid bitterness' commotion.

Heart, spirit, brain,
naked, naked,
enraptured nakedness
  of radiant emotion.

    Sea-smouldering,
    moor-grass glowing,
    rough hills flame-mourning,
      glorious your motion.

On the skyline far off, a lofty landmark,
I see the movement of the Coolin's antlers:
over seas of sorrow, a swamp agony,
I see the high peaks' white calmness.

Who goes there on an evil night?
Who goes marching across the height?
Steps of a spirit here at my side,
the gentle steps of my love, my pride.

Steps, steps on the hills ascending,
the thud of steps swelling and blending;
steps gentle and steps wild,
stealthy steps, disciplined, mild.

Who's there on a night of unrest?
Who goes marching on the summit crest?
The wraith of a bare naked brain,
cold with agony's chilling pain.

Who goes there on the spirit's night?
The wraith of a heart, naked and slight,
a phantom alone with its thoughts and hopes,
a fleshless skeleton on the stone-slopes.

Who goes there on the night of the heart?
A thing unreachable by any art,
the ghost seen by the soul's devotion,
a Coolin rising beyond the ocean.

Who goes there on the soul's night,
following the shifts of the wandering light?
Only the voyager, travelling free,
seeking the Coolin over the sea.

Who goes there on the night of humanity?
The spirit's ghost, a thing of vanity,
a lone soul on the peaks contending,   340
yearning for the Coolin and it ascending.

Beyond mankind's blood in lakes,
the battlefield's rotting, the climb's aches,
poverty, consumption, fever, stress,
brutality, fraud, violence, distress,
misery, despair, malice, meanness,
crime and filth, rising in keenness
the Coolin is seen, with heroic glow
rising on the far side of woe.

    ****

explicit feliciter prid. id. Feb. MCMXLIII.

Notes

In the instances where poems have been previously collected, *Auntran Blads* and *A Braird o Thristle* are cited as the sources for these poems. Sources have also been provided for the previously uncollected and unpublished poems, of which there is a significant number.

Young translated poems into Scots and English from many different languages. Where possible, sources for the poems in their original language and/or in English translation have been cited. These sources are either recent editions of the poems or the editions which would most likely have been consulted by Young himself during his translation work.

Some political, historical, social and geographical background on the poems has been given in this section; while these notes are by no means exhaustive, it is the editor's intention that they will aid in contextualising Young's poems.

Poems by Douglas Young

Thesaurus Paleo-Scoticus
Source: *Auntran Blads*: 11.

(l. 12) 'Jamieson's muckle buik' is John Jamieson's *Etymological Dictionary of the Scottish Language*,[21] which was first published in two volumes. It later became a valuable reference work for many of the Scottish Literary Renaissance writers.

Traveller's Tale
Source: *Auntran Blads*: 28.

Attic Noon
Source: *Scots Magazine* Vol XXXII, No. 4 (January 1940): 280-281

On the Akropolis at Skoplje, July 1936
Source: *Auntran Blads*: 29-30.

Skoplje is the capital of the Republic of Macedonia. It was conquered by the Ottoman Turks in 1392 and remained under Ottoman control for over 500 years.

(ll.12,13) 'Pashas' are high ranking officials in the Ottoman Empire. In 1912 the city was liberated by the Kingdom of Serbia during the Balkan Wars and after World War I it became part of the newly formed Kingdom of Serbs, Croats and Slovenes.

(l.19) The Vardar is the longest river in Macedonia and a major river in Greece.

Austrian Scene
Source: 'The Black Book'

The Erste Donau Dampfschiffahrtsgesellschaft (DDSG), the First Danube Steamboat Shipping Company, was founded in 1829 by the Austrian Government. A few years after this poem was composed the DDSG's role was influenced by the Nazis, when the company worked with the SS to transport Jews after Kristallnacht.

---

21 Jamieson 1808.

(l. 10) Passau is a town in lower Bavaria, Linz is the capital of the state of Upper Austria and Melk is a city in Lower Austria.

To Gillian in Vienna
Source: Edin NLS Acc 6419 Box 75 (4).

Gillian Stewart (1911-95) was born in London. She was a student at St Andrews University from 1929 to 1932. She acted as secretary of the Scottish Nationalists Society when Douglas Young was the President. Young and Stewart enjoyed a fleeting romance at university. Eventually, through Young, she met and married the classicist, Otto Skutch, who was a German Jewish refugee.

The Belvedere, built by Prince Eugene of Savoy, consists of two Baroque palaces (The Upper and Lower Belvedere), the Orangery and the Palace Stables. In 1903, the Lower Belvedere was opened as a modern gallery, housing works by Vincent van Gogh, Claude Monet, Pierre-Auguste Renoir and Paul Cézanne.

(l. 12) "It is now closed"

On the Death of Wallace Martin Lindsay
Source: Edin NLS Acc 6419 Box 75 (4).

This poem is also included in Young's Black Book, in which the poem's composition is dated to 24 February 1937.

Wallace Martin Lindsay (1858-1937) was Professor of Humanity (Latin) at St Andrews University from 1899 to 1937. He was a scholar of international repute, specialising in the classics and palaeography. He was killed in a road traffic accident in St Andrews.

(l. 4) The Lairig Ghru is a mountain pass through the Cairngorms.

(l.10) George Buchanan (1506-1582) was a Scottish humanist scholar and historian.

Lines on a Gaelic Poet at an Oxford Party
Source: Edin NLS Acc 7085 Box 15 (1).

Composed for the Gaelic poet, George Campbell Hay (1915-1984). Young became friends with Hay during their time at Oxford University. Both men left Oxford in 1938.

22 St Giles Street, Oxford. February Midnight.
Source: Edin NLS Acc 6419 Box 75 (4).

This poem is also included in Young's Black Book, in which it is dated February 1937, with a footnote reading 'Unsatisfactoriness of the green-dressing-gown *Weltanschauung*'.

Sonnet Peu Probable
Source: *A Braird o Thristles*: 27.

After Lunch, Ekali
Source: *A Braird o Thristles*: 26-27.

Ekali is a suburb of Athens. In *Chasing an Ancient Greek,* Young writes that 'When Hitler invaded Poland I happened to be in Greece, and I did not reach Britain till nearly mid-September of 1939'.[22]

(ll. 21-22) "I have now taken the decision to eradicate the Poles."
(l. 23) "very drunk"
(ll. 33-34) "Thank God. You are Scottish. You are not an enemy."
(l. 37) "You will come back after the war"
(l. 39) "In a short time, I hope,"
(ll. 41-44) In an Adriatic Bay, among the dry-stane walls of Hekale
A Scot, I got friendly with Germans.
But this is a terrible time; it stands on a knife-edge -.
War or Peace? But friendship will win through.

The exchange with the German host, during which she states that Young is not an enemy because he is Scottish (ll. 33-34), and Young's subsequent musing to himself that this is not entirely true due to the Treaty of Union in 1707 (l. 35), hints at his later anti-conscription stance when back in Britain. This poem and 'Leaving Athens', illustrate how World War II interrupted Young's Classical studies.

Leaving Athens
Source: *A Braird o Thristles*: 28-29.

(l. 1) Parnes, Pentelikon and Hymettos are mountains in Attica (central Greece).

(l. 14) Servius Sulpicius Rufus (c. 106 BC – 43 BC) was a Roman jurist and orator, whose words in a letter of condolence to his teacher, Cicero, on the death of his daughter and the transient nature of all things are reproduced in Young's poem (ll. 19-20: *Shall we poor mortals be indignant if one of us dies or is slain, when our lives ought rather to be shorter than they are, since the skeletons of so many towns lie prostrate and neglected on one spot?*) and given new life in the present circumstances of World War II.[23]

---

22 Young 1950: 57.
23 See Cicero 1909-14.

For Deòrsa and his *Calum Thonder*
Source: Edin NLS Acc 6419 Box 75 (4).

George Campbell Hay's 'To a Loch Fyne Fisherman' ('Calum Yonder') was set to music in June 1939 by the composer, F.G. Scott.[24] According to Michel Byrne, Calum Johnson was the skipper of the fishing boat on which Hay worked in the 1930s.[25]

London Midnight
Source: *A Braird o Thristles*: 29.

Maurice Lindsay (1918-2009), to whom this poem is dedicated, was a Glasgow-born poet, writer and broadcaster. He was writer and co-editor of *Poetry Scotland* and oversaw the publication of *Modern Scottish Poetry: An Anthology of the Scottish Renaissance 1920-1945*.

While the wider political situation is only insinuated in the last line of the poem, it is likely that this poem follows on chronologically from 'After Lunch, Ekali' and 'Leaving Athens', with Young's return to London in mid-September 1939. In *Chasing an Ancient Greek* he writes 'Arriving in London in a black-out, and disliking the melancholy singing of hymns kept up pretty constantly by the staff in the hotel I had gone to, I took a run down to Oxford...'[26]

Fife Equinox
Source: *Auntran Blads*: 25

(ll. 9-10) These were the words of a servant girl at Ardlogie, which were overheard by Young. The poem was composed around this memory.

December Night: The Aesthete in the House
Source: Edin NLS Acc 7085 Box 15 (1).

Composed on 23 December 1939, this poem was intended as a companion poem to 'Ardlogie, Christmas Eve, 1939', which was originally called 'The Aesthete in the Garden: Ardlogie, Christmas Eve 1939'. The poem can also be found in Edin NLS Acc 6419 Box 75 in a more incomplete form with a slightly different final line – 'but when to expect the crack of doom?'

---

24 Scott 1939: 25-28.
25 Hay 2003: 547.
26 Young 1950: 57.

(l. 6) The Dutch painter, Johannes Vermeer's (1632-1675), 'The Artist's Studio' (or 'The Allegory of Painting') is a realistic depiction of the artist's workplace, with the subject, whom the artist in the picture is painting, thought to be a symbol of Clio, the Muse of History.

(l. 7) John Constable (1776-1837), the English Romantic painter, was famous for his depictions of the landscape of Dedham Vale.

(l. 16) Young is referring to the terror bombing of Chongqing in China by the Imperial Japanese Army Air Service, which began in February 1938 and lasted until August 1943, and the bombing of Helsinki by the Soviet Air Force during the Winter War between the Soviet Union and Finland, which began on 30 November 1939 and led to the Soviet Union being expelled from the League of Nations on 14 December 1939.

(ll. 18-20) "It will be wonderful when the war is finished./ Down with war and goose-stepping./ It's best at home, close to the fire."

Ardlogie, Christmas Eve, 1939
Source: *Auntran Blads*: 32-33.

Winter Pool
Source: *Poetry Scotland* 1, 1944 (Glasgow, William MacLellan): 31

Quatorzain in an Entr'acte
His Majesty's Theatre Aberdeen. 2nd February 1940
Source: Edin NLS Acc 6419 Box 75 (4).

A quatorzain is a 14 line poem. An entr'acte is the interval between two acts of a play.

Speculation
Source: *Auntran Blads*: 30-31.

'Speculation', and the two poems which follow it ('The Cat in the Rock-Garden' and 'August Night'), were written in sequence on 11 May 1940, after Young had read a report on 10 May 1940 in *The Times* of Hitler's invasion of the Low Counties.

The Cat in the Rock-Garden
Source: *Auntran Blads*: 31.

In sprung rhythm, imitating the metre of *Piers Plowman* by William Langland.

August Night
Source: *Auntran Blads*: 31-32.

Around 1930, Young experienced an incident reminiscent of the one described in the poem. The poem is also influenced by a Dracula film that he had seen.

Autumn Fire
Source: *Scots Magazine* Vol XXXII No. 4 (January 1940): 280-281

The dedicatee of the poem, Bernard Babington Smith (1905-1993) was a lecturer in the Department of Experimental Psychology at St Andrews University during the 1930s. His mother, Lady Elisabeth Babington Smith, was the daughter of the 9th Earl of Elgin, who was viceroy of India in the last decade of the 19th century. The occasion for the poem was a day spent by Young and Babington Smith battling to clear up the over-grown garden of Far End, Lady Elisabeth's house in St Andrews.

Letter to Hugh MacDiarmid, 1940
Source: *Poetry Scotland* 2, 1945 (Glasgow, William MacLellan): 25-29

MacDiarmid's poem, 'On Receiving the Gaelic Poems of Somhairle MacLean and George Campbell Hay' (1940) was later published as part of *Lucky Poet: A self-study in literature and political ideas*[27] and begins with the lines

> At last, at last I see her again
>   In our long lifeless glen
> Eidolon of our fallen grace,
> Shining in full renascent grace,
> She whose hair is plaited
> Like the generations of men,
> And for whom my heart has waited
>   Time out of ken.
> Hark! hark! The *fead chruinn chruaidh Chaoilte*,
> Hark! hark! tis the true, the joyful sound,
> Caoilte's shrill round whistle over the brae,
> the freeing once more of the winter-locked ground,
> the new springing of flowers, another rig turned over,

---

27 MacDiarmid 1943.

dearg-lasrach bho'n talamh dubh na h-Alba,
Another voice, and another, stirring, rippling, throbbing with life,
Scotland's long-starved ears have found.

(l. 1) By addressing Hugh MacDiarmid in Gaelic, 'A MhicDhiarmid', Young is possibly evoking the first line of Sorley MacLean's 'An Cuilithionn', in which MacDiarmid is also addressed in this fashion ('A Chrìsdein MhicGrèidhir, MhicDhiarmaid').[28] This is confirmed in the last line of the poem when Young employs the vocative of MacDiarmid again and this time name-checks MacLean – 'I'll say with MacGhillEathain'.

(l. 6) *But now I am indifferent in Aberdeen*

(l. 7) A play on the familiar saying, 'If the mountain will not come to Muhammad, then Muhammad must go to the mountain', with Young substituting hill/mountain for the Gaelic, 'cnocan'.

(l. 17) 'The Voice o Scotland' is MacDiarmid's quarterly magazine.

(l. 18) *the voice of the blood, of my blood*

(ll. 25-26) Young is referring to Theocritus, *Idyll* 7, 28-42.

(l. 29) *Caoilte's shrill round whistle*. This phrase in is taken from l. 9 of MacDiarmid's 'On Receiving the Gaelic Poems of Somhairle MacLean and George Campbell Hay' but can also be found in Watson's *Rosg Gaelic: Specimens of Gaelic Prose*.[29]

(l. 30) *Long live the Hellenic-Celtic union*

(l. 31) *A Drunk Man Looks at the Thistle* (1926), MacDiarmid's long poem, is specifically named here but its style and atmosphere is also recalled throughout the poem, in the way that Young describes his wandering thoughts regarding poetry and Scotland's future in the early hours of the morning in Waverley Station, Edinburgh.

(l. 36) *What a mishmash of babble. Mourned Democritus* (Young employs a mixture of French, German and Gaelic vocabulary in this line).

(l. 61-68) MacDiarmid's *Scots Unbound and Other Poems*[30] and George Campbell Hay are mentioned in relation to Young's memory of Oxford in 1936 when Young first introduced Hay to MacDiarmid's work.

(l. 98) *browse, leaf through* (Young employs a mixture of French and German vocabulary in this line).

---

28 See MacLean 2011b: 345.
29 Watson 1915.
30 MacDiarmid 1932.

(ll. 116-117) A quotation from ll. 3-4 of MacDiarmid's, 'On Receiving the Gaelic Poems of Somhairle MacLean and George Campbell Hay'. MacDiarmid's 'eidolon' or spirit-woman of Scotland draws heavily on the imagery of the Irish poet, Aogán Ó Rathaille's (c. 1675-1729) aisling poetry, specifically 'Gile na Gile' ('Brightness Most Bright').[31]

(l. 142) The italicised quotation, translated into English as 'each to be manful alone', is from George Campbell Hay's poem, 'Is Duilich an t-Slighe' ('Difficult is the Road'). The first six verses were composed in 1939, subsequently transcribed by Douglas Young, and entitled 'Final Lyric to Nationalist Who Refuse Conscription'. Late in April 1940, Young wrote to Hay to report that he had set these lines to music.[32]

(l. 147) *Therefore, MacDiarmid*

(l. 148) *farewell*

(l. 149) *great my shame*

Sonnet for a Phone-Call

Source: Edin NLS Acc 6419 Box 75 (4).

(ll. 19-20) After World War I, at Oxford University, New College, along with Merton and Rhodes House, acknowledged their German scholars who had died in the war. The plaque at New College reads 'In memory of the men of this college who coming from a foreign land entered into the inheritance of this place and returning fought and died for their country in the war 1914-1919.'

To a Friend on a Campaign

Source: *Poetry Scotland* 3, 1946 (Glasgow, William MacLellan): 26.

This poem addresses the Gaelic poet, George Campbell Hay, who initially resisted conscription on the same nationalist grounds as Young. The poem is a revision of 'Tae Deòrsa i the heather, back-end o 1940'[33]

For Alasdair

Source: *Auntran Blads*: 21.

This poem was composed while Young was fishing on the banks of the Calder at Lochwinnoch in 1941, in memory of a Highland student at Aberdeen, killed during the German advance into Libya.

---

31 See Ó Tuama and Kinsella 1981: 150-153.
32 Hay 2003: 562.
33 See Edin NLS Acc 6419 Box 75 (4).

For a Scotsman Slain
Source: *Auntran Blads*: 22.

Dulce et Decorum
Source: *Auntran Blads*: 22.

The title of the poem is an acknowledgement of Wilfred Owen's poem, 'Dulce et Decorum Est', which is also the beginning of a Latin saying, taken from an ode by Horace. In the last line of Owen's poem, the saying is given in full; 'Dulce et decorum est pro patria mori ('It is sweet and right to die for your country'), an often repeated sentiment at the beginning of World War I.

(l. 1) The 'black angel o Cupar' is the Cupar war memorial. It was designed by John Kinross in a classical style and was unveiled by Field Marshall Earl Haig in 1922.

Carmen In Patriam Suam
Source: *Auntran Blads*: 51.

For the Old Highlands
Source: *Auntran Blads*: 23.

'For the Old Highlands' is also included in Young's Black Book under the slightly different title, 'For the Dead Highlands', dated 14 November 1937.

This poem (particularly ll. 2-3) is inspired by the Blasket writer, Muiris Ó Súilleabháin's autobiography, *Fiche Blian ag Fás*[34], which was translated into English, and published under the title *Twenty Years A-Growing*[35] in the same year of its publication in Irish.

Winter Homily on the Calton Hill
Source: *Auntran Blads*: 23-24.

The Scottish National Monument, on Calton Hill in Edinburgh, is also known as 'Scotland's Disgrace'. The Scottish architect, William Henry Playfair (1790-1857), had envisaged it as another Parthenon and as a commemoration of the soldiers killed in the Napoleonic wars but work was stopped in 1829 due to lack of money and the monument was never completed.

---

[34] Ó Súilleabháin 1933.
[35] O' Sullivan 1933.

Simplon Tunnel
Source: *Scottish Verse 1851-1952* (Edinburgh: Thomas Nelson and Sons Ltd): 277-278.

Simplon Tunnel is an alpine railway tunnel which connects the Swiss town of Brig with the city, Domodossola in northern Italy.

(l. 3) Monte Rosa is the highest mountain in Switzerland.

(l. 6) The Anzasca Valley leads up the eastern face of Monte Rosa.

Epilogue to Theokritos
Source: *Auntran Blads*: 24.

(l. 15) Arsinoe's tableau of Aphrodite and Adonis is described by Theocritus in his *Idyll* 15.

(l. 15) 'Simaitha's havers' refers to the witch, Simaitha, and her incantation in Theocritus's second *Idyll*.

(l. 20) The Antinoe papyrus was found on the site of Antinoe, Upper Egypt in 1914, dating to the late 5th or 6th century. It included the *Idylls* of Theocritus.

'Sang by the Sea'
Source: *Auntran Blads*: 25

Whiles
Source: *Auntran Blads*: 26.

(l. 15) Sveti Naüm is the monastery near Ohrid in the Republic of Macedonia.

Sabbath i the Mearns
Source: *Auntran Blads*: 27.

(l. 1) The Howe o the Mearns is a district of Kincardineshire, now subsumed into south-east Aberdeenshire, and forms a basin, surrounded by hills, at the north eastern ends of the wide valley of Strathmore.

(l. 2) The Mownth or Mounth is the range of hills on the southern edge of Strathdee.

(l. 18) The Honours of Scotland were successfully smuggled out of the castle in 1651 and when Ogilvie finally surrendered in 1652, the Cromwellians found that the Honours had gone.

(l. 19) The Whigs' Vault was the dungeon at Dunnottar, in which 167 Covenanters were placed during the rebellion of the Earl of Argyll in 1685.

(l. 21) The last Earl Marischal, whose seat was at Dunnottar Castle, forfeited his titles by taking part in the Jacobite Rising of 1715. He returned in 1761 and bought back the castle only to sell it five years later to an Edinburgh lawyer, Alexander Keith.

Confluence
Source: Edin NLS Acc 6419 Box 75 (4).

W.B. Yeats
Source: *Auntran Blads*: 28.

Referring to W.B. Yeats' *Last Poems and Plays*[36]

(l. 13) 'do 'n iolaire iomaluath' ('to the multi-swift eagle') is a phrase from Sorley MacLean's 'An Cuilithionn', Part V, l. 100.[37]

Russian Thought
Source: *Scots Magazine* Vol XXXII No. 4 1940 (January 1940): 280-281

The Roots of Love
Source: Edin NLS Acc 6419 Box 75 (4).

This poem also comes under the name of 'The Growing of Love' on the same page of the manuscript.

May Nocturne
Source: Edin NLS Acc 6419 Box 75 (4).

A Love
Source: *Auntran Blads:* 32.

D. til H.
Source: Edin NLS Acc 6419 Box 75 (4).

A poem, composed on her birthday — 27 July 1943 — for Helena Auchterlonie. She and Douglas were married on 24 August 1943.

For Willie Soutar, October 1943
Source: *A Braird o Thristles*: 8.

William Soutar (1898-1943) was a Perth-born poet and diarist. After serving in the Royal Navy in World War I, he studied at the

---
36 Yeats 1939.
37 MacLean 2001b: 385.

University of Edinburgh. He made contact with C.M. Grieve (Hugh MacDiarmid) during this time and this friendship had a considerable influence on Soutar's writing. Soutar composed in both English and Scots and became known as a key voice of the Scottish Literary Renaissance. In 1924, he was diagnosed with ankylosing spondylitis and he was bedridden from 1930 onwards. He died of tuberculosis in 1943. The fourth stanza references two of his war-time publications, *In the Time of Tyrants*[38] and *But the Earth Abideth*[39].

For a Wife in Jizzen
Source: *A Braird o Thristles*: 7.

Obair-Bhrothaig
Source: Edin NLS Acc 6419 Box 75 (4).

On 9 March 1944, Douglas Young copied this poem to Sorley MacLean, and wrote to him that 'I have made some verses for the Arbroath Commemoration and want to know if they are Gaelic.'[40] It is clear that while the English verse and the Gaelic verse are in a very similar spirit, the two stanzas do not exactly correspond. Perhaps anticipating the likelihood of a reader's assumption that one verse is a direct translation of the other Young has written in the margin of the manuscript that the English is not a 'version' of the Gaelic.

For D. D-H
Source: *A Braird o Thristles*: 9.

Douglas Young composed this poem for Lord David Douglas-Hamilton (1912-1944). He was educated at Balliol College, Oxford and, from 18 December 1941 to 20 July 1942, he commanded No. 603 Squadron RAF. Between 1939 and 1944 he saw active service, flying Spitfires in Operation Torch over Malta. However, on his return to Britain he was killed whilst carrying out reconnaissance over the French coast. In *Chasing an Ancient Greek*, Young describes a visit to Professor Reut-Nicolussi at Innsbruck after World War II. Reut-Nicolussi was one of the leaders of the South Tyrolese movement and showed Young a book, *Gesellschaft der Freunde Suedtirols*, 'containing among much interesting literary and political matter a photograph that touched me particularly, of my friend David

---

38 Soutar 1939.
39 Soutar 1943.
40 Edin NLS MS 29540, f. 82.

Douglas-Hamilton, who was killed in the war, wearing the dress of the Tyrolese, whose case he had done a good deal to bring up in London political circles, Chatham House for instance.'[41]

Requiem
Source: *A Braird o Thristles*: 10.

Fermer's Deein
Source: *A Braird o Thristles*: 10.

Sainless
Source: *A Braird o Thristles*: 11.

Young was inspired to compose this poem by the sight of a sick foal in a farm in Fife.

Drumcarro (l. 7) and Lucklaw (l. 12) are both hills situated in north-east Fife.

This poem was one of the readings at Douglas Young's memorial service, held at the University Chapel, St. Andrews by the University of St. Andrews on Saturday 12 January 1974.

Ice-Flumes Owregie Their Lades
Source: *A Braird o Thristles*: 12-13.

The dedicatee of this poem, Archie Lamont (1907-85), was a Scottish nationalist, political pamphleteer and geologist.

(l. 2) The Oetztal (or Ötztal) is a 65 km long alpine valley in the Tyrol in Austria. (l. 11) The Wildspitz (1,580m above sea level) is a mountain in the Glarus Alps, Switzerland.

(l. 29) The Diablerets (3,210m) is a mountain in the Bernese Alps, Switzerland. (l. 30) The Zanfleuron (or Tsanfleuron) is a glacier in the Bernese Alps, measuring 3.5 km in length.

Hielant Colloguy
Source: *A Braird o Thristles*: 14

Last Lauch
Source: *A Braird o Thristles*: 15.

'Last Lauch' is probably Young's best known poem. The cypress tree was planted in the garden at Ardlogie, his parents' house near

---

[41] Young 1950: 88.

Cupar. The minister in question was the Rev. McHardy, his brother-in-law's father.

A Cameronian Cat
Source: Typescript discovered by Clara Young on 14 July 2015 among some artworks on paper at home.

A Ballad o Saughton Jail
Source: Edin NLS Acc 6419 Box 75 (4).

This poem was composed in 1945 and was revised on 23 February 1959. Young had personal experience of this particular prison; after being tried for refusal of military conscription on 13 April 1942 at Glasgow Sheriff Court, Young was imprisoned in Saughton for eight months. Young may be referring to an earlier version of this poem in *Chasing an Ancient Greek* when he writes

> In odd moments I also wrote a good deal of verse, some of it quite good, including a long series of Limericks on the Governor, Chaplain, warders, and inmates, which gained a considerable, if restricted, currency, and gave rise to a vast range of popular variants, mostly in the direction of hair-raising obscenity, which eventually found their way to me, often on pieces of paper designed by the manufacturer for humbler purposes than writing.[42]

Thochts Anent Bluid and Roses
Source: Edin NLS Acc 6419 Box 75 (4).

Robin Black was founder of the *Free Man*, a magazine which was not attached to any political party but was clearly sympathetic to the nationalist cause in Scotland. Young's poem takes Hugh MacDiarmid's 'The Little White Rose' as its starting point.

Thomas Joseph Williams.
Source: Edin NLS Acc 6419 Box 75 (4).

While this poem in manuscript form is entitled 'Francis Joseph Williams' it is almost certainly a misprint and the title of the poem has been changed to 'Thomas Joseph Williams' at the discretion of the editor. Thomas Joseph Williams (1923-1942) was a volunteer in

---
42 Young 1950: 61.

the 2nd Battalion of the Belfast brigade in the Irish Republican Army. He was hanged for his part in the murder of an RUC officer.

(l. 44) The 1916 Easter Rising, was an armed insurrection in Ireland during Easter week. It was staged by Irish republicans whose aim was to end British rule in Ireland. While this single act proved to be unsuccessful, with the rebellion being suppressed within six days and the leaders court-martialled and executed, the Easter Rising took on a meaning and a symbolism which went beyond the specific events of that week. In its aftermath, sympathy for nationalism was significantly strengthened in Ireland.

Du Bellay in Fife
Source: *A Braird o Thristles*: 15.

Joachim du Bellay (c. 1522-1560) was a French poet and critic and was influenced by Latin models in his poetry.

(l. 9) The house is Young's family home, Ardlogie, in Fife. Young employs poetic licence here since Ardlogie was not built by his forbears. It was an old Free Kirk manse purchased by Young's parents soon after their return from India in 1926.

(l. 12) Young compares Moutray Water in Fife to the Tiber, the third longest river in Italy and the main watercourse in the city of Rome, and Lucklawhill in Fife to the Palatine Hill, the centremost of the Seven Hills of Rome (l. 13).

Til the Andantino frae Gluck's Orpheus
Source: *A Braird o Thristles*: 16.

Reconciliation
Source: *A Braird o* Thristles: 17.

Luve
Source: *A Braird o Thristles*: 17.

On an Auld Map o Scotland
Source: *A Braird o Thristles*: 18.

The dedicatee of this poem, J.B. Salmond, was an author and historian. He served in the Black Watch during World War I and in 1927 he became the editor of the *Scots Magazine*.

(l. 1,11) Jan Jansson (Jan Janssonius) (1588-1664) was a Dutch cartographer, who worked in Amsterdam. In the 1630s he went into partnership with his brother-in-law, Henricus Hondius, and their atlases were published as Mercator/Hondius/Janssonius. By 1660 the atlases had stretched to eleven volumes.

(l. 13) *Amsterdam, with Jan Jansson*

(l. 17) *Red Fool, where is Inveraray?*

(l. 22) The Marquis of Montrose and Alasdair MacDonald defeated the Covenanter army at the Battle of Auldearn, east of Inverness, on 9 May 1645. The Battle of Philiphaugh, near Selkirk in the Scottish Borders took place on 13 September 1645, when the Covenanter army, led by Sir David Leslie, gained a decisive victory over the Marquis of Montrose's Royalist army.

(l. 23) *the Kingdom of Scotland*

On A North British Devolutionary
Source: *A Braird o Thristles*: 18.

Bairn-Music
Source: *A Braird o Thristles*: 19.

The dedicatee of the poem, Florence Marian McNeill (1885-1973), was born and brought up in Orkney. During her childhood she was exposed to many old customs and folklore and this early introduction was to fuel much of her work in later life. Her greatest achievement is the four-volume study of folklore and folk belief, *The Silver Bough*.[43] She travelled in Greece, Palestine and Egypt and, interested in the burgeoning Scottish Renaissance movement, she worked as a researcher for the Scottish National Dictionary after returning to Edinburgh in 1926.

Duncan the Joiner
Source: *A Braird o Thristles*: 20-21.

The Ballant o the Laird's Bath
Source: *A Braird o Thristles*: 22-23.

(l. 3) The White Book of Sarnen was compiled in 1474 by Hans Schriber. The collection of manuscripts contains the earliest surviving reference to the Swiss national hero, William Tell.

---

43 McNeill 1957-68.

Jessie o Balronald
Source: *A Braird o Thristles*: 24-25.

Kintra Couplin
Source: Edin NLS Acc 6419 Box 75 (4)

Aisling na h-Alba
Source: *A Braird o Thristles*: 30.

The dedicatee of this poem, Roland Eugene Muirhead (1868-1964), was a Scottish nationalist from Lochwinnoch. He was first chairman of the National Party of Scotland. He later funded the publication of the *Scots Independent* and during World War II he endorsed the anti-conscription campaign. In 1942 he was a supporter of the more radical members of the SNP who ousted the moderates led by John MacCormick.

An 'aisling' or 'vision' poem is a genre which originated in Ireland in the 17th century with 'Ireland' appearing to the poet as a woman, lamenting her situation and the state of the country and foretelling of her deliverance from hardship with the appearance of a Stuart redeemer. Aogán Ó Rathaille is perhaps the best-known poet of this genre.

Pious Ejaculation in Aberdeen
Source: *A Braird o Thristles*: 30.

Eternitie
Source: *A Braird o Thristles*: 31.

Vishnu
Source: *A Braird o Thristles*: 31.

Duncan the Joiner and the Laird of Jura
Source: *A Braird o Thristles*: 33.

Rabbie in Plastics
The Immortal Memory: A Metrical Toast to Robert Burns
Source: Edin NLS Acc 6419 Box 75 (4).

In the manuscript, Young provides two dates (24 January 1947 and 22 January 1957), giving the impression that this was composed and then performed on at least two occasions over a decade apart. 'Greenock' is written next to the later date. Young clearly meant this poem to be given a local flavour where possible, stating under the title on the manuscript that 'placenames in first and last stanzas may be substituted by others.'

Snaw Thochts
Source: *Poetry Scotland* 4, 1949 (Edinburgh, Serif Books): 5.

(l. 9) Clara is Young's elder daughter.

Thow Thochts
Source: Edin NLS Acc 6419 Box 75 (4).

The Shepherd's Dochter
Source: *Poetry Scotland* 4, 1949 (Edinburgh, Serif Books): 6

This death occurred in the severest winter in living memory in the early months of 1947.

For Edwin & Willa, Bannockburn Day 1947
Source: Edin NLS Acc 6419 Box 75 (4).

Edwin Muir (1887-1959) was an Orcadian poet, novelist, translator and critic. He married Willa Muir (1890-1970), a Scottish linguist, translator and novelist, in 1919. They were both notable contributors to literary modernism in Scotland.

(l. 10) PEN (an acronym – 'Poets, Essayists, Novelists'), now known as PEN International, was founded in London in 1921. PEN is a literary organisation, which defends freedom of speech. Young was president of Scottish PEN from 1958 to 1962.

'Naomi Mitchison'
Source: Edin NLS Acc 6419 Box 75 (4).

Naomi Mitchison (1897-1999) was a Scottish novelist and poet, as well as a socialist, an advocate for women's rights and an enthusiastic supporter of Gaelic. She was a friend to Douglas Young and their correspondence, now housed in the National Library of Scotland, is evidence of their mutual respect and common interests.

Young Kilkerran
Source: Edin NLS Acc 6419 Box 75 (4).

Sir James Fergusson of Kilkerran (1904-1973), 8th Baronet Fergusson of Kilkerran, was a publisher, journalist and scholar. He was a talks producer with the BBC from 1934 to 1940.

(l. 9) Fergusson was the author of *Alexander the Third: King of Scotland*[44] and *William Wallace: Guardian of Scotland*.[45] (l. 11) Young is referring to Fergusson's *Letters of George Dempster to Sir Adam Fergusson, 1756-1813: with some account of his life*.[46]

Maurice Lindsay
Source: Edin NLS Acc 6419 Box 75 (4).

Maurice Lindsay (1918-2009) was a Scottish writer, broadcaster and poet. He was one of the foremost writers on the Scottish Renaissance, chronicling the poets of this movement in *Modern Scottish Poetry: an anthology of the Scottish Renaissance 1920-1945*.[47]

(l. 13) Allan Ramsay (1686-1758) was a Scottish poet, playwright and publisher, who revived an interest in Scots vernacular poetry and acted as a link between the 15th and 16th century Scottish makars and Robert Burns and Robert Fergusson.

Hugh MacDiarmid
Source: Edin NLS Acc 6419 Box 75 (4).

Hugh MacDiarmid (C.M. Grieve) (1892-1978) was a Scottish poet and a founding father of the Scottish Renaissance. Douglas Young and MacDiarmid shared a number of similar interests and aims in relation to Scotland and its literature. Young was capable of composing reverential poems such as 'Letter to MacDiarmid' but Young did not always agree with MacDiarmid's stance, as evidenced in this acrostic poem. In a letter to Sorley MacLean on 26 November 1940, which may also be related to Young's complex view of MacDiarmid in the present context, he writes

> Also there is a lot to be said for occasional complete abstinence from books and all intellectual ideas, and dealing only with practical matters, however crude and repulsive. There has been too much cerebration since literary folk became so self-conscious.

---

44 Fergusson 1937.
45 Fergusson 1938.
46 Fergusson 1934.
47 Lindsay 1946.

Soutar is a bit jejune, of course, in view of his precarious tenure of life, with complete paralysis of most of his body. But it is that effort to hang on that gives him the integration and economy that Grieve has wholly lost. I agree with the hollowness of Grieve's anglomania.[48]

(l. 2) This line is a deliberate echo of the first line of Sorley MacLean's 'An Cuilithionn', in which MacLean addresses MacDiarmid as 'A Chrìsdein MhicGrèidhir, MhicDhiarmaid'.[49]

(l. 12) Thrice most blessed of those who have ever been blessed.

London, 1948
Source: Edin NLS Acc 6419 Box 75 (4).

Ane Acrostich Sonnet in the auld Scots for the Queen's Grace in Embro, on Bannockburn Day 1953
Source: Edin NLS Acc 6419 Box 75 (4).

Maister John Knox's First Blast o the Trumpet again the Yerl o Balcarres
Source: Edin NLS Acc 6419 Box 75 (4).

Mary, Countess of Crawford and Balcarres, is included in the list of subscribers to the Douglas Young Memorial Volume Fund.

A Ballad of the Plockton Hay-Drier
Source: Edin NLS Acc 6419 Box 75 (4).

Composed in 1952.

(l. 4) The Brahan Seer (or Coinneach Odhar) came from Uig, which was Seaforth land on the Isle of Lewis. During the 17th century he was thought to have predicted many later events such as the building of the Caledonian Canal and the bridges over the River Ness.

(l. 9) Tom Johnston (1881-1965) was a Scottish socialist and Labour Party politician, associated with 'Red Clydeside'. He was Secretary of State for Scotland during World War II. After the war, he withdrew from politics and served as Chairman for the North of Scotland Hydro-Electric Board from 1946 to 1959. He had previously presented the Hydro-Electric Development (Scotland) Act to the House of Commons and the Act was passed in 1943.

48 Edin NLS MS 29540, f. 46.
49 MacLean 2011b: 345.

(l. 21) In the mid 1950s the North of Scotland Hydro-Electric Board built a hay drying plant, situated near the railway station in Plockton. The hay would be placed on racks to be dried by electrically powered fans. It was a trial unit and remained in use for some years. Torquil Nicolson was the Area Manager for the Skye and Lochalsh Hydro-Electric Board. He was an electrical engineer and had moved from the Head Office in Edinburgh to Lochalsh, and was involved in the early stages of development with the hydro-electric schemes at Nostie Bridge and Storr Lochs.

(l. 29) The Café Royal in West Register, Edinburgh, was one of the meeting places of the Scottish Renaissance writers.

Garlic in Colinton Dell
Source: Edin NLS Acc 6419 Box 75 (4).

Composed in May 1958. Colinton Dell contains ancient woodland and extends along the Water of Leith from Colinton Parish Church towards Slateford. The dedicatee of this poem, Moray McLaren, was a Scottish Nationalist and a writer and editor of books on Scottish literature and history.

The Fleurs of Embro
Source: Edin NLS Acc 6419 Box 75 (4).

Van Gogh – *The Starry Night*
Source: Edin NLS Acc 6419 Box 75 (4).

Starry Night (*Die Sterrennacht*), painted by Vincent van Gogh (1853-1890) in 1889, depicts the view from his sanatorium window at Saint-Rémy-de-Provence. It has been housed in the New York City Museum of Modern Art since 1941.

Passing Poet
Source: Edin NLS Acc 6419 Box 75 (4).

These verse captions were intended to go alongside photos of places and landmarks in Fife for publication in *Scotland's Magazine*.

St Andrews Castle
Source: *Scots Magazine* Vol XXXII, No. 4, January 1940: 280-281.

Political and Social Comment in Verse Form by Douglas Young

Scotlann, Awauk
Source: Edin NLS Acc 6419 Box 75 (4).

Scotland's Complaynt to his Mistress Industry
Source: Edin NLS Acc 6419 Box 75 (4).

Scotsmen, Wake Up!
Source: *The Scots Independent*, April 1939: 16.

 This poem deals with the issue of Scottish Neutrality and anti-colonial feeling, which Young was espousing during this period. One of the main arguments within the SNP during World War II was the party's stance regarding conscription. In 1937 the SNP's official stance was that it was opposed to conscription and participation in the war effort until a Scottish government was in place. This was altered in May 1939 when the party had to reach a compromise due to inter-party conflict regarding the war issue. On 12 December 1939 the issue was debated at the insistence of Young, at a special conference, in which a motion from Young's Aberdeen branch stating that the SNP should not cooperate with the Government was eventually defeated. Subsequently, the SNP still offered moral support for anti-conscriptionists. Throughout the poem, Young is making the point that colonial concerns of Britain, France and Italy are not Scotland's business. For example, Djibouti ('Jibuti' in the poem) was obtained as a colony by France in 1862 and, during the Italian invasion and occupation of Ethiopia in the 1930s and World War II, there were a number of border skirmishes between the French and Italian forces. Sarawak, on the island of Borneo, was a British protectorate and St Kitt's (Saint Christopher Island) in the West Indies was a British colony and, in Young's opinion, of little interest to the Scottish people. The latter part of the poem is referencing the German occupation of Austria on 12 March 1938. The Versailles settlement was disregarded and Czechoslovakia was placed in a vulnerable position. Young is referring to the British reassessment of its policy towards Germany following the occupation of Austria and a speech made by the Prime Minister, Neville Chamberlain, in the House of Commons on 24 March 1938 on this subject.

Pious Canticle
Source: Edin NLS Acc 7085 Box 15 (1).

The French are surrounded
Source: Edin NLS Acc 7085 Box 15 (1).

(ll. 1-4) Early in World War II, France was in a difficult position. The Phoney War, a period of inaction between the major powers, followed the German invasion of Poland in September 1939. Hitler proposed an invasion of the Low Countries to prevent France occupying them and, in the Battle of France, Germany defeated the Allied forces. On 25 June 1940, France formally surrendered to Germany and Italy.

(ll. 5-8) Before Germany's launch of Operation Barbarossa against the Soviet Union in 1941, the position of the Soviet Union and Britain was rather more unstable; with the Soviet Union feeling vulnerable to possible threats from Germany, they signed the Nazi-Soviet Pact, which effectively divided up Eastern Europe between the two powers.

(l. 13) Lord Beaverbrook (1879-1964), the Anglo-Canadian politician and journalist, served as a Minister in the British Government during World War I and World War II. He was an advocate of economic isolation for Britain and the British Empire in the 1930s, believing that it should function as a self-sufficient unit, supplying the needs of its people on its own.

(ll. 17-20) Young mentions several colonies in this stanza, effectively demonstrating how countries are divided up into empires by Western powers. By 1922, Cameroon was officially shared between Britain and France. During the 1930s, German settlers of the plantations supported the Nazis and when World War II broke out these German plantations were confiscated. The Tanganyika Territory was the British share of the former German colony of German East Africa, which was taken by Britain under a League of Nations Mandate in 1922.

(l. 20) "Give me India." "Yes, dear Führer (Leader)."

(l. 23) Brummagem is the local name for the city of Birmingham. The 'brightest brain' refers to Neville Chamberlain.

Prognostication, April 1939
Source: Edin NLS Acc 7085 Box 15 (1).

(l. 2) Neville Chamberlain (1869-1940), the British Prime Minister from 1937 to 1940 was known for his foreign appeasement policies.

(l. 5) On 30 September 1938, Chamberlain signed the Munich Agreement, which permitted Germany to annexe portions of Czechoslovakia in which there were mainly German speakers. This appeasement was a failure and did not halt the war that Chamberlain was attempting to avoid. In mentioning Spain in this line, Young is also highlighting Chamberlain's non-interventionist stance in the Spanish Civil War, culminating in the British Government's signing of the Non-Intervention Agreement in August 1936.

(ll. 9-14) By mentioning the Anschluss of 1938, in which Nazi Germany occupied and annexed Austria, deliberately breaking the terms of the Treaty of Versailles, with no action taken by either Britain or France in retaliation to this, Young clearly did not hold out much hope for the British and French assurances to Poland, Romania, Turkey and Greece.

(ll. 19-20) The Conservative politician and Prime Minister Stanley Baldwin (1867-1947) coined a phrase 'the bomber will always get through', used in his 1932 'A Fear for the Future' speech to the British Parliament, in which he aired the belief that bombing by enemy aircraft could destroy cities, regardless of British air defences. The bombing of cities was a legitimate concern for Young and one which he discussed at length in his correspondence with the Gaelic poet, Sorley MacLean, in the early stages of World War II. On 29 July 1940 Young wrote to MacLean that

> Then it is obvious now that the bomber, as Baldwin used to say, can always get through, even if not back, except perhaps against very restricted targets very heavily defended by balloons, A-A guns etc. I can quite conceive that the Axis can hurl against England 100,000 bombers of sorts. At the moment they are waiting only to site guns, arrange invading troops etc., and doubtless hoping that the benighted Sassenachs will show some glimmerings of common sense even yet. When they decide that they can't waste time doing the thing gradually, then they will wreck all the aerodromes in Britain one fine day...[50]

---

50 Edin NLS MSS 29540, ff. 23-24.

Chain Stores
Source: *The Scots Independent*, May 1939: 5.

Timor belli ne nos conturbet
Source: Edin NLS Acc 7085 Box 15 (1).

'Timor belli ne nos contubert': 'Let not the fear of war disturb us'. William Dunbar's (c.1465-1520) 'Lament for the Makers', with its refrain – 'Timor Mortis conturbat me' ('Fear of death disturbs me') may have been the inspiration for Young's poem, in which he deftly alters Dunbar's phrase.

(l. 6) For a more detailed note on Neville Chamberlain and the Munich Agreement see note on 'Prognostication, April 1939'.

(l. 18) The Krupp family is synonymous with German ammunition and armament manufacturing. Alfried Krupp was a strong supporter of Adolf Hitler and his business was the main supplier for German armament during World War II. He used slave labour in this process, with particularly harsh treatment of Jews and Slavs.

It's Easy Sperin'
Source: *The Scots Independent*, November 1939: 12.

Britain declared war on Germany on 3 September 1939, following Germany's invasion of Poland on 1 September. In his radio broadcast to the British people, Neville Chamberlain described the situation as follows: 'This morning the British Ambassador in Berlin handed the German Government a final note stating that unless we heard from them by 11.00 a.m. that they were prepared at once to withdraw their troops from Poland, a state of war would exist between us.'

Crusade
Source: *The Scots Independent*, July 1940: 4.

(l. 2) Wilhelmina (1880-1962) refers to the Queen regnant of the Kingdom of the Netherlands. She was a figure of Dutch resistance during World War II, making radio broadcasts to the Dutch people and taking charge of the Dutch government in exile, after her evacuation to Britain in May 1940.

(l. 2) Haakon (1872-1957) refers to Haakon VII, King of Norway, who was also evacuated to Britain in June 1940, following Germany's invasion of Norway in April 1940. He became a figure of Norwegian resistance throughout World War II.

(ll. 5-8) Edvard Beneš (1884-1948) was the leader of the Czechoslovak independence movement, Minister of Foreign Affairs and the second President of Czechoslovakia. He was exiled to Britain during World War II and organised the Czechoslovak Government-in-Exile in London.

(ll. 5-8) Józef Beck (1884-1944) was a Polish politician, diplomat, military officer and Polish Foreign Minister in the 1930s. He called on France and Britain to enter the war after Germany invaded Poland. He withdrew to Romania during the occupation of Poland and was interned by the authorities there.

(ll. 9-10) The six names refer to individuals involved in politics before and during World War II. Otto von Habsburg (1912-2011), the Archduke Otto of Austria, was the last Crown Prince of Austria-Hungary and had strongly opposed the Anschluss of Austria to Nazi Germany. He was exiled to the United States. Leon Trotsky (1879-1940), the Russian Marxist Revolutionary and founder and first leader of the Red Army, was opposed to the Stalinist regime and was an advocate of the Red Army's intervention against European fascism. Zog I, Skanderbeg III of the Albanians (1895-1961), was exiled to Britain following the Italian invasion of Albania. Hubert Marie Eugène, Count Pierlot (1883-1963) was a Belgian politician and Prime Minister of Belgium between 1939 and 1945. He led the Government-in-Exile in London from 1940 onwards. Otto Strasser (1897-1974) was a German politician and member of the Nazi Party, who broke from the Party and formed the Black Front, a group which attempted to split the Nazis and remove Hitler. He spent World War II in exile and wrote articles on the Nazi leadership for British, American and Canadian newspapers. The Negus, Haile Selassie (1892-1975), the Emperor of Ethiopia, was exiled from 1936 to 1941 after Mussolini invaded Ethiopia. He became an anti-fascist figure and was reinstated after Ethiopia's liberation in 1941.

(l. 29) Paul Reynaud (1878-1966) was a liberal French politician. He was opposed to German military advancement in the interwar period. He refused to participate in the Vichy government and was a prisoner throughout World War II.

'Mr E. Brown's Highland Tour'
Source: *The Scots Independent*, September 1940: 5.

Ernest Brown (1881-1962) was a British politician who was appointed Secretary of State for Scotland by Winston Churchill in

1940, serving in that position for a year before becoming Minister of Health. Young is referring to Brown's visit to the Highlands in August 1940, during which he visited Inverness and Dingwall and answered questions put to him by representatives of local authorities on the subject of evacuation, civil defence and protected areas. He also visited Wester Ross and met with the branches of the Farmers' Union there.

The Bold Sloganeer
Source: *The Auld Aiberdeen Courant and neo-Caledonian Spasmodical: a political and literary gallimaufray*, 1940 (Aberdeen, privately published).

This publication is described as 'a politico-literary gallimafray, indyteit an furthset by Maister Douglas Young, his lane, at The Bothy, Auld Aberdeen. Onie siller won frae the Courant sall be gien owre till the International Reid Corss for the behoof o the Scots sodgers left ahint in France an noo incarcerate in Germanie. Pay as muckle as ye wull. Mid-December 1940.'

(l. 46) Ernest Bevin (1881-1951), the British Labour Party politician and Trade Union leader, served as general secretary of the Transport and General Workers Union from 1922 to 1940 and as the Minister of Labour in the wartime coalition Government. Alfred Duff Cooper, 1st Viscount Norwich (1890-1954) was a Conservative Party politician, diplomat and author. He was a critic of Neville Chamberlain's appeasement policy on the lead-up to the Munich Agreement.

Moral Problem
Source: Edin NLS Acc 6419 Box 75 (4).

This poem was composed in August 1941 and refers to the Ecuadorian-Peruvian War, which was a territorial war (5 July - 31 July 1941) over a disputed border.

The Umpteenth Forefront
Source: Edin NLS Acc 6419 Box 75 (4).

Composed on 31 March 1944.

To the Hymn Tune "Veni Immanuel"
Source: Edin NLS Acc 6419 Box 75 (4).

Emanuel 'Manny' Shinwell (1884-1986) was one of the leading figures of Red Clydeside, a British trade union official and Labour politician. After the 1945 Labour victory, he was Minister of Fuel and Power and presided over the nationalisation of the mining industry.

Lady Grant
Source: Edin NLS Acc 6419 Box 75 (4).

Lady Priscilla Grant of Monymusk was an MP for Aberdeen South. She entered Parliament in 1946 and left in 1966. Austin Walker was a member of the SNP. In the General Election of 1945 he came third (5.3%) in Aberdeen North.

Fiscal and Advocate
Source: Edin NLS Acc 6419 Box 75 (4).

The Glesca Muckers
An Againflytin tae George Todd's "The Embro Makars"
Source: Edin NLS Acc 6419 Box 75 (4).

Included alongside the poem in the manuscript is a short letter from Young to C.M. Grieve (Hugh MacDiarmid), the editor of *Voice of Scotland*.

> Dear Chris, have just seen the latest *V of S*, which is excellent on the whole, but I don't appreciate either from a literary or any other angle the utterance of G. Todd, therefore send a counterblast in haste.

(l. 16) For more detailed notes on Maurice Lindsay see the note on Young's poem, 'Maurice Lindsay'.

(l. 22) Robert Garioch (1909-1981) was a Scottish poet and translator. He composed his work almost exclusively in Scots.

(l. 23) Norman MacCaig (1910-1996) was a Scottish poet and teacher. He was a conscientious objector during World War II and was well-known for his pacifist stance.

(l. 24) MacNib was the pen name of Albert David Mackie (1904-1985), the Scottish Renaissance poet, journalist and playwright.

Anthem for the Primrose League
Source: Edin NLS Acc 6419 Box 75 (4).

The Primrose League was an organisation, founded in 1883, which spread and encouraged Conservative principles in Britain.

(l. 6) Clement Richard Attlee (1883-1967) was Prime Minister of the United Kingdom from 1945 until 1951 and was leader of the Labour Party from 1935 to 1955.

(ll. 17-18) Aneurin Bevan (1897-1960) was a Labour Party politician on the 'left-wing' of the party. He contested the Labour leadership after Attlee's retirement but was unsuccessful.

Labour's Call to Rally
Source: Edin NLS Acc 6419 Box 75 (4).

In the margin of the manuscript, the poem is dated 29 April 1957.

In the 1950s, the Labour Party was in opposition after losing the 1951 General Election. This was a period of internal party divisions and resulted in another defeat in the 1959 General Election.

Translations by Douglas Young

Translations from Gaelic

Sorley MacLean (Somhairle MacGill-Eain) (1911-1996) was a Gaelic poet, writer and schoolteacher. He was born on Raasay and gained a First Class degree in English Language and Literature at the University of Edinburgh in 1933. He counted Hugh MacDiarmid and other writers of the Scottish Literary Renaissance as close friends and literary peers. The literature that he produced modernised Gaelic poetry in the 20th century. During World War II he was conscripted into the Signal Corp and was wounded at the Battle of El Alamein on 2 November 1942. It was during World War II that Douglas Young's friendship with MacLean strengthened, often through correspondence, while MacLean was on active duty. Young championed MacLean's work, helping to prepare *Dàin do Eimhir* (and MacLean's long political poem, 'An Cuilithionn') for publication, and negotiating with publishers in MacLean's absence. The majority of MacLean's poems that Young translated into Scots are from *Dàin do Eimhir agus Dàin Eile*;[51] a collection of poems to 'Eimhir' (a muse-like figure for the poet), which also comprised a number of 'Dàin Eile' ('Other Poems') on social and political themes.

Dàin do Eimhir XXVIII – The Ghaists
Source: *Auntran Blads*: 14-15.[52]

Dàin do Eimhir XXXIII – The weird o makars
Source: *Auntran Blads*: 15.[53]

Dàin do Eimhir XXXIV - When I am talkan o the face and natur...
Source: *Auntran Blads*: 16.[54]

---

51 MacLean 1943.
52 For the original Gaelic with English translation see MacLean 2011b: 130-133.
53 For the original Gaelic with English translation see MacLean 2011b: 136-137.
54 For the original Gaelic with English translation see MacLean 2011b: 136-137.

Dàin do Eimhir XLII - Were we thegither, me and you...
Source: *Auntran Blads*: 19.⁵⁵

Dàin do Eimhir XLIII - Were't no for ye
Source: *Auntran Blads*: 12-13.⁵⁶

Dàin do Eimhir LI - I the connachan time
Source: *Auntran Blads*: 13-14.⁵⁷

Dàin do Eimhir LIII - I fashna masel for the grand revolution...
Source: *Auntran Blads*: 16.⁵⁸

Dàin do Eimhir LIV - Ye were the dawn
Source: *Auntran Blads*: 11-12.⁵⁹

Dàin do Eimhir LV - I dinna ken the sense o ma trauchlan...
Source: *Auntran Blads*: 17.⁶⁰

Dàin do Eimhir LVII
Source: *A Braird o Thristles*: 34-37.⁶¹

Young's translation of LVII was praised by MacLean, writing to Young on 9 September 1941 that 'The version of LVII is remarkably good, I think the best of your versions of my stuff which I have seen... I showed it and the original to Deòrsa [George Campbell Hay] who liked it immensely...'⁶² On 31 March 1943 Young wrote to MacLean on the subject of his Scots translations of MacLean's *Dàin do Eimhir*, noting that the publisher, William MacLellan, 'is printing a good many in my [Auntran] *Blad*[s], nearly finished now; but not LVII, which is miles the best, and most unintelligible.'⁶³ Young's translation of LVII was later published in *A Braird o Thristles*.

---

55 For the original Gaelic with English translation see MacLean 2011b: 140-143.
56 For the original Gaelic with English translation see MacLean 2011b: 142-143.
57 For the original Gaelic with English translation see MacLean 2011b: 152-153.
58 For the original Gaelic with English translation see MacLean 2011b: 156-157.
59 For the original Gaelic with English translation see MacLean 2011b: 156-157.
60 For the original Gaelic with English translation see MacLean 2011b: 156-157.
61 For the original Gaelic with English translation see MacLean 2011b: 158-165.
62 Edin NLS Acc 6419 Box 38b.
63 Edin NLS MS 29540, f. 65.

(l. 25) Patrick Mòr and Patrick Òg MacCrimmon were two of the most famous pipers of the MacCrimmon family, who were hereditary pipers to the MacLeods of Dunvegan, Skye.

Dàin Eile XVII - Wald ye be atween a lassie's houghs
Source: *Auntran Blads*: 14.[64]

Hielant Woman
Source: *Auntran Blads*: 18.
'Ban-Ghàidheal'.[65]

My een are nae on Calvary
Source: *Auntran Blads*: 12.
'Calbharaigh'.[66]

Gealach Ùr: A Communist Sicht o the New Mune
Source: *Auntran Blads*: 17.
'Gealach Ùr'.[67]

Reothairt
Source: *A Braird o Thristles*: 33.
'Reothairt'.[68]

***

George Campbell Hay (Deòrsa Mac Iain Dheòrsa) (1915-1984) was born in Elderslie, Renfrewshire, and was brought up in Tarbert, where he learned Gaelic from the last generation of native speakers in that area. Hay composed poetry in Gaelic, Scots, English, French, Italian and Norwegian. He was also a translator. He was educated at Fettes College in Edinburgh and then afterwards he took a degree in Classics at Oxford University. Hay was a Scottish nationalist who refused conscription, hiding in the hills of Argyll from October 1940 to May 1941, before being caught and briefly

---

[64] For the original Gaelic with English translation see MacLean 2011b: 48-49.
[65] For the original Gaelic with English translation see MacLean 2011b: 16-17.
[66] For the original Gaelic with English translation see MacLean 2011b: 20-21.
[67] For the original Gaelic with English translation see MacLean 2011b: 52-55.
[68] For the original Gaelic with English translation see MacLean 2011b: 182-183.

imprisoned. He later capitulated and joined the Royal Army Ordnance Corps in June 1942, serving in Algeria and Tunisia, and then in Italy from June 1944. In January 1946, as part of the Army Education Corps, he was sent to northern Greece. He was invalided out of the Army with 'nervous trouble'. This condition meant that he never took up full employment again and spent periods in the Royal Edinburgh Hospital. His ambitious poem, *Mochtàr is Dùghall*, was not published until 1982, many years after its composition, and much of his poetry was not published until after his death.

Douglas Young and George Campbell Hay met at the University of Oxford (they both attended between 1934 and 1938). It was Young who was responsible for introducing Hay to the work of Hugh MacDiarmid and their friendship was fuelled by discussion of nationalist politics and literature. By his own admission, Young felt that it was Hay who encouraged him to continue with his anti-conscription stance during World War II. While Hay was on active service, Young held copies of his poetry and, in November 1943, began to seriously plan the publication of a collection of Hay's poetry, appealing to the McCaig Trust for financial support with the venture. There was also discussion of a possible collaboration between Hay and Young in the same vein as Sorley MacLean and Robert Garioch's book, *17 Poems for 6d*.[69]

Thonder They ligg
Source: *Auntran Blads*: 20-21.

'Grunnd na Mara'.[70] Hay may have originally intended this poem to be part of his political sequence 'Dealbh na h-Eòrpa'. Douglas Young's translation was included in Hay's collection, *Fuaran Slèibh*.[71]

Guestless Howff
Source: *A Braird o Thristles*: 31.

'Aonarain na Cille'.[72]

Lass wi the Keekin-Gless
Source: *A Braird o Thristles*: 32.

'An Gaol Cha d'Fhiosraich Mi'.[73]

---

69 MacLean and Garioch 1940.
70 For the original Gaelic and English translation see Hay 2003: 62-63.
71 Hay 1948.
72 For the original Gaelic and English translation see Hay 2003: 74.
73 For the original Gaelic and English translation see Hay 2003: 57-58.

***

William Livingstone of Islay (Uilleam MacDhunlèibhe) (1808-1870) was a Gaelic poet with a keen interest in Classical and modern languages, including Latin, Greek, French and Welsh. His poetry included dramatic reconstructions and reimaginings of Scottish history, including the struggle between Gaels and Norsemen, as well as imaginary pseudo-historical and legendary themes. He was also concerned with the plight of the Gael in the 19th century and the state of Scotland, harking back to a perceived 'golden age' before evictions and betrayals by landlords.

Eirinn ag Gul. Ireland Greitan
Source: *Auntran Blads*: 33-34.

Translation into Scots of William Livingston's poem, 'Eirinn ag Gul'.[74]

***

Do Threasgair an Saol
Source: *Auntran Blads*: 35.

Translation into Scots of an Irish poem. Young may have come into contact with these lines from a variety of sources, one of the most likely being Daniel Corkery's *The Hounds of Banba*[75]

***

An t-Iarla Diurach – *by a MacLaine Lady of Lochbuie to a Campbell of Jura.*
Source: *Auntran Blads*: 35.[76]

***

"Raasay Lament – Cumha Mhic 'ille Chaluim"
Source: *A Braird o Thristles*: 39.

On 29 June 1940, Young wrote to Sorley MacLean on the subject of the translation of this poem:

> Enclosed are also other sundry pieces. There is a version for singing of one of the 'Cumha Mhic 'ille Chaluim', doubtless

---

[74] Livingston 1882: 205-206.
[75] Corkery 1922: 33.
[76] Kennedy-Fraser and MacLeod 1909: 141.

well known to yourself in Raasay. It is taken from Kenneth Macleod's version in the *Songs of the Hebrides*, and is to the tune as there given for the Gaelic, his English version, as often, dividing the phrases amiss. It is highly instructive to try in English the Gaelic rhyme-scheme. I have failed to register the same rhyme through the whole poem in the second and fourth lines of each stanza, for I never noticed it was the same till I had finished. These apparently simple things have their share of subtlety.[77]

Classical Translations

Douglas Young's translations of Sappho's poetry are taken from the original Aeolic dialect. **Sappho** was born on Lesbos around 630 BC. She belonged to a socially and politically prominent family and it is thought that she was well-known for her poetry, even within her own lifetime. She died after 570 BC, but as late as the 1st century BC her poetry was an influence on the flowering of the Latin lyric poetry of Catullus and on the Odes of Horace.

Thon time we aa wonned
Source: *Auntran Blads*: 36.[78]

Til Anaktoria
Source: *Auntran Blads*: 36-37.[79]

Aa that was lowsit
Source: *A Braird o Thristles*: 54.[80]

Minnie, I canna caa my wheel
Source: *A Braird o Thristles*: 54.[81]

---

77 Edin NLS MS 29540, f. 22.
78 For the original Greek see Sappho 1955: 96.1-20 and for an English translation see Sappho 2007: 24.
79 For the original Greek see Sappho 1955: 31 and for an English translation see Sappho 2007: 11
80 For the original Greek see Sappho 1955: 104 and for an English translation see Sappho 2007: 26.
81 For the original Greek see Sappho 1955: 102 and for an English translation see Sappho 2007: 26.

The mune has gane doun
Source: *A Braird o Thristles*: 54.[82]

Caller rain frae abune
Source: *A Braird o Thristles*: 54.[83]

The starns around the bonnie mune
Source: *A Braird o Thristles*: 54.[84]

Deid sall ye ligg, and ne'er a memorie
Source: *A Braird o Thristles*: 54.
'To Andrómeda'.[85] Young also provides a Latin translation of the poem directly under his Scots translation.

***

The partan tellt the ether
Source: *A Braird o Thristles*: 55.
A Greek fable from the late 6th or early 5th century BC.[86]

***

Theognis of Megara was a lyric poet during the 6th century BC. He was a moralist and composed in an elegiac style about ethical and practical matters of life.

I've been a gangrel bodie...
Source: *Auntran Blads*: 37.
Theognis 783-788[87]

---

82 For the original Greek see Sappho 1971: 168B and for an English translation see Sappho 2007: 40.
83 For the original Greek see Sappho 1955: 2 and for an English translation see Sappho 2007: 4.
84 For the original Greek see Sappho 1955: 34 and for an English translation see Sappho 2007: 12.
85 For the original Greek see Sappho 1955: 55 and for an English translation see Sappho 2007: 18.
86 For an English translation of this Attic scholium see Adrados, Ray and Dijk 1999.
87 See Young 1971: 49 and Edmonds 1931: 322-323.

They pledge me nae mair in wine...
Source: *Auntran Blads*: 37.
  Theognis 261-266[88]

Yill's ma guid frien...
Source: *Auntran Blads*: 37.
  Theognis 841-844[89]

Drinkan, I heedna puirtith...
Source: *Auntran Blads*: 37.
  Theognis 1129-1132[90]

The lyon dinesna aye on flesch...
Source: *A Braird o Thristles*: 55.
  Theognis 293-294[91]

***

Hektor's Twynan frae Andromacha
Source: *Auntran Blads*: 38-41.

The Iliad is attributed to the poet, **Homer**, and was composed in the latter part of the 8th century BC. It is the first literary achievement of Greek civilisation but has its roots in a much older tradition of oral poetry. The poem tells of the events in the last year of the Trojan War (*The Iliad* opens with the Trojan War in its tenth year), which lead to Achilles' killing of Hektor and the eventual fate of Troy. Book VI, 392-496, which Douglas Young has translated from Greek into Scots, deals with Hektor's visit to his wife Andromache. During the couple's exchange, Andromache advises Hektor to stay in Troy rather than fight. It is a symbolic meeting-point, which forms a boundary between war and peace, as both Hektor and Andromache meet at a place outside their own natural spheres. [92]

In Young's translation, Scots hexameters mimic the original Greek

---

[88] See Young 1971: 19 and Edmonds 1931: 260-261.
[89] See Young 1971: 52 and Edmonds 1931: 328-329.
[90] See Young 1971: 68 and Edmonds 1931: 364-365.
[91] See Young 1971: 20 and Edmonds 1931: 262-263.
[92] For the original Greek text see Homer 1920 and for an English translation see Homer 1987.

version composed in dactylic hexameters. On 29 June 1940, Young wrote to Sorley MacLean that he has sent to him

> a lump of the *Iliad* in Scots, in the original metre more or less. It illustrates the fact that dactyls in Scots are colloquial, whereas iambic would be stately; in Greek the emphasis is the other way. I believe it shows the capacity of Scots; I was never at a loss for a word over a fair extent of diction, and of course I don't know much Scots. A translation can on occasion put the original in a new perspective; Willa Muir said this version completely revitalised Homer for her. And I find myself that the Greek word 'phaidimos' is somehow enriched when you learn that it is the Scots 'begesserant', and vice versa.[93]

***

Gaius Valerius Catullus (c. 84 BC – c. 54 BC) was a Latin poet of the Republican period. He was born in Verona but spent most of his young adult years in Rome. It was in Rome that he fell in love with the 'Lesbia' of his poems (Clodia, the wife of a statesman). The poems of Catullus are preserved in an anthology of 116 *carmina*, which include erotic poems, invectives and condolences. His poems to 'Lesbia' describe the range of his experiences and feelings during his relationship with Clodia.

Lassie, c'wa
Source: *Auntran Blads*: 41-42.

Catullus, V. This poem may have been composed in the early stages of his relationship with Clodia.[94]

Catullus man, ye maunna
Source: *Auntran Blads*: 42.

Catullus, VIII. This poem describes his misery at being rejected by his lover and his attempt to lift himself out of his depression.[95]

***

---

93 Edin NLS MS 29540, f. 22.
94 For the original Latin see Catullus 1970: 3 and for an English translation see Catullus 1978: 28.
95 For the original Latin see Catullus 1970: 5 and for an English translation see Catullus 1978: 30-31.

Sulpicia was the author of some of the elegies attributed to the Roman poet, Tibullus (ca. 55 BC-19 BC).

I wish, my jo
Source: Edin NLS Acc 6419 Box 75 (4)

Elegidion VI. This is a poem of apology, dealing with Sulpicia's strength of feelings after she has left her lover, Cerinthus, at their meeting place.[96]

***

Sextus Propertius (c. 50/45 BC-15 BC) was a Latin elegiac poet. His four books of elegies (around 92 poems in total) were dominated by a single woman, 'Cynthia'.

Ithers may scryve
Source: Edin NLS Acc 6419 Box 75 (4)

Elegies II, xi.[97]

***

Emperor ***Gallienus*** (A.D. 253-268) is believed to have been a gifted orator, who composed verses in Latin and Greek. These verses included love poems or 'wedding songs'.

Lasses and Lads[98]
Source: Edin NLS Acc 6419 Box 75 (4)

***

Aeschylus (c. 525/4 BC–c. 456/5 BC) was an ancient Greek playwright, often known as the father of tragedy, who alongside the other Greek tragedians, Sophocles and Euripides, shaped and influenced the development of this genre.

Choric Threnody
Source: Edin NLS Acc 6419 Box 75 (4)

From *Agamemnon*, 429-455.[99]

---

[96] For the original Latin see Tibullus 1909: 257-258.
[97] For the original Latin and English translation see Propertius 1972: 316-317, 80.
[98] For a detailed discussion of these verses see Clover 2002: 192-208.
[99] For the original Greek with facing English translation, see Aeschylus 1950: 116-119.

***

Aristophanes (c. 446 BC-c. 386 BC) was a playwright from Athens, best known for his comedic plays. His play, *The Birds,* was first performed in 414 BC.

Aristophanes in Scots: ***Frae Choruses o The Birdies***
Source: Edin NLS Acc 6419 Box 75 (4)

This translation is taken from ll. 1482-93 and ll. 1694-1705 of *The Birds*. Young's Scots translation includes Scottish placenames.

He later completed a full version of the play in 1959, *The Burdies,* which made its debut at the Edinburgh Fringe Festival.[100]

Translations from Italian

Durante degli Alighieri (Dante) (c. 1265-1321) was an Italian poet, most famous for his *Divine Comedy*. His *La Vita Nuova*, compiled in 1293-1294, is an expression of courtly love and is in the form of verse and prose. He composed it in Italian rather than Latin. It contains 42 brief chapters with commentaries on 25 sonnets, one ballata and four canzoi.

'Mentre io pensava la mia frale vita...'
Source: *Auntran Blads*: 43.

From Capitolo XXIII. This excerpt, translated into Scots, is lines 29-56 of the second canzone of *La Vita Nuova* (a canzone is an Italian or Provençal song or ballad).[101]

Translations from French

Paul Valéry (1871-1945) was a French poet, essayist and philosopher. He also kept an intellectual diary, *Cahiers* (*Notebooks*), which covered a range of subjects including mathematics and science.

---

[100] See Young 1959a and 1966. For the original Greek play, with an English translation, see Aristophanes 1987.

[101] For the original Italian see Dante 1903. For a translation into English of this section of *La Vita Nuova* see Dante 1992: 49.

His poetry was influenced by the Symbolists and he was a friend of the poet, Stéphane Mallarmé.

The Couthy Wuid
Source: *Auntran Blads*: 44.
A translation into Scots of 'Le Bois Amical'.[102]

The Kirkyaird by the Sea
Source: *A Braird o Thristles*: 41-45.

A translation into Scots of 'Le Cimetière Marin'.[103] The poem is an elegiac meditation in the presence of the sea, sun and sky and is a reflection of Valéry's experience from his childhood in Sète, a theme which this Scots translation highlights effectively with Young's native Fife as a focus in place of Sète.

Translations from German

Hugo von Hofmannsthal (1874-1929) was an Austrian poet, essayist, librettist and dramatist. Born in Vienna, he held a government post during World War I, writing speeches which encouraged the war effort and the cultural traditions of Austria-Hungary. He later co-founded the Salzburg Festival with Max Reinhardt. He viewed the artist as someone who should be able to incorporate both politics and art in their work.

Whaur monie a wee bit spruce and craig
Source: *Auntran Blads*: 44.
A translation into Scots of 'Wo kleine Felsen, kleine Fichten'.[104]

***

Theodor Storm (1817-1888) was a German writer of literary realism, born in the small town of Husum on the west coast of Schleswig. Husum was an independent duchy ruled by the king of Denmark and later came under Prussian rule.

---

102 For an English translation of the poem see Valéry 1971: 22-23.
103 For an English translation of the poem see Valéry 1971: 212-221.
104 For the original German poem, see Hofmannsthal 1919: 13.

Grey are the sands
Source: *Auntran Blads*: 45.

A translation of 'Die Stadt', a poem about Husum.[105]

***

Emanuel Geibel (1815-1884) was a German poet and playwright and one of the members of a literary circle, *Die Krokodile* (Crocodile Society), who were concerned with traditional forms and styles, and were drawn together in Munich by Maximilian II of Bavaria. He was interested in Classical philology and in 1840 he published a volume of Greek translations.

The mowdie
Source: *Auntran Blads*: 45.

A translation into Scots of 'Der Maulwurf hört in seinem Loch'.[106]

***

Erich Fried (1921-1988) was an Austrian poet, writer and translator who was born to Jewish parents and fled to England after the annexation of Austria by Nazi Germany in 1938. He was a supporter of the left-wing and a critic of the Zionist movement and was best known for his political poetry.

Hame frae Stalingrad
Source: *A Braird o Thristles*: 50.

A translation into Scots of 'Soldatenlied im Osten'.[107]

The Bairns' Slauchter o Bethlehem
Source: *A Braird o Thristles*: 51.

A translation into Scots of 'Der Bethlehemitische Kindermord' from 'Pieter Breughel'.[108]

***

On the Daith o a Young German Scholar
Source: *A Braird o Thristles*: 52.

---

105 For the original German poem, see Bruns 1921: 93.
106 For the original German poem, see Geibel 2013: 60.
107 For the original poem, see Fried 1944: 21.
108 For the original poem see Fried 1945: 6.

***

Ludwig Uhland (1787-1862) was a German poet, philologist and literary historian.

On a Bairn's Daith
Source: *A Braird o Thristles*: 52-53.

Translations of 'Auf den tod eines kindes'.[109]

The dedicatee of this poem, David Murison (1913-1997), was Young's long-time friend. He was a Scottish lexicographer and editor of the Scottish National Dictionary from 1946 to 1976.

***

Paul Heyse (1830-1914) was a German writer and translator. He was a member of *Die Krokodile* (see also Emanuel Geibel above) and he was awarded the Nobel Prize for Literature in 1910.

Eftir the Daith o a Bairn
Source: *Honour'd Shade: An Anthology of New Scottish Poetry* (Edinburgh, W.R. Chambers Ltd): 130.[110]

This poem is significant as it is the first poem in Scots to be included in the Black Book.

***

Christian Morgenstern (1871-1914) was a German writer from Munich, known for his lyrical and nonsense verse. His methods have been compared to those of Lewis Carroll. He also translated various Norwegian and French poems and plays into German, including the work of Henrik Ibsen.

A black birdie flees owre the warld
Source: *A Braird o Thristles*: 55.

A translation into Scots of 'Vöglein Schwermut'.[111]

---

[109] For the original German poem, see Uhland 1892: 81.
[110] For the original German poem, see Heyse 2013: 98.
[111] For the original German poem, see Morgenstern 2013: 14.

How the Stillness oer the Width of Water hitherwandering comes
Source: A Braird o Thristles: 55.[112]

***

Christian Johann Heinrich Heine (1797-1856) was a German poet, journalist and literary critic. He held radical political views and, greatly encouraged by the French Revolution in 1830, he moved to Paris, where he spent the last 25 years of his life.

I loe a fleur
Source: Edin NLS Acc 6419 Box 75 (4)
   This poem, "Ich liebt eine blume, doch weiss ich nicht welche...", is No. 4 in the poem cycle, *Neuer Frühling*. It was first published in *Der Salon: Zweiter Teil* in 1835.[113]

***

Johann Wolfgang von Goethe (1749-1832) was a German politician, novelist, playwright, poet and natural philosopher.

Travesty in Lallans: Mignon's Song, "Kennst du das Land..."
Source: Edin NLS Acc 6419 Box 75 (4)
   From *Wilhelm Meisters Lehrjahre*. In the novel, this poem is voiced by the child, Mignon, who recalls her Italian homeland after being forcibly removed to Germany. Wilhelm Meister becomes her protector.[114]

Translations from Lithuanian[115]

Kościuszko's son
Source: *Auntran Blads*: 46.

---

112 For the original German poem, see Morgenstern 2013: 14.
113 For the German original see Heine 1982a: 10. For an English translation, see Heine 1982b: 315.
114 For the German original, see Goethe 1998: 117. For Thomas Carlyle's English translation see Goethe 1899: 176.
115 See Landsbergis and Mills 1962, for an introduction to Lithuanian poetry, particularly *dainos* such as Kościuszko's Son'.

The Gods' buss, epple-ringie
Source: *Auntran Blads*: 46-47.

Britherly Fareweel
Source: *A Braird o Thristles*: 40.

Translations from Chinese

The *Shi King* is a collection of ancient Chinese poetry, recounting the habits, customs and feelings of all classes of people in China 3000 years ago. While the *Shi King* predates Confucius by three centuries, he is often credited with organising it into its present form around 520 BC, selecting the poems that best illustrate propriety and righteousness from a much greater number of poems. The collection is organised into four parts: the Characteristics of the State, the Minor Festal Odes, The Greater Festal Odes and Festal Hymns and Songs.

Rowans are rowthie
Source: *Auntran Blads*: 47
Young's translation into Scots of the second of the Odes of T'Ang.[116]

The Hermit Bonze
Source: *A Braird o Thristles*: 56.
Young's translation into Scots of the second of the Odes of Wei.[117] This poem may have been directed against Duke Chwang (756-734 BC); during his rule men of virtue and talent withdrew from public service to live in obscurity.

The Rich Spinster's Sang
Source: Edin NLS Acc 6419 Box 75 (4)
Young's translation into Scots of the ninth of the Odes of Wei.[118] In an accompanying note to this poem, Jennings writes

---

116 For an English translation – 'Enjoy Life's Good Things While You May' – see Jennings 1969: 128-129.
117 For an English translation – 'The Happy Recluse' – see Jennings 1969: 82.
118 For an English translation – 'Wifeless and Forlorn' – see Jennings 1969: 88-89.

in a time of anarchy and confusion in Wei, there were many who could not marry. Here a widow or unmarried woman has met a vagabond male, and his forlorn condition has so roused her matronly instincts that she is willing to marry him and look after him... in the ancient Preface to the Book of Poetry it is said to be directed against the time. 'The males and females of Wei were losing the time for marriage... Anciently, when a State was suffering from the misery of famine, the rules were relaxed so that there might be many marriages; and men and women who had no partners were brought together, in order to promote the increase of people.'[119]

The phaisant cock has flown awa
Source: Edin NLS Acc 6419 Box 75 (4)

Young's translation into Scots of the eighth of the Odes of P'ei,[120] dealing with the wife of an officer, who describes their mutual regret at his absence on foreign service.

Translations from Russian

Alexander Sergeyevich Pushkin (1799-1837) was a Romantic-era Russian poet and writer, often described as the founder of modern Russian literature. He was committed to social reform, became a literary radical and took inspiration from the Greek Revolution. His earlier political poems caused him to be censored for a time by the government after the Decembrist Revolt of 1825. His best-known works include the play, *Boris Godunov* and his novel in verse, *Eugene Onegin*. He was fatally injured during a duel.

I loed ye yince
Source: *Auntran Blads*: 48.

Young's translation into Scots and German of Pushkin's 1829 poem.[121]

---

119 Jennings 1969: 88-89.
120 For an English translation – 'Separation' – see Jennings 1969: 61.
121 For the original Russian poem and English translation see Pushkin 1972: 37, 232-233.

The Black Shawl
Source: *A Braird o Thristles*: 48-49.
Young's translation into Scots of 'The Black Shawl'. [122]

Dearer the fleurs o hairst's dwynin
Source: *A Braird o Thristles*: 49.
Young's translation into Scots of Pushkin's 1825 poem. [123]

Amang the fullyerie's shadow-ferlies
Source: *A Braird o Thristles*: 49 [124]

'To A. P. Kyern'
Source: Edin NLS Acc 6419 Box 75 (4)
Young's translation of 'To A. P. Kyern'. [125]

***

Kondrati Fyedorovitch Rileyev (or Kondraty Fyodorovich Ryleyev) (1795-1826) was a Russian poet and publisher who became a leader of the Decembrist Revolt, which attempted to overthrow the Russian monarchy in 1825. He was later arrested and executed for his role in the revolt. [126]

Octobrist Manifesto
Source: *A Braird o Thristles*: 47

***

Nikolay Alexeyevich Nyekrasov (or Nekrasov) (1821-1878) was a Russian poet, critic and publisher. He was sympathetic to the Russian peasantry and composed folk poems, works for children and socio-political poems dealing with themes such as the difficulties of Russian life and events including the Decembrist Revolt.

---

122 For an English translation of this poem see Pushkin 2012: 135-136.
123 For the original Russian poem and English translation see Pushkin 1972: 20, 199.
124 For the original Russian poem and English translation see Pushkin 1972: 20, 199.
125 For a more recent English translation of this poem see Pushkin 2012: 19-20, 22-23.
126 For a selection of his original Russian poems see Ryleyev 1934, and for English translations see Ryleyev 1887.

A Mother's Tears
Source: *A Braird o Thristles*: 47[127]

Translations from Welsh

D. Gwenallt Jones (David James Jones) (1899-1968) was a Welsh poet, critic and an influential figure of the 20th century Welsh language revival. He was a conscientious objector during World War I and was incarcerated for his beliefs during this time.

Wales
Source: *A Braird o Thristles*: 38.[128]

Translations from Hebrew

The 23rd Psalm o King Dauvit
Source: *A Braird o Thristles*: 46.

Young composed this translation on St Andrew's Day, 1942, in Edinburgh Prison. In the *Scots Independent* the origin of this translation is described:

> Douglas Young has now been in prison for four months for refusing in the name of the constitutional laws and liberties of Scotland to be conscripted for the British Imperial Armed Forces. Our appreciation of his courage and determination can best be shown by redoubled efforts to achieve a Scottish Democratic Government and the freedom this war is being fought for. Writing from prison, he warmly thanks all those who have contributed generously to the Douglas Young Defence Fund. He continues: 'On Wallace Day I amused myself by owresetting in Lallans the 23rd Psalm o Dauvit.[129]

Moray McLaren writes that

> A Scottish writer who was speaking in support of a Scottish Nationalist political candidate at a rural district in the East Lowlands found himself at an informal meeting of farmers

---

[127] For an earlier English translation of this poem see Nekrassov 1929: 187.
[128] For the original Welsh, see Jones 2001: 70-71. For an English translation of this poem see Jones 2000: 98-99.
[129] *Scots Independent* (November 1942) 4.

and small town business men. They asked him whether all this revival of the Scottish language was not 'so much nonsense', and whether anything that he had written in this kind could really be understood by them – plain ordinary Scots folk. For an answer this rather peculiar looking literary man, black-bearded and immensely elongated, drew himself up to his full six and a half feet and recited to them his own translation of the Twenty-third Psalm in Scots. When he had finished there was a long silence; and the present writer can vouch for it that one or two of these practical East Coast Lowland farmers were near to tears.[130]

This translation was also a reading at Douglas Young's memorial service, held at the University Chapel, St. Andrews by the University of St. Andrews on Saturday 12 January 1974.

**

The Coolin: An Assonantal Projection
Source: Private papers, The Saughton Manuscript.

Young's projection of Sorley MacLean's long political poem, 'An Cuilithionn', is previously unpublished.[131] The original version of MacLean's 'An Cuilithionn' has only recently been published for the first time.[132] Young's projection is based on the 1939 version of the poem. It is clear that MacLean admired Young's English version, writing to Young on 30 March 1943 that 'I like your 'projection' very much. It is far better than I could expect anyone to do.'[133] There was a very real possibility of Young's translation being published, most probably as a separate pamphlet to MacLean's original poem. One expression of interest in funding this project is mentioned to MacLean by Young in a letter dated 10 June 1943.[134] However, MacLean's reservations about 'An Cuilithionn', which are well documented in Whyte's introduction to the 1939 edition, is likely to be the main reason that Young's version has remained unpublished until now.

Young's projection is presented here as it is set out in the original manuscript and therefore there are inconsistencies between the

---
130 McLaren 1951.
131 See Edin NLS MS 29561.
132 MacLean 2011a.
133 Edin NLS Acc 6419 Box 38b.
134 Edin NLS MS 29540, f. 68.

original Gaelic poem and this text. For example, in the First Movement, there is a verse missing, which should follow on from line 193 of Young's translation ('Agus gach eile a bha a' caoidh/ na beinne brice is creachainn àird,/ is fòirneart shanntach luchd an Dùin/ a chuir an cùl-san ris an tràigh.'). In the Sixth Movement two lines are missing from the 'China stanza' following on from ll. 168-169 and in the Seventh Movement two stanzas dealing with T.S. Eliot and Hugh MacDiarmid have also been omitted, which should follow on from l. 67.

Other alterations and corrections would most certainly have been made to Young's projection, had it been published in the 1940s. In a letter dated 9 April 1943, MacLean expressed his dislike of the phonetic forms of Gaelic placenames given by Young[135] but these have been deliberately retained here because they show Young's attempt to aid his intended readership in attaining as much of the flavour of the Gaelic original as possible.

During the editing of *Naething Dauntit*, Young's daughter, Clara, found the original manuscript of 'The Coolin', composed in Saughton Jail, at Makarsbield. It contained some minor changes to punctuation and vocabulary. This copy has been merged with the NLS typescript in order to display Young's translation in its best possible form. The original 'Saughton' manuscript also contained extensive footnotes, which Young presumably planned to include in the proposed publication of his translation. Christopher Whyte's edited edition of 'An Cuilithionn' is also an excellent resource for the numerous names and placenames included in the poem.

On 14 January 1943, while Young was incarcerated in Saughton Jail, he wrote a letter to C.M. Grieve in which he mentions his work on 'An Cuilithionn'.

> I have three wonderful letters from Somhairle, the last Oct. 6th, and on Dec. 18th, I think, I had a vivid sensation of his being present & impelling me to get ahead with work on his poems. Please write him by airgraph (Sig. S.M. 2331381, Signal Troop, 1st R.H.A., M.E.F.) that in the last five days I have drafted a near-literal assonantal projection into English of the first part of An Cuilthionn, & hope to have the whole done before I emerge (8 weeks). I choose English, not Lallans, to reach a wider public, but it is like transliquidating whisky into ditch-water.[136]

---

135 Edin NLS Acc 6419 Box 38b.
136 Manson 2011.

Appendix

Foreword to *Auntran Blads*
By Hugh MacDiarmid

This is a significant book.

Readers who have a good knowledge of the literary history of Scotland, and of its recent developments in the so-called Scottish Renaissance movement of the 1919-1939 inter-war period, will note at once that these selected poems of Mr. Douglas Young manifest all the chief characteristics of the independent Scottish tradition in its differences from English tradition.

The declared purpose of the Scottish Renaissance movement was to revive these elements which had been more and more lost in the process of assimilation to English standards, to which Scotland has been subject since the Union. The elements in question may be listed as internationalism; wide-ranging linguistic and scholarly interests; an intense concern with the crucial problems, needs and potentialities of Scotland; and, along with that, a thorough knowledge of Scottish history, psychology, and the whole of the country from Maidenkirk to John o' Groats. With these characteristics went a thorough-going critical revaluation of the Scottish past in all its aspects, and a new insistence on the Scots Lallans language in the first place and, beyond that, on the need to restore Gaelic as the national language of Scotland and to resume in the fullest way the great traditions of our lost heritage of Gaelic culture, and to apply these to new creative purpose.

Several of these elements were obviously such that pursuit of them was bound to involve the writers and scholars concerned more and more in practical politics. It was not long, therefore, before these cultural activities found a political counterpart in a revived Scottish Nationalism with a multiplicity of organisations, of which the best known is the Scottish National Party. The underground strength of the forces generated in this revived Nationalism was not adequately reflected in the sphere of practical politics, and the positions reached by the S.N.P. and other organisations gave no true indication of the power, temper and tendency of what was really strongest and most significant in these new developments. That indication was only to be found in the work of the younger Scottish poets, critics and scholars, in the increasing divergence of that work, alike in content and in form, from the work of their English and Anglo-Scottish contemporaries, and in the extent to which that work represented a re-embodiment of the salient characteristics of the independent Scottish tradition prior to the Union with, or rather *under* England.

Part of Mr. Douglas Young's significance is to be discerned in the fact that recently an important new development, which may make the Scottish National Party really worthy of its name, has taken place under his leadership, that he is now Chairman of the Party, and has the enthusiastic support, not only of all the best contemporary Scottish writers, but of a large and increasing body of the younger Scottish people and of intelligent Scots generally, despite the fact that his attitude to the Second World War is so deeply at variance with that of the Westminster Government and the so called "national unity" of our war-effort generally, that his political opponents in the Anglo-Scottish capitalist Press have (falsely) denounced him as a Pacifist and attempted to prejudice on this ground the new Scottish Nationalist developments with which he is so prominently associated. Mr. Douglas Young holds that, for the defence of Scotland and the discharge of Scotland's part in the enlargement of national and personal liberty throughout the world, the Scots must be embodied in Scottish armed forces under the control of a democratic Scottish government; for refusing to comply with the British Government's conscription scheme the British authorities sentenced him to 12 months' gaol.

Incidentally it may be here pointed out that most, if not all, the significant poets in Scotland fully share Mr. Young's attitude to the war, to Anglo-American Imperialism, and to the Money Power, and that, whatever may be said on the other side, its exponents do not seem able to express their myopic toe-the-line all-in patrioteering in any worthwhile prose or poetry, or in art or music either, since what is true of our poets and prose-writers in this matter is equally true of our painters and composers.

The significance of this literary and political leadership is best seen in the light of the speeches given from the dock by many of the unsuccessful Scots protestors against British conscription in the

Courts. These young men manifested a spirit which has been sadly lacking in Scotland since the time of Wallace, and many of their speeches ring with a passionate denunciation of any but a Scottish government daring to conscribe Scottish youth, a denunciation which has no counterpart in modern literature, except perhaps Vanzetti's last speech at the infamous trial at which Sacco and he were condemned to the electric chair. It is this passion which lies behind Scottish poetry and Scottish nationalist politics today, and it is in its many-sided fruitful relation to that that Mr. Young's personality and work, poetical and political, should be gauged.

These political positions – this awareness of and passionate concern with Scottish social and economic problems – this regained knowledge of the differentiae of Scottish literature, in all its phases, Gaelic, Scots, Latin and of the whole history of our country – this knowledge and loving use of our neglected Scottish languages – this vivid sense of our very different historical, psychological and practical affiliations from those of the English people with the other peoples of Europe, are all clearly reflected in the poems in this volume.

The late M. Henri Hubert, the great French Celtic authority, in his monumental works on the rise and decline of the Celts, pointed out, inter alia, that Celtic literature, had always been a learned literature, the work of highly-trained experts in elaborate and intricate forms, and, so far as poetry was concerned, had nothing to do with mere "lyrical outpourings". It is a long overdue return to this intellectual position (pedantic position, if you will) from the analphabetic versifiers of post-Burnsian Scotland that the new tendencies of the Scottish literary movement of the past twenty years set out to encompass. And the new voices in Scottish poetry today – notably Mr. Douglas Young himself, and the two young Gaelic poets of whose work (not yet fully available in volume form) he gives excellent translations, Sorley MacLean (Somhairle MacGhill' Eathain) and George Campbell Hay – show that these tendencies are still gathering force, reaching further and further away from the English and Anglo-Scottish literary norm, and achieving work of great aesthetic and intellectual promise bridging the gulf between the poor parvanimous products of the Scottish poets (with few exceptions) in the intervening centuries and the scholarship and technical expertise of the great Scots poets of the fifteenth and sixteenth centuries (Dunbar, Gawain Douglas, Henryson and others) on the one hand, and of the Golden Age of classical Gaelic poetry (recaptured in one splendid outburst two hundred years ago by Alexander Macdonald, Duncan Ban MacIntyre, and the other great Gaelic poets of the 'Forty-Five; only, alas, to sink again into a dreary rut of pietistic *bardachd* from which it is only today at long last showing signs of re-emerging).

M. Henri Hubert, in the same great volumes, points out that "difficult", elaborate, intricate and highly scholarly as Gaelic poetry always was, it was always popular as hardly any other literature has ever been – popular, that is to say in its appeal to all classes of the community; and it is by that essential republicanism that work such as Mr. Young's, conjoined to practical political activity, hopes and seems likely to bridge the appalling gulf between Poetry and the People which has yawned ever wider during the past century and a half.

I need say nothing here of the great range of scholarly and aesthetic interest manifested by the poems in this volume. They revive in some sort the traditions of the "Wandering Scholars"; they have wit as well as learning, and by their exemplification of the fact that, as Nietzsche said, "everything great moves on light feet," they seem likely to play and important part in leavening the sad dough to which modern Scottish mentality has been brought under and increasing assimilation to the standards of an utterly different and incompatible people. That aeration may well be one of the great services which Mr. Douglas Young and his colleagues render to Scottish letters and to Scottish life, and its influence will not be limited to Scotland. Mr. Young's internationalism, his wide knowledge and appreciation of languages and literatures, will evoke the grateful responses and reciprocal activities of younger writers and scholars in all the countries concerned, and play its part in securing once again that fruitful friendly interanimation which is the hope of the Mind of man, a restoration of the Abbey of Thelema in which indeed Scotland, the stone which the builders have despised and rejected, may well prove a corner-stone, when the unsightly scaffolding behind which the future of Humanity is being erected is removed, and the revelation of what has been built shows the great significance of what was belittled or unsuspected up to then by those bemused by the claims to major moment of forces arrogating a great place to themselves in public life today, yet destined to "leave not a wrack behind" and, in the long run, to be discerned as having contributed nothing whatever to "the temple not made with hands."

In a word, Mr. Douglas Young and the other young Scottish poets to whom I refer and whom he translates, have regained for themselves, and seek to regain for their misled and maltreated country as a whole, that lost tradition of Scotland to which Louis Pasteur paid tribute when, on the occasion of the tercentenary of Edinburgh University in 1884, he said, "The city of Edinburgh is now presenting a spectacle of which she may well be proud. All the great scientific organisations, assembling here, seem an immense gathering of hopes and mutual encouragement. The honour reflected by this international concourse rightly belongs to you, for centuries ago the fortunes of Scotland were joined with those of the human mind. She was one of the earliest nations to realise that intellect rules the world. And the world of intellect, gladly responding to your call, places a well-deserved homage at your feet. Yesterday, when the renowned Professor Robert Flint, in his address to Edinburgh University students from the pulpit of St. Giles, uttered the words, "Remember the past and work for the future," all the delegates, sitting like judges at a great tribunal, called forth a vision of bygone centuries and united in a unanimous desire for a still more glorious future."

This is the atmosphere in which these poems of Mr. Douglas Young live and move and have their being, and I confidently predict that they will play their part in producing a like effect.

Bibliography

Unpublished sources

National Library of Scotland
MS 29540 Letters from Douglas Young to Sorley MacLean 1940-1968
Accession 6419 Box 75 Mss and typescripts of poems by Douglas Young
Accession 6419 Box 38b Letters from Sorley MacLean to Douglas Young
Accession 7085 Box 15 Mss and typescripts of poems by Douglas Young

Private papers

'The Saughton Manuscript' (Makarsbield): Douglas Young's original manuscript of 'The Coolin'

> This version of An Cuilthionn by Somhairle MacLean was made by Douglas Young between January 8th and February 12th, 1943, in Saughton Jail, Edinburgh. The pencil variants are mainly from one the Revd. James Morton, I believe an acquaintance of S. MacLean's, and are mainly negligible.

'The Black Book': Begun in 1931 and containing early poems by Young, hand-written copies of poems he admired in a variety of languages and favourite poems copied into the book by friends.

Published sources

1: By Douglas Young

Young 1939a 'Scotsmen, Wake Up!' *The Scots Independent* (April 1939): 16
Young 1939b 'Chain Stores' *The Scots Independent* (May 1939): 5
Young 1939c 'It's Easy Sperin'' *The Scots Independent* (November 1939): 12

Young 1940a 'Attic Noon' in *Scots Magazine* Vol XXXII, No. 4 (January 1940): 280-281

Young 1940b 'Autumn Fire' *Scots Magazine* Vol XXXII No. 4 (January 1940): 280-281

Young 1940c 'Russian Thought' *Scots Magazine* Vol XXXII No. 4 (January 1940): 280-281

Young 1940d 'St Andrew's Castle' *Scots Magazine* Vol XXXII No. 4 (January 1940): 280-281

Young 1940e 'Crusade' *The Scots Independent* (July 1940): 4

Young 1940f 'Mr E. Brown's Highland Tour' *The Scots Independent* (September 1940): 5

Young ed. 1940g *The Auld Aiberdeen Courant and neo-Caledonian Spasmodical: a political and literary gallimaufray* (Aberdeen, privately published)

Young 1942 *The free-minded Scot: trial and defence of Douglas Young* (Glasgow, The Caledonian Press)

Young 1943 *Auntran Blads: an outwale o verses* (Glasgow, William MacLellan)

Young 1944 'Winter Pool' *Poetry Scotland* 1 (Glasgow, William MacLellan): 31

Young 1945 'Letter to Hugh MacDiarmid, 1940' *Poetry Scotland* 2 (Glasgow, William MacLellan): 25-29

Young 1946 'To a Friend on a Campaign' *Poetry Scotland* 3 (Glasgow, William MacLellan): 26

Young 1947a *A Braird o Thristles: Scots Poems* (Glasgow, William MacLellan)

Young 1947b *Plastic Scots and the Scottish Literary Tradition: an authoritative introduction to a controversy* (Glasgow, William MacLellan)

Young 1949a 'Snaw Thochts' *Poetry Scotland* 4 (Edinburgh, Serif Books): 5

Young 1949b 'The Shepherd's Dochter' *Poetry Scotland* 4 (Edinburgh, Serif Books): 6

Young 1950 *Chasing an Ancient Greek: Discursive Reminiscences of an European Journey* (London, Hollis and Carter)

Young 1952 'Simplon Tunnel' *Scottish Verse 1851-1951, selected for the general reader by Douglas Young* (Edinburgh, Thomas Nelson and Sons Ltd): 277-278

Young 1959a, rev. 1966 *The Burdies: a Comedy in Scots verse by Aristophanes and Douglas Young* (Tayport, privately published)

Young 1959b 'Eftir the Daith o a Bairn' *Honour'd Shade: An Anthology of New Scottish Poetry*, edited by Norman MacCaig (Edinburgh, W.R. Chambers Ltd): 130.

Young ed. 1971 *Theognis. Ps.-Pythagoras. Ps.-Phocylides. Chares. Anonymi Aulodia. Fragmentum teliambicum post, Ernestum Diehl.* (Leipzig, Teubner)

Young 1977 *A Clear Voice: Douglas Young, Poet and Polymath*, a selection from his writing with a memoir by David Murison and Clara Young (Loanhead, MacDonald Publishers)

2: Other works

Adrados, Francisco Rodríguez, Ray, Leslie A. and Dijk, Gert-Jan van eds. 1999 *History of the Graeco-Latin Fable: Introduction and from the Origins to the Hellenistic Age* (Boston, Brill)

Aeschylus 1950 *Agamemnon*, Vol. 1, edited by Edward Fraenkel (Oxford, Clarendon Press)

Aristophanes 1987 *The Comedies of Aristophanes*, Vol 6, edited by Alan H. Sommerstein (Wiltshire, Aris and Phillips)

Bowd, Gavin 2013 *Fascist Scotland: Caledonia and the Far Right* (Edinburgh, Birlinn)

Bruns, Friedrich ed. 1921 *A Book of German Lyrics* (Boston, D.C. Heath & Co.)

Byrne, Michel 2002 'Tails o the Comet? MacLean, Hay, Young and MacDiarmid's Renaissance' ScotLit 26, Spring 2002 http://www.arts.gla.ac.uk/scotlit/asls/Tails_o_the_comet.html

Catullus, Gaius Valerius 1970 *Catullus: The Poems*, edited by Kenneth Quinn (London, MacMillan)

Catullus, Gaius Valerius 1978 *The Poems of Catullus*, translated by Frederic Raphael and Kenneth McLeish (London, Jonathan Cape)

Cicero 1909-14 *Letters* (The Harvard Classics edition), translated by E. S. Shuckburgh (New York, P.F. Collier and Son)

Clover, Frank M. 2002 'An Epithalamium Attributed to Emperor Gallienus' *Hermes*, 130 (2nd Qtr): 192-208.

Corkery, Daniel 1922 *The Hounds of Banba* (New York, B.W. Huebsch)

Dante Alighieri 1903 *Vita Nuova di Dante* with illustrations by Dante Gabriele Rossetti (Torino, Casa Editrice Nazionale)

Dante Alighieri 1992 *Vita Nuova* edited and translated by Mark Musa (Oxford, Oxford University Press)

Edmonds, J.M. ed. 1931 *Elegy and Iambus, Vol I, Elegaic Poets from Callinus to Critias* (London, William Heinemann Ltd)

Fergusson, James 1934 *Letters of George Dempster to Sir Adam Fergusson,1756-1813: with some account of his life* (London, Macmillan)

Fergusson, James 1937 *Alexander the Third: King of Scotland* (London, A. MacLehose)

Fergusson, James 1938 *William Wallace: Guardian of Scotland* (London, A. MacLehose)

Findlay, Bill 2005 'Towards a Reassessment of Douglas Young: Motivation and his Aristophanic Translations' *Études écossaises* 10: 175-186
Fried, Erich 1944 *Deutschland: Gedichte* (London, Austrian PEN)
Fried, Erich 1945 'Pieter Breughel', *Die Zeitung* (2 February): 6
Geibel, Emanuel 2013 *Gedichte und Gedenkblätter* (CreateSpace Independent Publishing Platform)
Gibbon, Lewis Grassic 1932 *Sunset Song* (London, Jarrolds)
Goethe, Johann Wolfgang von 1899 *Wilhelm Meister's Apprenticeship and Travels*, Vol I, translated by Thomas Carlyle (London, Chapman and Hall)
Goethe, Johann Wolfgang von 1998 *Wilhelm Meisters Lehrjahre* (Husum/ Nordsee, Hamburger Lesehefte Verlag)
Hay, George Campbell 1948 *Fuaran Slèibh* (Glasgow, William MacLellan)
Hay, George Campbell 2003 *Collected Poems and Songs of George Campbell Hay*, edited by Michel Byrne (Edinburgh, Edinburgh University Press)
Heine, Heinrich 1982a *Neue Gedichte* (Berlin, Eulenspiegel Verlag)
Heine, Heinrich 1982b *The Complete Poems of Heinrich Heine: A Modern English Version,* edited by Hal Draper (Boston, Insel Publishers)
Heyse, Paul 2013 *Paul Heyse: Gedichte* edited by Michael Holzinger (CreateSpace Independent Publishing Platform)
Hofmannsthal, Hugo von 1919 *Die Gedichte und Kleinen Dramen von Hugo von Hofmannsthal* (Leipzig, Insel-Verlag)
Homer 1920 *The Iliad,* (Oxford Classical Texts Series, 3rd edition) edited by D.B. Monro and T.W. Allen's (Oxford, Clarendon Press)
Homer 1987 *The Iliad,* edited by Martin Hammond (London, Penguin)
Jamieson, John 1808 *An Etymological Dictionary of the Scottish Language* (Edinburgh, University Press)
Jennings, William ed. and trans. 1969 *The Shi King, the Old "Poetry Classic" of the Chinese. A Close Metrical Translation, with Annotations,* (New York, Paragon Book Reprint Corp.)
Jones, Gwenallt 2000 *Sensuous Glory: the Poetic Vision of D. Gwenallt Jones,* edited by Donald Allchin, D. Densil Morgan and Patrick Thomas (Norwich, Canterbury Press)
Jones, Gwenallt 2001 *Cerddi Gwenallt: Y Casgliad Cyflawn,* edited by Christine James (Gomer, Llandysul)
Kennedy-Fraser, Marjory and MacLeod, Kenneth eds. 1909 *Songs of the Hebrides and Other Celtic Songs from the Highlands of Scotland*, Vol I (London, Boosey & Co.)
Landsbergis, Algirdas and Mills, Clark eds. 1962 *The Green Oak: Selected Lithuanian Poetry* (New York, Voyages Press)
Langland, William 1975 *Piers Plowman,* edited by Stella Brook (Manchester, Manchester University Press)

Lindsay, Maurice ed. 1946 *Modern Scottish Poetry: an anthology of the Scottish Renaissance 1920-1945 (London, Faber)*
Livingston, William 1882 *Duain agus Orain le Uilleam Mac Dhunèibhe: am Bard Ileach* (Glasgow, A. Sinclair)
MacDiarmid, Hugh 1926 *A Drunk Man Looks at the Thistle* (Edinburgh, W. Blackwood)
MacDiarmid, Hugh 1932 *Scots Unbound and Other Poems* (Stirling, Eneas Mackay)
MacDiarmid, Hugh 1940 *The Golden Treasury of Scottish Poetry* (London, MacMillan)
MacDiarmid, Hugh 1943 *Lucky Poet: A self-study in literature and political ideas* (London, Methuen)
MacDiarmid, Hugh 1978 *Complete Poems 1920-1976* 2 vols edited by Michael Grieve and W.R. Aitken (London, Martin Brian and O' Keeffe)
Mac Dhunèibhe, Uilleam *see* Livingston, William
Mackay, Peter 2011 'Townland, desert, cave: Irish and Scottish Second World War Poetry' in Fran Brearton, Edna Longley and Peter Mackay eds. *Modern Irish and Scottish Poetry* (Cambridge, Cambridge University Press): 87-101
MacLean, Sorley and Garioch, Robert 1940 *17 Poems for 6d* (Edinburgh, The Chalmers Press)
MacLean 1943 *Dàin do Eimhir agus Dàin eile* (Glasgow, William MacLellan)
MacLean, Sorley 2011a *An Cuilithionn 1939/ The Cuillin 1939 and Unpublished Poems,* edited by Christopher Whyte (Glasgow, The Association for Scottish Literary Studies)
MacLean, Sorley 2011b *Caoir Gheal Leumraich/ White Leaping Flame: Sorley MacLean Collected Poems,* edited by Christopher Whyte and Emma Dymock (Edinburgh, Polygon)
Manson, John ed. 2011 *Dear Grieve: Letters to Hugh MacDiarmid (C.M. Grieve)*(Glasgow, Kennedy and Boyd)
McCaffery, Richie 2015 'The Adjacent Kingdom of England': England, Scotland, and World War Two in the Poetry of Douglas Young (1913–1973) *Études écossaises 17: 87-101*
McClure, J. Derrick 2000 *Language, Poetry and Nationhood: Scots as a Poetic Language from 1878 to the Present* (East Linton, Tuckwell Press)
McClure, J. Derrick 2004 'The Puddocks and The Burdies by Aristophanes and Douglas Young' in Bill Findlay ed. *Frae Ither Tongues: Essays on Modern Translations into Scots* (Clevedon, Multilingual Matters Lts) :215-230
McLaren, Moray 1951 *The Scots* (Harmondsworth, Pelican)
McNeill, Marian 1957-68 *The Silver Bough* (Glasgow, William MacLellan)
Morgenstern, Christian 2013 *Auf vielen Wegen* (CreateSpace Independent Publishing Platform)

Nekrassov, Nicholas 1929 *Poems by Nicholas Nekrassov* translated by Juliet M. Soskice (London, Oxford University Press)

Ó Súilleabháin, Muiris 1933 *Fiche Blian ag Fás* (Baile Átha Cliath, Clólucht an Talbóidigh)

O' Sullivan, Maurice 1933 *Twenty Years A-Growing* (New York: Viking Books)

Ó Tuama, Seán and Kinsella, Thomas eds. 1981 *An Duanaire 1690-1900: Poems of the Dispossessed* (Buckinghamshire, Colin Smythe Ltd)

Propertius, Sextus 1972 *The Poems of Sextus Propertius: A Bilingual Edition*, edited by J.P. McCulloch (London, University of California Press)

Pushkin, Alexander 1972 *Pushkin Threefold: Narrative, Lyric, Polemic, and Ribald Verse. The Originals with Linear and Metric Translations*, edited and translated by Walter Arndt (London, George Allen and Unwin Ltd)

Pushkin, Alexander 2012 *The Works of Alexander Pushkin*, edited and translated by Ivan Panin (Delphi Classics, ebook)

Ryleyev, K.F. 1887 *The Poems of K.F. Relaieff*, translated by T. Hart-Davies (London, Remington and Co.)

Ryleyev, K. F. 1934 *Polnoye sobraniye sochineniy* (Leningrad)

Sappho 1955 *Poetarum Lesbiorum Fragmenta*, edited by Edgar Lobel and Denys Page (Oxford, Oxford University Press)

Sappho 1971 *Sappho et Alcaeus: Fragmenta*, edited by Eva-Maria Voigt (Amsterdam, Athenaeum)

Sappho 2007 *The Poetry of Sappho*, edited and translated by Jim Powell (Oxford, Oxford University Press)

Scott, F.G. 1939 *Scottish Lyrics,* Book V (London and Glasgow, Bayley and Ferguson)

Soutar, William 1939 *In the Time of Tyrants* (Perth, privately printed)

Soutar, William 1943 *But the Earth Abideth* (London, Andrew Dakers)

Theocritus 2008 *Idylls* (Oxford World's Classics) translated by Anthony Verity with introduction and notes by Richard Hunter (Oxford, Oxford University Press)

Tibullus 1909 *Tibulle et les auteurs du Corpus Tibullianum*, edited by A. Cartault (Paris, Librairre Armand Colin)

Uhland, Ludwig 1892 *Gedichte von Ludwig Uhland,* edited by Friedrich Brandes (Leipzig, Philipp Reclan jun.)

Valéry, Paul 1971 *Poems of Paul Valéry*, edited by James R. Lawler, Vol. I (London, Routledge and Kegan Paul)

Watson, William J. ed. 1915 *Rosg Gaelic: Specimens of Gaelic Prose* (Inverness, An Comunn Gaidhealach)

Yeats, W.B. 1939 *Last Poems and Plays* (Churchtown, Cuala Press)

Index

Rules to maintain consistency within the Index of Titles and First Lines:
Titles in single quotation marks.
First lines without quotation marks.
When title and first line are the same, the full line without quotation marks.

Symbols

22 St Giles Street, Oxford. February Midnight.	15, 290
Βόσκε τάς ἠγάς τού νουν ἀν κολώνας,	181
ʾΗλθές ποτα μολθάκως σύ,	214
ʿΡίμφα μάλʾ ἦλθες ἀπώχεό τʾ αὖ μαλακοῖσι πόδεσσι	214
῟Υστατου ἁμέ φίλαμα μένει, χωρισμόσ επεστιʾ	182

A

Aa owre the hale o Grewe whaur they gaed out	198
Aa that was lowsit by the bricht day's mou	185, 324
'A Ballad of the Plockton Hay-Drier'	119, 308
'A Ballad o Saughton Jail'	73, 302
A barefaced trousered keelie	150
A black birdie flees owre the warld	217, 332
'A Cameronian Cat'	72, 302
Ae day and ae nicht a yowden-druft	24
'Ae Fond Kiss'	182
Ae time that I our flownrie life appraisit	200
A face aye hauntan me	163
'After Lunch, Ekali'	xxii, 18, 291, 292
'Aisling na h-Alba'	96, 305
'A Love'	57, 299
Although, my love, you always betrayed me	179
Amang the fullyerie's shadow-ferlies	229, 336
A MhicDhiarmaid, ye wish me and the lave	33
'A Mother's Tears'	xxiv, 232, 337
An auld man in an auld touer	53
'Ane Acrostich Sonnet in the auld Scots for the Queen's Grace in Embro, on Bannockburn Day 1953'	116, 308
'Anthem for the Primrose League'	151, 318
'An t-Iarla Diurach – by a MacLaine Lady of Lochbuie to a Campbell of Jura'	179, 323
'Ardlogie, Christmas Eve, 1939'	26, 292, 293
'Aristophanes in Scots: Frae Choruses o The Birdies'	199, 329

A rumour flees round frae the verra Heidquarters	146
A seventeenth-century Dutchman made it	83
A thrush screams in the night	56
'Attic Noon'	vii, 7, 289, 348
'August Night'	31, 293, 294
'Austrian Scene'	10, 289
'Autumn Fire'	32, 294, 348
Ay, shair eneuch, that's Crail ye're seein nou	124

B

'Bairn-Music'	85, 304
Bethlehem is a Fleming toun	212
Biggan his bothy by the muirland burn	224
Black on whyte i the paper, Dauvit's deid	63
Blyth that stravaigs the warld braid and fair	79
"Bright city, violet-wreathed and songful," chanted	7
'Britherly Fareweel'	222, 334
Brown vermouth in a glaucous glass	15

C

'Caa the Yowes'	181
Caller rain frae abune	185, 325
'Carmen In Patriam Suam'	44, 297
Catullus man, ye maunna gang sae gyte	194, 327
'Chain Stores'	138, 314, 347
Chaste and pure were the things we thocht	202
'Choric Threnody'	198, 329
Christopher Grieve, "MacDiarmid"	237
Cicalas burst the air, a heat-haze quivers	18
Classical Translations	183, 324
Confluence	52, 299
Crail Harbour	124
'Crusade'	141, 314, 348

D

Dàin do Eimhir LI	159, 320
Dàin do Eimhir LIII	160, 320
Dàin do Eimhir LIV	161, 320
Dàin do Eimhir LV	162, 320
Dàin do Eimhir LVII	163, 320
Dàin do Eimhir XLII	157, 320
Dàin do Eimhir XLIII	158, 320
Dàin do Eimhir XXVIII	154, 319

Dàin do Eimhir XXXIII	155, 319
Dàin do Eimhir XXXIV	156, 319
Dàin Eile XVII	167, 321
Day-light-long in the woodland penumbra	32
Dearer the fleurs o hairst's dwynin	229, 336
'December Night: The Aesthete in the House'	25, 292
Deid sall ye ligg, and ne-er a memorie	186, 325
Deòrsa, the peat-fire	16
Do Dingwall farmers curse and frown	142
'Do Threasgair an Saol'	178, 323
Drinkan, I heedna puirtith that eats the hert	188, 326
'D. til H'	60, 299
'Du Bellay in Fife'	79, 303
'Dulce et Decorum'	xxv, 43, 297
'Duncan the Joiner'	87, 100, 304, 305
'Duncan the Joiner and the Laird of Jura'	100, 305
Dunfermline Abbey	126

E

Earth hath not many things to show less fair	115
'Eftir the Daith o a Bairn'	216, 332, 348
'Eirinn ag Gul. Ireland Greitan'	176, 323
'Epilogue to Theokritos'	xxiii, 48, 298
'Eternitie'	98, 305

F

Falkland Palace	125
Far is the flicht frae Prague to canny Fife	110
'Fermer's Deein'	65, 301
'Fife Equinox'	xxvii, 24, 292
Fiscal and Advocate, you're monsters baith	149, 317
Five year owre the sea at the war	73
'For Alasdair'	xvii, xxv, 41, 296
'For a Scotsman Slain'	42, 297
'For a Wife in Jizzen'	xxix, 61, 300
'For D. D-H'	63, 300
'For Deòrsa and his Calum Thonder'	22, 292
'For Edwin & Willa, Bannockburn Day 1947'	110, 306
'For the Old Highlands'	45, 297
'For Willie Soutar, October 1943'	59, 299
'Fowr Epigrams'	188
Frae a German owreset by Lili du Bois-Reymond o an English Sonnet o the First World War whas autour isna kent	213

Frae Catullus, VIII, "Miser Catulle, Desinas Ineptire..."	194
Frae Catullus, V. "Vivamus, Mea Lesbia, Atque Amemus..."	193
Frae Christian Morgenstern	217
Frae Homer's Iliad, VI, 392-496	189
Frae Hugo Von Hofmannsthal: "Wo kleine Felsen, kleine Fichten..."	208
Frae Paul Heyse	216
Frae Propertius. Elegies II, xi.	196
Frae the Aiolic o Psappho	183, 185
Frae the Erse, Eichteenth Yearhunder	178
Frae the French o Paul Valéry, "Le Bois Amical"	202
Frae the French o Paul Valéry, "Le Cimetière Marin"	203
Frae the Gaelic	179
Frae the Gaelic o George Campbell Hay	172
Frae the German o Emanuel Geibel	210
Frae the German o Erich Fried	211, 212
Frae the German o Goethe	219
Frae the German o Hein	218
Frae the German o Ludwig Uhland	214
Frae the Greek	187, 188, 198
Frae the Greek of Aeschylus, Agamemnon 429-455	198
Frae the Greek o Theognis o Megara	188
Frae the Hebrew	235
Frae the Lallans o Burns	181
Frae the Latin o Emperor Gallienus	197
Frae the Latin o Sulpicia, Elegidion VI	195
Frae Theodor Storm: "Die Stadt"	209
Frae the Russian o Kondrati Fyedorovitch Rileyev	231
Frae the Russian o Nyekrasov	232
Frae the Russian o Pushkin	227
Frae the Scots Gaelic o William Livingstone	176
Frae the Second Canzone o Dante's "Vita Nuova"	200
Frae the traditional Gaelic	180
Frae the Welsh hymn by D. Gwenallt Jones	233
Freedom! Your proud inspiration	231

G

Gairs o green gerss again i the policies	106
Gangan hamewith throu the snaw	105
Gangan my lane amang the caulkstane alps	67
'Garlic in Colinton Dell'	121, 309
'Gealach Ùr'	170, 321
Gie aa, and aa comes back	82
Gin the firmament was nearer	29
Grey are the sands, and grey the sea	209, 331

Grey-green the Danube flows, grey-green the willows	10
'Guestless Howff'	174, 322

H

Hae ye seen her, ye unco Jew	168
'Hame frae Stalingrad'	211, 331
Ha! the blue trumpets blowing triumphantly	30
'Hektor's Twynan frae Andromacha'	xxiv, 189, 326
Here on the hillside garden the dusk closes	8
He turns awa frae life	65
'Hielant Colloguy'	70, 301
'Hielant Woman'	168, 321
Hold tight, Tory diehards	151
Home Rule be ours and we shall see	135
Hou sall a makar makarize your name	114
How shall we adore and adorn thee, Scotland, our mother and bride	96
How the Stillness oer the Width of Water hitherwandering comes	217, 333
Hugh MacDiarmid	xviii, xix, xx, xxviii, xxxvii, 33, 37, 114, 294, 295, 300, 302, 307, 317, 319, 322, 339, 341, 348, 351

I

I am the thinker and the thocht	99
I canna woo ye, lass, sae stark	60
I can't lie still in my bed	23
'Ice-Flumes Owregie Their Lades'	viii, xxvi, 67, 301
Ich liebte dich. Mag sein dass jene Liebe	227
I dinna ken the sense o ma trauchlan	48, 162, 320
I ever seated at the sea-ford	180
I fashna masel for the grand revolution	160, 320
I hae stuid an hour o the lown midsummer nicht	66
I knew that learned man when he was old	13
I'll pit a haundle on the heuk o the mune	170
I loe a fleur, but I kenna whilk ane	218, 333
I loed ye yince, and aiblins i ma hert	227, 335
I mind when I was a bairnie hou ma mither	5
In Athens once a Macedonian Jew	6
In England's hour o need	42
In Switzerland lang syne befell	89
In the theatre-bar three officers laughing and drinking	28
I remember the marvellous meeting	230
It came unsought for, undesired	57
I tell ye a tale o a simmer nicht	87
I the connachan time o the sterns	159, 320

Ithers may scryve, or lea ye ligg unkent   196, 328
I the Wild West there's a region   199
I thocht I heard ye chap upo the door   216
'It's Easy Sperin'   140, 314, 347
It's nae juist canny, whiles, readan Plato   50
I've been a gangrel bodie, I've been to Sicilie   188, 325
I wish, my jo, ye'll never mair   195, 328

J

'Jessie o Balronald'   91, 305
Je vois les eaux qui se frottent dans le désableur   20

K

Ken ye the countrie whaur the citrons grow   219
'Kintra Couplin'   95, 305
Kościuszko's son liggs i the wuid shot deid   220, 333

L

'Labour's Call to Rally   152, 318
'Lady Grant'   148, 317
Lasses and lads, crouse and herty   197, 328
Lassie, can ye say   61
Lassie, c'wa   193, 327
Lassie, c'wa, let 's live in houghmagandie   193
Lassie, gin ye'd made me your lad   154
'Lass wi the Keekin-Gless'   175, 322
'Last Lauch'   xvii, xxvi, xl, 71, 301
Lay her and lea her here i the gantan grund   109
'Leaving Athens'   xxiii, 20, 291, 292
'Letter to Hugh MacDiarmid, 1940'   33, 294, 348
'Lines on a Gaelic Poet at an Oxford Party'   16, 290
'London, 1948'   115, 308
'London Midnight'   23, 292
Love grows in the heart   55
'Luve'   82, 175, 200, 206, 303
Luve I never was acquent wi   175

M

Maik o the gods he seems to me   184
'Maister John Knox's First Blast o the Trumpet again the Yerl o Balcarres'   117, 308
'Maurice Lindsay'   xxxviii, 23, 113, 292, 307, 317
Maurice, musician, makar, moniefauld   113

'May Nocturne'	56, 299
"Mentre Io Pensava La Mia Frale Vita…"	200, 329
Minnie, I canna caa my wheel	185, 324
'Moral Problem'	145, 316
Mox tu morte jaces. remanent oblivia longa	186
'Mr E. Brown's Highland Tour, or Muckle Cry and Little Oo'	142, 315, 348
My een are nae on Calvary	169, 321
My Lord Balcarres, tak tent til your ways	117

N

Nae bore o blue i the lither lyft	49
'Naomi Mitchison'	111, 306
Naomi Mitchison, but umquhile Haldane	111
Nineteen year auld he dee'd for Ireland's cause	76
Noucht upon erde heir stands siccar	139
Nou it's Peru and Ecuador	145
Nou three crousie cockerels craw	222

O

'Obair-Bhrothaig'	62, 300
O come, o come Emmanuel	147
'Octobrist Manifesto'	231, 336
O hoo can ye gang, lassie, hoo can ye gang?	132
'On a Bairn's Death'	214, 332
'On an Auld Map o Scotland'	83, 303
'On A North British Devolutionary'	86, 304
'On the Akropolis at Skoplje, July 1936'	8, 289
'On the Daith o a Young German Scholar'	213, 332
'On the Death of Wallace Martin Lindsay'	13, 290
Our prospects may be fearful	143
Outside is cold and rain and gloom	25
Owned by the Lunnon boss they stann	138

P

Parnes, Pentelikon, Hymettos, glowing	21
'Passing Poet'	124, 309
Photo from Pitlour Towards East Lomond	125
'Pious Canticle'	135, 312
'Pious Ejaculation in Aberdeen'	97, 305
'Prognostication, April 1939'	137, 313, 314
Puir friendless tod	225

Q

'Quatorzain in an Entr'acte'	28, 293
Queemly the Queen fares furth; the pipers play	116

R

'Raasay Lament – "Cumha Mhic' ille Chaluim"'	180, 323
'Rabbie in Plastics'	101, 305
'Reconciliation'	81, 303
'Reothairt	171, 321
'Requiem'	xxvi, 64, 301
Rowans are rowthie heich on the braes	223, 334
'Russian Thought'	54, 299, 348

S

'Sabbath i the Mearns'	51, 298
Saftlie ye cam and gaed. Awa frae men	214
'Sainless'	xli, 66, 301
'Sang by the Sea'	49, 298
Saunts o lang syne ligg in stour nou	233
Scotia, patria mea carissima	44
'Scotland's Complaynt to his Mistress Industry	132, 311
'Scotlann, Awauk'	131, 311
Scotlann, awauk, be again a nation	131
'Scotsmen, Wake Up!'	133, 311, 347
Scotsmen, wake up, and face the facts	133
See here the castel whaur they killed the Cardinal	124
"Shi King": The Ninth o the Odes o Wei	225
"Shi King": The Second o the Odes o T'Ang	223
"Shi King": The Second o the Odes o Wei	224
'Simplon Tunnel'	47, 298, 348
Sleep saft and sound	85
'Snaw Thochts'	105, 306, 348
Some folk seem to be cold inside	54
'Sonnet for a Phone-Call'	39, 296
'Sonnet Peu Probable'	17, 291
'Speculation'	29, 293
Standan here on a fogg-yirdit stane	41
St Andrews Castle	124, 127, 309
Steady, Labour comrades	152
Syne when he cam to the Skaian yetts as he gaed throu the burgh	189

T

Thar bheanntan na h-Eachdraidh	62
That old lonely lovely way of living	45
That pleasant voice nearly sawed me asunder	39
'The 23rd Psalm o King Dauvit'	235, 337
The Auchtand o the Odes o P'ei	226
'The Bairns' Slauchter o Bethlehem'	212, 331
'The Ballant o the Laird's Bath'	89, 304
The bens are nae ayebydan. Frost and sun	47
'The Black Shawl'	228, 336
'The Bold Sloganeer'	xxv, 143, 316
'The Cat in the Rock-Garden'	30, 293
'The Coolin: An Assonantal Projection into English, from the original Gaelic of Sorley MacLean's 'An Cuilithionn' '	237
'The Couthy Wuid'	202, 330
The English are going to be down the drain	137
The English at last have gaen tae war	140
The fleurs of Embro sae blythlie leaman	122, 309
The French are surrounded on every frontier	136, 312
The geans are fleuran whyte i the green Howe o the Mearns	51
'The Ghaists'	154, 319
'The Glesca Muckers'	150, 317
The gloaman comes owre the muirland	211
The Gods' buss, epple-ringie, blaws	221, 334
'The Hermit Bonze'	224, 334
'The Kirkyaird by the Sea'	203, 330
The Lady Grant	148
The Laird o Jura raised a troop	100
The Lord's my herd, I sall nocht want	235
The lyon dinesna aye on flesch, strang tho he be	188, 326
The mild midwinter evening ebbs, leaving	26
The Minister said it wad dee	xxvii, 71
The mowdie fae his couthie neuk	210, 331
The mune has gane doun	185, 325
The partan tellt the ether	187, 325
The phaisant cock has flown awa	226, 335
The pool in the dark rocks reflects the sky no longer	27
The refugee royalties	141
There is no poem in language like Deòrsa's poem for Calum	17
There's a steer amang the shadaws	81
There's nae place whaur ye can feel the Auld Alliance,	125
There was a Cameronian cat	72
There was a lad was born in Kyle	101

'The Rich Spinster's Sang'	225, 334
'The Roots of Love'	55, 299
'Thesaurus Paleo-Scoticus'	xxix, 5, 289
These chill pillars of fluted stone	46
'The Shepherd's Dochter'	109, 306, 348
The starns around the bonnie mune	186, 325
The swaws o the firth whammle and freeze til a wyce daith	64
'The Umpteenth Forefront'	146, 316
The waas o the muckle haa in Portree	91
The warld whummlit them aa, the wind soopit them aff	178
The waves' unwearied washing on the walls	127
The wee whyte rose o Scotland that braks the hairt	75
The weird o makars	155, 319
They libbit William Wallace	86
They pledge me nae mair in wine, for nou anither	188, 326
They're bonnie bens the Lomonds, Aist and Wast	125
Thirty years on: now I tread the same garlic	121
This lown riggin-side, whaur whyte doos gang	203
thocht I heard ye chap upo the door	216
'Thochts Anent Bluid and Roses'	75, 302
'Thomas Joseph Williams'	76, 302
Thonder they ligg on the grund o the sea	172, 322
Thon time we aa wonned thegither	183, 324
'Thow Thochts'	106, 306
'Til Anaktoria'	184, 324
'Til the Andantino frae Gluck's Orpheus'	80, 303
'Timor belli ne nos conturbet'	139, 314
'To a Friend on a Campaign'	40, 296, 348
'To A. P. Kyern'	230, 336
'To Gillian in Vienna'	12, 290
'To the Hymn Tune "Veni Immanuel"'	147, 317
Translation from the Hebrew	235
Translation from the Welsh	233
Translations from Chinese	223, 334
Translations from French	202, 330
Translations from German	208, 330
Translations from Italian	200, 329
Translations from Lithuanian	220, 333
Translations from Russian	227, 335
'Traveller's Tale'	6, 289
'Travesty in Lallans: Mignon's Song, "Kennst du das Land…"'	219, 333
Twenty year beddit, and nou	59

U

"Using the rain to dry the hay"	119
Uttermost isle of Europe	176

V

Van Gogh paints night with her milky ways	123
'Van Gogh – The Starry Night'	123, 309
Viewing the terrors of the strife	232
'Vishnu'	99, 305

W

Wae for the lanelie kirkyaird fowk	174
Wald ye be atween a lassie's houghs	167, 321
'Wales'	140, 233, 337
'W.B. Yeats'	38, 53, 299
We ken we maun hae our ain seuch	97
Were't no for ye	158, 320
Were we thegither, me and you	157, 320
We walked together in the Belvedere	12
Whan ye can see a yirdit suin	98
What can ye shaw me here, i this land o the Scots	70
What is thatt? What iz it? Swish-swishing about me in the dark	31
Whaur monie a wee bit spruce and craig	208, 330
Wha wald hae thocht that gowden hair	80
When he beguid tae chap the wuid	95
When I am talkan o the face and natur	156, 319
While eftir while, and me broken	171
'Whiles'	48, 50, 67, 77, 298
'Winter Homily on the Calton Hill'	46, 297
'Winter Pool'	27, 293, 348
Wudlike I luik on the black satin shawl	228, 229

Y

Ye are my theme nou, tremble, young Kilkerran	112
Ye're aff and awa, meikle the dreid	40
Ye were my fier, albeid we never met	213
Ye were the dawn on the hills o the Cuillin	161, 320
Yill's ma guid frien, but ae thing that's agee	188, 326
Yonder a black flood pouring among green beeches	52
'Young Kilkerran'	xxx, 112, 306

www.ingramcontent.com/pod-product-compliance
Lightning Source LLC
Chambersburg PA
CBHW021148230426
43667CB00006B/304